# THE TIME'S DISCIPLINE
## The Beatitudes and Nuclear Resistance

Philip Berrigan and
Elizabeth McAlister

WIPF & STOCK · Eugene, Oregon

Wipf and Stock Publishers
199 W 8th Ave, Suite 3
Eugene, OR 97401

The Time's Discipline
The Beatitudes and Nuclear Resistance
By Berrigan, Philip and McAlister, Elizabeth
Copyright©1989 by Catholic Worker
ISBN 13: 978-1-60899-057-3
Publication date 5/2/2010
Previously published by Fortkamp -- Cath Worker, 1989

We dedicate this book to
two valiant women
our Mothers
Frida Berrigan
Elizabeth McAlister

# ACKNOWLEDGMENTS

The direct quotations from Scripture throughout the text are in italics. Except for quotations from the Psalms, the Bible text is from the Revised Standard Version of the Bible, Copyright 1946, 1952, 1971, by the Division of Christian Education of the National Council of Churches of Christ in the United States of America and is used by permission.

The quotations from the Psalms are from PSALMS ANEW: IN INCLUSIVE LANGUAGE by Nancy Schreck, OSF, and Maureen Leach, OSF, Saint Mary's Press, Winona, Minnesota, with permission.

The Appendix on resources for resistance is reprinted with minor changes and some additions from SWORDS INTO PLOWSHARES: NONVIOLENT DIRECT ACTION FOR DISARMAMENT, Edited by Arthur J. Laffin and Anne Montgomery, Harper & Row Publishers, San Francisco, with permission.

The quotations from the poetry of Wendell Berry are from COLLECTED POEMS, 1957-1982, by Wendell Berry, Copyright © 1985 by Wendell Berry, North Point Press, Berkeley, California, with permission.

The authors are grateful to Johnny Baranski and Sunburst Press for permission to reprint the first part of Philip's "Chronicle of Hope" which first appeared in OF BEASTS AND BEASTLY IMAGES.

The authors are also very grateful to Roger Ludwig for his diligent researching of obscure quotations and to George Hanst for his practiced, professional proofreading.

# A Discipline
## by Wendell Berry

Turn toward the holocaust, it approaches
on every side, there is no other place
to turn. Dawning in your veins
is the light of the blast
that will print your shadow on stone
in a last antic of despair
to survive you in the dark.
Man has put his history to sleep
in the engine of doom. It flies
over his dreams in the night,
a blazing cocoon. O gaze into the fire
and be consumed with man's despair,
and be still, and wait. And then see
the world go on with the patient work
of seasons, embroidering birdsong
upon itself as for a wedding, and feel
your heart set out in the morning
like a young traveler, arguing the world
from the kiss of a pretty girl.
It is the time's discipline to think
of the death of all living, and yet live.

# Contents

Foreword ..................................................... xi

Introduction ................................................ xvii

Chapter 1.
   The Poor in Spirit .......................................... 1

Chapter 2.
   Those Who Mourn ........................................ 28

Chapter 3.
   The Meek ................................................ 51

Chapter 4.
   Those Who Hunger and Thirst for Justice ............... 73

Chapter 5.
   The Merciful ............................................. 91

Chapter 6.
   The Pure in Heart ...................................... 118

Chapter 7.
   The Peacemakers ....................................... 150

Chapter 8.
   Those Who Are Persecuted ............................. 175

Appendix A.
   Advent Reflections ..................................... 199

Appendix B.
    The Chronicle of Hope..................................... 225

Appendix C.
    Resources.................................................. 267

Appendix D.
    Suggested Readings ........................................ 283

# FOREWORD

## by Daniel Berrigan S.J.

One day, many years ago, a bishop summoned me to headquarters. I had made bold to propose in writing (everything ecclesiastic in those days was presented in writing; it was as though we were conducting banking or forensic affairs)—had proposed the founding of a Catholic Worker house in his (and my) city. The project as a matter of course required the imprimatur of the chief of his (and my) diocese.

I was, on a chief point, shortly disabused. It transpired that "his" by no means included "my."

A dumber pate than mine would have known, the moment I took my uneasy seat, that the proposal had been ill received.

His eminence was rendered splenetic; unaccountably at first. Then, as our converse wobbled on, a number of sore points emerged.

Chief among them was this: the young man who had volunteered to run the house, dispensing meals and lodging to the poor, was a pacifist.

"A pacifist!" sputtered his eminence. "And you, a professor of theology, don't know that the holy father has vindicated the right of nations to wage just wars?" There was more of this, in the brimstone mode. But perhaps enough for now.

Another tic, another nerve.

"I ask you, Father B. What guarantee you can offer (supposing for the moment that I'd approve this venture in My Diocese)—what indication is there that such a place would last, say, forty or fifty years?"

He had in mind of course, the marmoreal pilings and architraves of his (and not my) diocese; or for that matter, my (and not his) Order, the Jesuits.

Pacifism, improvisation. Two sticking points.

. . . . . . . . . .

One can only conclude (in virtue of an inside-out logic named by the world, foolishness, and by Christians, the Cross)—we have here two ideas inviting a long long look. Beyond doubt ideas so unpopular must contain an unnerving hidden charge. Dynamite, Peter Maurin would call them, the dynamite named faith.

Someone, so to speak, has pissed on the dynamite.

. . . . . . . . . .

The episcopal disfavor rested first on pacifism, a term much abused certainly, and by no means only by him. An ambiguous term, bandied about, half understood, somewhat abstract, passive, a theory perhaps? In any case, side by side with a history all but terminally violent.

Violence; our history; our North America, our world reality. And according to conventional politics presently hustled on all sides, our ironbound future.

In light of this, pacifism seems not a wholly satisfactory term.

The Bible, Jesus, prefers another term; peacemaking.

"The makers of peace." In the Greek, we have a kind of hyphenated coinage: *eireno-poioi*. The Biblical lexicon gives as first meaning of the verb *poiein*, "to produce, form, fashion, construct, create." One is attracted to the solidity and sweat implied.

There are rich nuances. The lexicon goes on: "to labor, to do work, to exercise activity."

And in reference to time (and patience and starting over!) "To continue."

And again, a consolation prize of sorts: "to be the author of, to cause."

We are digging in rich soil. One is tempted to linger over the rural-legal passage in Mark. Commended to us is an ecological sense, highly moral. Nature rightly understood, is on our side; ears of grain are for the hungry. And the law is our lethal adversary: *Why are they doing what is not lawful on the sabbath?* Mark, 2: 24.

The disciples are described amid the standing grain. The verb, *hodopoiein;* to make a path for themselves by plucking the heads, or *As they made their way his disciples began to pluck heads of grain.* Mark, 2: 23.—illegally, of course. The peacemakers, in this usage, clear the way for others; but only by acting against the law.

Again that verb, delightfully concrete and variant: "to make something out of something else." (As, for notable instance, plowshares out of swords.)

Also a living work, a work on behalf of life: "To cause, bring about; to produce, bear, shoot forth."

Yet again, simply, "To do; to follow and express by deeds, the feelings and thoughts of the mind." Talk about orthopraxis as true to, and one with, orthodoxy!

And finally, cheerfully: "To celebrate, to keep, as a festival or banquet."

Thus the rich grammar of peacemaking, indeed a grammar of assent.

. . . . . . . . . .

Peacemaking, not pacifism. Scripture rather than theory. The life and work of Jonah House, recounted in this book, were undertaken long years prior to their recording, undertaken in obedience to another Book, seldom out of hand.

In this "diary on the run," numbers of devoted friends across the land and elsewhere, will meet, or meet once more, the Jonah House community, an irreformable peacemaking tribe, within or outside the law as circumstance requires.

And standing firm all the while in the ambit of the "great law" of love. Despite all.

The form of the book is, as they say, the message. One thinks of notes hastily set down, a diary of events, headlong, original insights tested over and over, as the furnace of law is stoked red hot to receive The Singing Youths.[1] Life together, life in the breach, and scarcely time to take breath.

The breath is however, taken. There are the spaces created by a common discipline, the prayer and Bible reflection and eucharist. Making sense of it all, when very little in the world offers much beyond a pimp's wage, entitlement to the dance of death.

. . . . . . . . . .

The burden of the book is peace. The peace sought and labored after is neither silly nor psycho. In Camus' inelegant phrase, it "pays up." It is socially, politically, personally laborious, hot, dangerous. It is governed by the verb *poiein*, the "to make" implicit in Isaiah and Jesus. The one underscoring the sweat and tears, and yes, the blood, at risk and often out poured. The other proffering like a wounded hand, celebration: *Blessed are the poor.* Matthew, 5: 3-12.

Peacemaking, an effortful life; living simply, feeding the poor. Wide hospitality. Earning a living, carpentry and housepainting. Then responsibility to the wider public, so victimized by cowardly media, so ignorant of our common plight. Translating the meaning of the community, its vision, and work, the actions (that scandalous lawbreaking, that odious blood pouring.) Travel, conference, retreats. Never easy, never dull.

There is a precious biology at work too. A biology of peace; *poiein*, to bring forth. Children are born in the house, they are a pledge that something other than a wantonly wrecked creation is our legacy, something better than duplicity, dishonor, despair can be passed to them.

The house is in fact a kind of "small universe" where humans do their best; to tread softly, in accord with that other Isaian

---

[1] The reference is to the three youths in the fiery furnace in the book of Daniel, chapter three.

image, neither quenching the flame nor crushing the fragile reed. (The reference is to Isaiah, chapter forty-two.)

. . . . . . . . . .

To revert, there was that other nervous matter twitching at the bishop's mind; something to do with continuity.

To translate, and as I hope, to do no injustice, he was offered a gift; a community prepared to work among the poor. But I venture he could think only of—an institution.

This has been our bane. When authorities utter the word "Church," they summon at the back of the mind, institutions in the manner of curias, schools, temples, centers of this or that good dispensed; and then the perks and privileges that mortise the walls (and seal us in); investments, favor of the wealthy, exemptions from tax laws, political cronyism.

These become the point of Church itself; the flourishing of worldly fortune, a mark of divine favor.

More, and worse. The institutions must, if truth were told, be preferred above—people. To the point that, crises arriving, choices impending, *diakonia,* the service of others, named by Christ as the sign of His community, vanishes. "Lording over," the conduct of the "dwellers on earth," becomes the Church logo as well.

There is the undoubted continuity of institutions, and the improvisation, the so-so, the making do, ups and downs, of communities.

Sometimes a nice mix prevails in the former—for a time. Prior to the era of the big spenders and getters, as in the history of religious orders, the action takes place both in the upper room, pentecostal, and in the street; equally pentecostal.

Thus we hear of early Jesuits with their tatters and begging bowls, their caring for the homeless, the plague-stricken, the prostitutes. The brothers were, for all purposes, indistinguishable from Franciscans of an earlier time. And so on.

Improvising with a vengeance.

Subsequently of course, law, order, and property reared their anxious heads. With effects we need no instruction in.

So we have in Jonah House, God be praised, a continuity of sorts, institutionally free, the Upper-Room kind, the Street-kind. It honors the rhythms of the Holy Spirit, prayer, and praxis. It is free to move, and free to be still. It is unprotected, at mercy. Has a single eye for essentials, modesty, the "good work" which defines true art, including the art of peacemaking.

It is handed on, one house to another, one city to another, one generation to another. It is like the passing of a genetic code, a message sotto voce, Paul's "mysterion." Christ.

The good work continues. That Jonah House has achieved little as the world reckons; that the stockpiled weapons loom higher than fabled Babel—and far crazier; that few come to the work and of those a number soon depart; that farcical trials and summary jailing proliferate like the frogs of Egypt; that that that—

All this, given the times, given the wars, given the waste, given the unimaginably low voltage of public passion, must be declared beside the point. Painful indeed, hard to live with, but beside.

The point? Continuity, the Spirit, the good work at hand, unquenched courage, patience, all these and more. The goodness and truthfulness of what is to be done.

Let me dare say, and kiss my hand to those I love; the point is the sheer joy of it.

# INTRODUCTION

Jonah House came into being in 1973 from the merger of two communities, one in resistance, the other in prison for resistance. Communication between the two communities was possible because Liz and Phil[1] saw each other frequently, and firm friendships existed within and without prison walls. Long reflection, numberless meetings, prayer, study, and some experience brought us to joint conclusions:

first, our country's addiction to war was long-term, maybe terminal;
second, resistance would become needed more desperately than even during the most genocidal years of the Indochina War;
third, the resistance communities of the Sixties and Seventies were too shallow and ad hoc to serve as models for a lasting community;
fourth, some of us would have to accept God's Word as a handbook and try to embody it.

We sensed something further: if we didn't begin with community, Big Brother and his culture would digest us as free lunch. And, if our community were not grounded in faith, we risked abandoning resistance altogether.

This book is a record of that community's actions and insights over its first fifteen years. Much that is here comes from prison

---

[1] We use the first person whenever one or the other of us is clearly speaking, and speaking from an understanding of where our lives are at the time of writing. We use the third person (Phil, Liz) to describe something that we did or thought in the past; it may or may not reflect what we would do or think in the present; the future is in the hands of God, our friends, and unforeseeable events.

writing, compilation, editing. It is primarily a work of community. To write of fifteen years in community logically, neatly, tidily, with any hint of "the last word" is not only impossible but also faithless. Living in a tent is neither neat nor neatly recordable; living in a neighborhood of often hopeless destitution is not neat; holding property in common is not neat; demonstrating around the calendar against war addiction is not neat; traveling the judicial railroads (loosely called courts of justice) and going to prison are not neat.

To explain such a vision, to outline such an experiment, is to structure a floating crap game! So, in these pages, we report questions more than answers; we tally failures and as many (or more) joys; we remember incessant strivings, unwillingness to quit. We say this not as an apologia, nor excuse for "unfocused" work, nor, strictly speaking, as a rationale or explanation. It is an effort to be true to sisters and brothers, in and out of chains, who have rescued us time and again from egotism, fear, and triviality. It is an effort to be faithful to what truth we learned as we learned it, as one always learns it, by doing.

We have learned that community, when properly understood, is not merely a vivid foretaste of the people of God, not only the most formidable critic and opponent of a criminal state. It is also a constant test of personal and interpersonal integrity. In no other setting are we held so closely accountable to God, to the victims, and to one another.

When Liz wrote from Alderson Penitentiary in 1986 that she was using the Beatitudes as a framework for organizing material from our community experience (Biblical reflections, lectures on nonviolence and community, writings from prison, political polemics, resistance chronicles), Phil thought her choice inspired. It reminded him again that prisoners of conscience have, if they desire it, special access to the Spirit of God.

The people of Jonah House dared to try to realize the Beatitudes—sometimes fumbling, always fragile, two steps forward and three back, kicking and screaming. Yet curiously persistent. She saw our effort as a question of spirit.

Liz knew the Beatitudes described why Christ was blessed,

pleasing, chosen by God. She also knew what we must do to be blessed, pleasing, chosen (choosing to be chosen). Christ certainly revealed himself in the Beatitudes; but he taught them to the disciples, the crowds, and to us. These descriptions or definitions of the embodied Word become possible in faith. To the person who believes, anything is possible. (A paraphrase of Mark, 9:23.)[2]

We make the Beatitudes into ideals and we judge them, whimsically, as possible or impossible. But Christ taught them as imperatives, as needs of creatures born in God. We recall one scholar writing that what the Gospel teaches is comprehensible to a twelve-year-old. The problem, though, is not comprehension; the problem is our unwillingness to believe, to act, to live, to become what we are, creatures born in God. Because we cling so passionately to unbelief, we lose even the understanding of the twelve-year-old.

Liz also knew that the Beatitudes were ignored or mistaught in their socio-political dimensions. Do they not portray Christians as those who, like God, hear the cry of the poor? Do they not reveal Christians as those who are responsible for the enemy, the starved, the hostage, the weak, or any current target of the hatemonger within and around us? Do they not state that God measures Christians finally by their defense of the victims and by their resistance to the executioners, who, all too often, wear official hats and titles?

How does one, for example, live a common distribution (first beatitude) of spiritual and material goods without a nonviolent rebellion against the conspicuous consumption of a decadent

---

[2] Scripture quotations, when rendered in italics, are taken from the *Common Bible, The Revised Standard Version*. Collins Press. New York. 1973. The Psalms, however, are taken from *Psalms Anew: In Inclusive Language*. Nancy Schreck, OSF, and Maureen Leach, OSF. Saint Mary's Press. Christian Brothers Publicatons. Winona, Minnesota. 1986. We are unable, because of copyright laws, to substitute non-sexist pronouns as we would like to do, so, where the Biblical language is exclusive of women, we have sought to paraphrase it and indicate the passage as paraphrased.

culture, one which devours not only resources, goods, and services, but also consciences, genius, talents, and skills? How does one hunger and thirst for justice or righteousness (fourth beatitude) without confronting the systems of war, economic rip-off, sexism, racism? How does one become a peacemaker (seventh beatitude) without resisting the makers of war? If the first seven beatitudes were not concerned with the respectable murderers and their corporate and political threats to life, the eighth beatitude would promise banquets, gold watches, and other testimonials from a grateful Big Brother rather than the persecution it foretells.

Humankind, it seems, has always been overdue to see God's Word as subversive of a human dis-order largely disobedient, rebellious, and perverted—one close to self-destruction from toxic fouling of our nest, or from weapons designed to protect our *mammon*, the money of exploitation. The Word of God revolutionizes this social chaos nonviolently, replacing the politics of greed, blood lust, and violence with politics designed for children.

The crown of God's Word is the Beatitudes—a condensation or kernel of God's speech to us. They refer implicity to God's compassion for those needlessly suffering; they condescend to include us as instruments of God's justice in Jesus Christ. They reveal the Cross, in both its socio-political and interpersonal aspects, as salvation and life.

Years into the experiment called Jonah House, about 1985, notes on Mark's Gospel written by a young friend and scholar, Ched Myers, helped to clarify our quest. According to Ched, Mark established authority for his Gospel in the first chapter. The Gospel is *the gospel of Jesus Christ, the Son of God.* Mark, 1:1. It is the *gospel of God.* Mark, 1:14. It is affirmed by the Hebrew prophets, Isaiah and Malachi. Mark, 1:2-3. It is authorized when *a voice came from heaven.* Mark, 1:11. God is the author of (which is to say, the authority for) the Good News of Jesus Christ.

Mark makes reference to the "way" first through the metaphor of sandals. John the Baptist says *the thong of whose sandals I am not worthy to stoop down and untie.* Mark, 1:7. Later on, as he sends out the disciples, Christ tells them to *wear sandals*, Mark, 6:9, for the work of God's realm, leading to Jerusalem and the Cross.

The *way* leads to Baptism, a renunciation of more than an artisan's privilege, family, and constituency. Baptism meant an unconditional acceptance of the Cross; it meant seeking out the Strong Person, Mark, 3:27—the state, Satan—as the Stronger Person and overcoming the demonic with suffering love. The Cross meant denial of self, exposing the criminal state, limiting its destructiveness, following Jesus. Baptism, the cleansing by water and by God's Spirit of justice, is neither understood nor fulfilled without the Cross.

Finally, Mark introduces the factor of community by the command "Follow Me!" Why not an invitation? We find the command outrageous. We would rather have a choice in the matter, that is, to say "No!" or "Maybe!" or "Perhaps!" or "Later!" Yet, all the time, we take commands from our ego, or from "the mainstream," or from "elected representatives" in a kind of coglike rhythm: mindlessly, slavishly. But a command from Christ to become a true member of the family, the race, the people of God, is quite another matter. We think our freedom compromised by such a command; but in reality, our freedom depends on obedience to it.

Return to Mark's authority for a moment. Does God have the authority to command us? Of course, God is loving Author—no one else has final authority. Does our good depend on obedience to that command? Of course, we cannot be God's children without being sister and brother one to another. What else is community; what else is behind Christ's "Follow Me?"

And what of the nuts and bolts of "way" and "Baptism?" Who will keep us on the "way" except the grace of God and the love, counsel, friendship, and example of one another? Who will help us to accept Baptism and its consequences of ridicule, ostracism, indifference from Church and media, and the harshest of penalties from the state?

Mark's singular treatment of authority, way, Baptism, and community as footing for his Gospel prepared us to view life at Jonah House as an experiment in the Beatitudes.

Above all, however, this book asks the question: *But who do you say that I am?* Mark, 8:29. Neither the disciples nor we can answer that question: Christ had to answer it himself. He had to point to the Cross as the means to break into the Strong Man's house, the means to overcome him, tie him up, and restore his loot to God. Because he did that, we can also; we can follow, however fearfully, fitfully, and faithlessly. But still follow. The assault on the Strong Man's house by the Stronger Person (Christ) reveals the Christian mission as simply nonviolent assault upon the strongholds of the world.

Redeemed by the Beatitudes—less so by our experiment and our record—our book offers selections of the common life of faith, prayer, equality of relationship, risk, care of the poor, protest, and resistance.

In any case, we wrote it for love of those who will pick up and read. May they find it true to the Good News of Jesus Christ, true to the Cross. And may they, in turn, become better followers than we are.

*Blessed are the poor in spirit,
for theirs is the kingdom of heaven.*
Matthew, 5: 3.

## CHAPTER ONE
# THE POOR IN SPIRIT

The Gospel of Matthew 5:3 gives us this reading: *Blessed are the poor in spirit, for theirs is the kingdom of heaven.* Luke 6:20 renders the same beatitude: *Blessed are you poor, for yours is the kingdom of God.*

The difference between these two accounts has enabled those endowed with worldly goods to own Matthew, those deprived of necessities to own Luke, and both to rest with some composure. But ownership—be it of things, of ideas, of truth, of people—is part of the problem the beatitude seeks to right. The Gospel calls us to stand, as indeed we are, empty and needy before God; it hints that there is nothing more powerful or creative than the very emptiness from which we flee with all our hearts. Flee or stand empty: that is our deepest real choice as human beings; needy we are.

It was Thomas Merton's insight that sin belongs in the realm of ontology rather than morality. Evil raises its head when we forget who we are—people created in God's image, people on a journey back to God, the first step of which is the recognition of our need of God—a first step, incidentally, that recurs at each twist and turn in the journey.

Any of us who would be ministers of God's Word meet our first stumbling block in understanding and living the spirit of poverty. There is always lack of someone to proclaim the good news, not just by preaching, but by embodying both its implicit and explicit call to poverty. Try as we might to rationalize it— to get around, under, over it—we know what poverty is; we know what need is.

The image of those who know their need of God is before us at every turn. The ragged child looks into our hearts out of the pages of slick magazines. The toothless, the lined, the aged are staring us down from the pages of Mission journals. Translated into art by good black-and-white photos, they evoke our esteem and our pity.

In the context of the first beatitude, these are our models, archetypes of our vulnerability. The poor call to our hearts, to our shared humanity, to our dependency on and interdependency with the earth. They speak in whispers of what is best in us, people who are part of one world. At times with urgency, at times with gentle coaxing, they call us to go where it hurts, to enter those places where pain is part of life, to share the anguish, the fear, to become, in a word, vulnerable.

The men and women who rummage through garbage cans on our streets, who mumble or shout, incoherently or threateningly, are different; or so it seems. They strike us as violent, as mad; they might smell. We raise our hackles in fear or disgust and walk on; but their poverty follows us, a profound challenge to Christian conscience. We silence it to our ruin.

Does Christ call us to this kind of poverty?

Maybe and maybe not. But he definitely calls us to know our need, to serve those in need, to displacement, to moving from our "ordinary," our "proper" place in this culture. Usually we have chosen the place for ourselves, as opposed to being called. Usually we have aspired toward the place, labored to attain it. Usually it implies that we have "made it," culturally speaking, that we have "come of age."

For most of us attempting to live the good news of the first beatitude, a genuine exodus results:

—out of mindless consumption, into attentiveness to the needs of others.

—out of a solitary, selfish life into community.

—out of laziness of mind and body into a willingness to learn and to understand (which, as Dan Berrigan likes to say, is to stand under, which is to look up to, which is to be judged by) God's Word.

—out of arrogance into an appreciation of the mystery of our interdependence.

We of Jonah House do not suggest that all must take our same road. In the following pages we merely share what has been our journey so those who wish may test it for themselves. In any case, in retrospect, these seem to have been our first steps.

## OUT OF MINDLESS CONSUMPTION INTO ATTENTIVENESS TO THE NEEDS OF OTHERS

Often the exodus involves unlearning much that life and the culture have taught us. Maybe Phil was blessed in having less to unlearn. His childhood and youth were marked by some of the values we seek to relearn at Jonah House.

As Phil recalls from some personal notes:

> I was six when the "Crash" happened, and the Great Depression began. Virtually everyone we knew was "poor"—having a job put a family in a different class somehow.
>
> I grew up at Jerryknoll (dubbed so by Father for unknown reasons), an eight-acre summer place owned by the Sisters of Charity, who ran an orphanage in Syracuse. They gave us the place rent free, on the condition that we "keep it up."
>
> When we arrived from Minnesota in 1925, the house possessed neither running water nor means for heating. I

imagine that Mother cooked on a wood/coal range in those early days. The water we pumped from a well next door, grudgingly allowed us by the caretaker. To the rear of the house was a customary outhouse, supplemented by a chamber pot in every bedroom.

The house itself was brick, a huge three-story affair crowned by a cupola. We heated two rooms with stoves, and relied upon the stovepipe to warm a bedroom above. There most of us boys slept in winter, two in a bed, the mattresses insulated by newspapers. I recall long johns, vapor-rub, frozen chamber pots, windows encrusted with ice. I recall colds, bronchitis, streptococcus, whooping cough, and several cases of pneumonia.

Resourceful and thrifty from her frontier background, Mother, for several years in the late Twenties and early Thirties, did cooking, washing, sewing, and nursing for a family of eight without running water or refrigeration or gas or oil heat. In retrospect, her achievements were extraordinary, even heroic.

I remember the meals during those years of growing up. Mother cooked what was at hand, priding herself on providing "enough;" though in the lean years of the early Thirties, "enough" often meant cornmeal mush for days on end. Later on, about 1935 or 1936, with Father and some older brothers off working, with a cow, some chickens and pigs—and a garden from which to can vegetables and berries—Mother provided a more prosperous table.

Frida Fromhart, Mother, came to this country from Germany when she was twelve, homesteading with her family on the Minnesota frontier northwest of Duluth. Ely, Hibbing, and Two Harbors were familiar names. Her neighbors were largely Finlanders and Swedes—tough, practical people who adapted easily to the raw demands of frontier culture. Drinking, strife, prejudice, violence were commonplace.

After high school, she kept books for a local lumber company, walking long miles to and from work. Both family and friends encouraged her to carry a gun as protection against roving bears or wolves, or "drunken Indians." She always refused. I recall her telling of befriending the hapless native Americans who were afflicted with the white man's booze, Bible, and diseases.

In Minnesota, Frida met Father, who was railroading for the Oliver Mining Co., a subsidiary of U.S. Steel. Tom Berrigan was an engineer on the ore trains which transported iron ore to Duluth and the ore boats headed for Chicago, Gary, Cleveland, and Buffalo. Infrequently, at lighter moments, Frida would confide that Father was considered a "catch" in those days.

Like our mother, Tom Berrigan came from a background of deprivation and struggle. Fatherless at five, he spent his childhood and teens on a tiny family farm south of Syracuse. Imagine a second-generation Irish Catholic amid hostile Yankees, who controlled local economics, politics and pecking-orders. In his late teens, he drifted west, worked in steel mills, tried college (Valparaiso), and landed finally with the railroad in Minnesota.

Always a staunch union man with socialist sympathies, he was fired and blacklisted by the Oliver Mining Company after marriage to Frida, and soon after the birth of Thomas, our oldest brother. In the space of ten to twelve years, all six of us were born in Minnesota. The economics of a growing family finally forced the move east, with an uneasy reliance upon elements of Father's family. These Irish relatives were generally agreed that Father had married "beneath" himself, and that our mother was unintelligent, inept, and insensitive. She "kept him down," as they said; kept him from his true potential.

In any case, Frida and Tom were strangers to ease or security in the bleak Depression years. Our little farm sat squarely on a main northern route from Syracuse; and thousands of unemployed men were riding the rails or on the road, mostly looking for work, some fleeing families they couldn't support, some running from the law. They'd come to our back door: "Lady, could ya gimme a bite to eat? I'll work for it, split wood, do anything!" Frida would never refuse, not if there was food. Others would come at dusk, exhausted, asking to sleep in the barn. Tom would let them, asking only that they not smoke there.

Frida and Tom took the Gospel to heart—to a depth unprovided by a lifetime of conventional Catholicism. Their faith was due undoubtedly to experience with desperate need, deprivation, misery, discrimination, oppression. Their analysis of social injustice might prove lacking; but they understood profoundly the command to care for "the least of these." This they did with a rare and tenacious faith. They saw this one hurt, another hungry, a third desperate. And they responded with what they had.

Nor did their magnanimity lack contrast. For nearly twenty years, we lived next door to the estate of Thomas Gale, a retired salt baron and millionaire, who had built his fortune from the salt springs and mines on the shores of Onondaga Lake. And, it should be said, from the backs of his workers. Tom Gale had the reputation of being a hard, capitalist boss, a "skinflint" in the estimation of those who knew him.

Gale would winter in Florida, returning to his somber holdings (every building a dark brown) for short weeks in the summer. During this time sacralized by his presence, the caretaker would forbid us the water pump, and order us off the fences. "Stay off the propitty!" he would warn us. The great man had no time for us; less time yet for those wandering the roads.

Frida was not awed by Tom Gale, nor by any of his fierce lackeys. Instead, she mustered a great pity for him. "Old Tom," she'd say, "is planning to take it all with him. Well, others have tried that!"

Our parents never had property, and had little ambition to acquire it. (The original Berrigan home, built and inhabited by the clan for two generations, was willed to Tom in the early Forties.) They knew that property had little to do with Christian living, except, frequently, to inhibit it. They also knew that if they had more than they needed, it belonged to those in need. Frida would give prodigally to the poor overseas through the "missions;" and Tom had thousands of dollars owed him by co-workers down on their luck. He took exorbitant pride in giving, sensing that it was a high human moment. "Put me down for fifty cents," he'd boom when neighbors would solicit for this or that charity.

We were all perfectly aware and deeply pained by the imperfections of Frida and Tom—their marriage was sometimes stormy, contentious, unhappy. But toward others, especially the poor and outcast, they were people of towering compassion and justice.

Their example, never formal, never a matter of preachment, penetrated the lives of all six of us, by a kind of subtle, moral osmosis. None of us has ever shown interest in "making it," making peace with the idols of the culture. Four of us have worked consistently with the poor; and that same four have resisted a social dis-order that the war game is. Furthermore, we have joined the poor in jail—a most unpopular place for the unpoor.

Our parents taught us that, properly speaking, only God "owns." Yet God acts as though owning nothing—always giving, always sharing. We humans have nothing we have not received—from God, from family, friends, community. We possess only what we give away—materiality, learning, skill, virtue, any aspect of our being. Paul reminds us that we are not our own; that we belong twice to God (twice to the human family)—once by creation, once by ransom.

All this flies in the teeth of the North American obsession with property, a sickness, a social disease. The disease exposes itself, above all, in the means we take to defend what we possess—38,000 nuclear warheads, a Rapid Deployment Force (Central Command), scores of overt and covert wars of intervention, more money invested in war in the last forty years than the military investments of the rest of the world combined. If the North American disease is the addiction to property, the disease is also the means to defend it. The disease is like the worst of addictions; we are on a high over "things;" we are on a high over killing to protect these things.

By implication, our parents taught us that wealthy Americans (often avowed Christians) do not hesitate to rewrite the Bible, making it possible to possess God and mammon, the fruit of exploitation, at the same time. Ross Perot, the Texas billionaire, reportedly remarked that it was nice to have God on your side, but nicer to have him on your payroll.[1]

Finally they taught us that one cannot honor the first beatitude without resisting the state, the patron of those who aspire to own the earth, and crush the poor. We have learned, and we resist.

From the beginning of our Jonah House community in 1973, we have tried to honor and preserve these values of poverty and resistance to the causes of poverty.

## OUT OF THE SOLITARY, SELFISH LIFE INTO COMMUNITY

A ceramic sculpture of the prophet Jonah, made by two Latin American artists, sits on the mantel in the living room at 1933 Park Avenue, Baltimore, Maryland. Half of "Jonah" is Jonah's head. A sour expression clouds his face. He holds the city of Ninevah on his arm. The whale grins at his feet, glad, we assume, to be relieved of its burdensome cargo.

Jonah was a gift from Dan Berrigan in May 1973. The ceramic came to Baltimore with us in June. "Jonah" was enthroned some three weeks before he gave his name to the new community effort and to the place that was his home. Jon Bach, a remarkable young brother who shared the Danbury prison years

---

[1] Ivins, Molly. "Small Favors." *The Progressive*. February 1987. p.18.

with Dan and Phil, together with Liz and Phil formed the new Baltimore community. Jon first suggested that we call the new community JONAH HOUSE. "Jonah could be our mascot. After all, if God could use Jonah for his work, there is hope for us, too!" (Jon, a year or so later, was to call his new community in Hartford, Connecticut, "The Whale's Tale" to express its complementarity to Jonah House.)

The idea for Jonah House was conceived at least a year earlier by a dozen or more people who came together in New York City.[2] All had been deeply involved in the Harrisburg Trial;[3] each was searching for a new direction. All came from recent experiences with civil disobedience (as we then termed it) and prison.

From the "Baltimore Four" action of defacing draft files with blood in October 1967 to the "Camden 28" in August 1971, there were 200 or more acts of civil disobedience, direct actions against the Selective Service System, government offices, and war corporations. Each was performed by a distinct community of people; each community had its own style and personality. The relationship among these communities, which the federal government tried so hard to pin down during the Harrisburg trial, was of a common spirit and outlook. We were indeed

---

[2] Phil was still in Danbury prison serving a six-year sentence for destroying draft files in the "Customs House" action and the "Catonsville 9" action. It was Liz who met with this group and whose recollections serve here.

[3] In November 1970, J. Edgar Hoover, making a claim to Congress for additional F.B.I. funding, spoke of the need for additional monies because of a threat to this country coming from "The East Coast Conspiracy to Save Lives," a radical Catholic group headed by the Berrigans who, Hoover claimed, planned to kidnap a high government official and blow up selected targets in Washington, D.C. An indictment to the same effect was handed down in January 1971; it was superseded in March 1971; in January 1972, seven people including Phil and Liz went on trial in Harrisburg, Pennsylvania, on charges of conspiring to destroy draft files in seven states and thirteen cities. The trial lasted five months and ended in a hung jury.

conspirators, but in a sense that J. Edgar Hoover never understood.

To one degree or another, the people who came together in New York City had been moved by that spirit. Initial meetings were spent reflecting on recent events and on the choices and challenges before us. In weekly meetings we studied our options:

> George McGovern was running for president on the promise to end the war in Indochina. We contributed to that effort in whatever way each of us could while conscious that our support involved a great deal of compromise with both religious and political convictions. Conventional politics, we knew, could never be more than an aside in our lives.
>
> Two or three of our friends were at that time paid staff with one of the national peace organizations. The struggles and compromises they made daily in their work clarified the situation: while such work was good and qualified as service, it did not meet the yearning that had brought us together. We had some experience of displacement; we needed a life that would be faithful to that experience of poverty, a life that would carry us more deeply into solidarity with the poor rather than entrench us further in the values of the culture.
>
> It would be fine to invest our time speaking with groups, leading retreats, even writing about our experiences; but such teaching would be authentic only if we continued to struggle and to act. Such was our instinct. We needed to stand back, to reflect more deeply, to understand more clearly what our lives had meant to date. There was much that was still too new, too close to understand.

The character of that circle was unique; all were marginalized people. For one reason or another, the old order had both failed us and squeezed us out. We recognized that as gift and grace. We also sensed the need for some breakthrough, some new source of energy and direction for ourselves and, in time, perhaps, for others—a future not determined by or even derived from the present.

We chose to explore building a nonviolent movement in our country. That meant developing resistance communities whose members would learn nonviolence as it applied to their own lives as well as to the public arena. Communities, the vision went, would study the sources of nonviolence and resistance, would look at current events and appropriate responses, would explore resources, personal and communal, for confronting or diminishing violence. Such communities would relearn our cultural heritage and find ways to reduce complicity in institutionalized violence.

In fine, we made a commitment to come out of isolation and learn together; to become, at least for the time being, an intentional community.

The study began. We sought to feel in our own flesh and spirit the violence of our culture. As we did so, the need for a community or communities of nonviolent resistance became real to us.

North Americans, we learned, have inherited a legacy of violence. We came to understand that My Lai was no aberration; it took its place in a litany with so many other names and places: Orangeburg, Kent State, Attica, and back through Selma, Wounded Knee, Haymarket, to the very foundations of our nation.

Even as we met, Americans were living under an ongoing war and war economy; war and war preparations constituted some sixty percent of the national budget, militarism and consumerism at peak; twelve percent of the work force earned at least part of its livelihood from war-related work. Moreover, people willingly referred to themselves (which is to say accepted their identity) as consumers. A sense of powerlessness gnawed at many good and decent people.

A consensus formed: people are crushed when there is no community to mediate the needs of the world and to respond to those needs. The evidence mounted as we continued our meetings. The evidence underscored a need for something new, for the empowering of people. How could men and women live humanly in these times? "The American Way," like a magnet, drew people into itself and wasted them. The only hope seemed to be the creation of a counter force called community. As soon as people can speak of a "WE," they transcend individual limitations and begin to answer the needs, the pain of others.

Resistance, we thought, given the times, was not a luxury but a necessity for decent human life. More and more clearly we saw our responsibility to experiment with aspects of sanity against the insanity of life under the bomb.

As we went on, our fledgling community committed itself to the tasks of helping to form other resistance groups, of submitting ideas about process, and of serving as a resource as long as our help seemed useful. Our credentials for this work were simply our lives: our experiences with nonviolence, with resistance, with community, and our reflections on those experiences. But we also made the commitment to continue both action and reflection.

Meanwhile, a similar process was occurring in Danbury prison, where Dan and Phil met regularly with their brother prisoners. Naturally, their meetings were more intense than were those of us on the outside. The prison community at Danbury relied on Bible study, prayer, political meetings, and action. During 1972, the community of ten to twelve prisoners met four or five times weekly. Action included protests such as anti-war fasts, refusal to work in war-related prison industries, and a nonviolent work-strike that neutralized the prison for eight days. (All these actions were punishable by solitary confinement, punitive transport, and possible loss of parole.)

As these men were released, many hoped to continue the process on the street. Phil was released in December 1972, and he began a parallel process of community building in Baltimore. It was there that the efforts of the Danbury group and the New York group converged.

We called our effort "Community Development." Though we thought it a new concept, we learned of the development of base communities throughout Latin America, communities that have been the backbone of "conscientization." Then Liz read Eric Fromm's *Let Man Prevail: A Socialist Manifesto and Program*,[4] in which he advocated a process like the one we had undertaken. It is Fromm's conviction that base communities are indispensable to sanity. Ideas and insights converged. We felt affirmed in the rightness of and the need for just such a process.

In the early meetings at Jonah House, a few theoretical and practical principles were hammered out:

—Nonviolence, resistance, and community are interchangeable—their effects are identical.
—Contemplation (in whatever form—prayer, meditation, reflection, analysis) gives sustenance to spirit and resistance.
—Holding property in common is essential to justice.
—The Scriptures hold the vision of a society faithful to God whose members are loving toward each other, reverent toward all of life.

Before we made the move into a community house, certain practical questions had to be faced. These had to do with location, the issues of privately owned versus rental property, urban versus rural setting, and whether to adopt a single community house or a cluster concept. Those who met in New York were certain that the City was not the place for us to begin. The expense was forbidding, as was the exhaustion endemic to life there. Baltimore was less costly; inexpensive housing was still abundant; there were good friends; there was room to work. Further, Phil was limited to Baltimore by his parole conditions. Altering his location could focus more attention on our effort than was desirable.

After some soul-searching on the issue of ownership, we chose rental property. As a strictly economic consideration,

---

[4] Fromm, Eric. *Let Man Prevail: A Socialist Manifesto and Program*. A Doubleday Anchor Book. New York. 1961.

ownership would have been preferable. But the question was also one of spirit and of resistance. Property, as we saw, readily takes a hold on the soul. The roles too easily reverse themselves; owned becomes owner. Furthermore, what we don't own, the government can't seize.

Some longed for a rural setting, dreamed of gardens, animals, fresh air; others preferred an urban community. That issue resolved itself. Rural property with proximity to cities where resistance was required was either unavailable or too costly. So we settled in Baltimore, among the urban poor of Baltimore. In the inner city of Baltimore, we hoped, we could make God's compassionate presence visible. Here the "why" of our life is still ever present, unavoidable.

## OUT OF LAZINESS OF MIND AND BODY INTO LEARNING AND UNDERSTANDING GOD'S WORD

A vision that binds people together is often put on paper before it can be lived. As a dream is talked through, both unity and differences emerge. The splits and spin-offs begin. That, as we came to understand, is healthy. If it is handled well, conflict can be a source of clarification and growth.

The New York community became two communities about four months into the clarification process. Some from the original circle were still struggling with the vision; others heard of the process and joined because the vision was already, even if vaguely, a part of them. The former would continue searching; the latter would take concrete steps toward community development.

Within the latter group the vision became crystalized; but only a few were ready for the radical displacement that a move into community entailed. Further differences surfaced as we began to act on the vision. The early years were painful. The journey into community took unexpected turns and involved us in profound solitude and loneliness.

Those who began their journey with us were shortly to be tested. Liz and Phil were excommunicated from the Roman Catholic Church after their marriage in 1973. The censure was automatic. They learned of it through the press.

A priest who had shared—spearheaded even—the process toward community received pressure from his bishop and his family to distance himself from Jonah House. That pressure, joined to his need for prayer and solitude, led him to leave the community. His departure was the first of many comings and goings, each involving some degree of judgment, anger, hurt.

There is a human tendency—we know it well in ourselves—to rationalize these "failures," to blame the other: he or she didn't pray enough, didn't measure up to expectations, wasn't really committed. But the truth we've had to stand under repeatedly is that we are irritable, demanding, hard to live with. There were times which exceeded all healthy self-criticism; we were tempted to rewrite our lives, as it were. We wished we had handled some relationships differently. There were days, weeks, months even, when friends refused to meet, when people who had shared the same faith showed only distrust and hostility, when no one came near us.

Simultaneously, the war in Southeast Asia ground on, the war against which the community had formed. Resistance had "lost its sex appeal," as the journalists put it. Editors agreed: the age of protest was a phenomenon of the Sixties. It seemed that nothing could alter the conclusion.

Through the summer of 1973, people prayed daily at the White House over the escalating air war in Vietnam. There were daily arrests; people were tried; many were jailed for brief periods. With friends from the Community for Creative Nonviolence (CCNV) in Washington, D.C., we from Jonah House brought a globe, carved like a turkey, to Henry Kissinger's home on Thanksgiving Day. At Christmas, we enacted a medieval morality play, "Herod and the Kings," at the White House, connecting the feasts of Christmas and the Massacre of the

Innocents.[5] Dolls, broken and bloodied, were deposited on Nixon's lawn to recall the continuing massacre of the innocents.

Through Lent of that year, our two communities mounted a series of direct actions connecting the war in Indochina with North America's support of tyrants abroad and with the war against the poor at home. (Allende had been assassinated with CIA and NSA[6] support. This we exposed in the only demonstration held at NSA headquarters.) Holy Week brought the first action in which actors faced serious consequences (longer jail terms) at the Vietnamese Overseas Procurement Office. Holy Week also brought the birth of Frida Berrigan, our first child.

Friends began to consider and counsel other, less costly forms of commitment. Indeed, Liz was also drawn apart; weariness and cowardice entered. Her mother urged a teaching position, quiet. "You've done your part," she said. In any case, Mother's suggestion was no longer an option for us. We had walked too far along the road of resistance to be able to turn back.

Our marriage was a grace. Seldom, if ever, did we face discouragement and dread simultaneously. We were able to keep each other's courage up, to gain new perspectives, new energy. Love called us to reject inertia, to begin again. And Dan offered light, encouragement, and hope more often than we can remember. In Syracuse, Jerry and Carol Berrigan's home was a second home for us where we could unpack the baggage we carried, where we could probe better ideas and recover strength.

Prayer—personal and communal—put our problems in perspective. The Eucharist, which we celebrated together at least weekly, reminded us anew of both the promise and the demands of justice, and the freedom and fellowship toward which we struggled.

---

[5] The Feast of the Massacre of the Innocents recalls Herod's order to kill all the boy babies two years of age or under in and around Bethlehem in his effort to kill the child born "King of the Jews." Matthew, 2:16-18. These children are the first martyrs, the innocents destroyed by the powerful.

[6] NSA is National Security Agency, at Fort Meade in Maryland.

During those early years there was never a question of simple progress in one direction. There were layers upon layers of solitude and loneliness, profound yearning for community, moments when we were blessed with a sense of community, only to undergo a bitter cycle again. Maybe in all of this we learned to be a little less baffled by recurring loneliness, trusting in God's designs through it all.

There were big decisions, moments in which nothing was clear except the decision that must be made. In 1974, James Schlesinger announced the alteration of America's nuclear policy from the stance of MAD (Mutually Assured Destruction)[7] to FTO (Flexible and Strategic Targeting Options.)[8] Here and there news analysts unpacked and translated this change. It meant that nuclear war was both more probable and more imminent because limited nuclear war seems a more acceptable option than all-out nuclear war; because aiming at military targets sounds like the way a war should be waged; because it seems more humane than obliterating population areas. As members of our community and friends read and reflected on these accounts, we became acutely aware that the nuclear arms race had escalated, while our attention and that of virtually all the anti-war element in this country had been focused on Indochina.

Meetings were set up. Communities were encouraged to educate themselves about this new threat and to begin exploring ways to stand against it.

Then another split. The CCNV community, with whom we had worked so closely, opted to focus on world hunger. Jonah

---

[7] This policy implied the threat of mutual annihilation that was supposed to keep both the U.S. and the U.S.S.R. from first use of nuclear weapons. It was this principle upon which the first Strategic Arms Limitation Talks (SALT) were based.

[8] FTO is the basis of our Counterforce Policy with regard to nuclear weapons. It involves the targeting of Soviet weapons, bases, and munitions plants rather than cities; it involves the threat to use nuclear weapons in what has become known as "limited nuclear war scenarios."

House would remain with the Vietnam focus, while preparing through prayer, study, and reflection to address the nuclear threat.

The ouster of American troops from Indochina in April 1975 coincided with the birth of our son, Jerome, and with the initiation of our community's anti-nuclear work. We began with silent vigils at the homes of Schlesinger, Kissinger, and Donald Rumsfeld. Then we acted at the White House with the call "DISARM OR DIG GRAVES." Then we began to direct our resistance to the Pentagon, which remains a primary focus for us.

Insights are won slowly, if at all. Do we make connections? Or do connections make us into the people we are to be? The difference may be subtle or great. In any case, hindsight teaches that nothing is accidental, nothing is a chance throw of the dice. Even the "bad news" is often an occasion through which the Lord relentlessly pursues those whom he will draw to himself.

On January 20, 1977, Phil was again in prison. Reading The Washington Post was, he said, like gazing at the entrails of the society. "Plans for Evacuation in Nuclear War Studied." An augury of things to come. Phil made this entry in his journal:

> The article stated that the Pentagon expected to spend $50 million for "Crisis Relocation Planning" in the next four years, to heat up the Cold War, to counteract an alleged Soviet investment of $1 billion a year and a "vast Soviet evacuation plan." So, in the event of a nuclear war, with D.C. as a prime target, residents would be routed out to counties in Virginia and West Virginia as far as 200 miles away.
> 
> The article failed to mention or evaluate another Pentagon proposal to use abandoned mine shafts as fallout shelters, an old idea every bit as absurd as this new one. Nor did the journalist seek to understand or explain the evacuation plans as yet another Pentagon ploy to heat up the stew of cold war and spoon-feed the public with it.

At least once a year—sometimes several times a year—for thirty-two years to this date, Pentagon officials come out with a new crisis and ring up thumping sales. Their pitch has not only kept our "defensive arms" strong, but it also has been a sure-fire way of creating an enemy.

The propaganda aired in this article fashioned two assumptions into facts: that the Russians aim beyond weapons parity to weapons superiority; and that Russian civil-defense efforts are evidence of their preparations for nuclear war.

Despite the opportunism of the Soviets and the tendency of their national-security managers to think like their North American counterparts, American military and news media tiresomely and grossly abuse the facts. The facts are: the Russian military effort has been, by and large, a desperate attempt to keep pace with the phobic American development; weapons superiority, from whichever side, means nothing in light of incalculable overkill and the vulnerability of retaliatory systems; and Russian civil-defense systems, futile on whatever scale of development, are a reaction to American nuclear saber rattling, especially to the first-strike capability America now seeks.

The absurdity of the civil-defense concept is never analyzed. In crises, the Pentagon relies on two to three days to evacuate our cities. The Cuban Missile Crisis is commonly used as an historical example of that time span. But it is seldom said that there was no evacuation of American cities during the Cuban crisis. Moreover, the two to three days might have been consistent with "Mutually Assured Destruction" in vogue in 1963, but it is utterly inconsistent with the FTO announced by Schlesinger in 1974. In light of FTO, such an evacuation would give evidence to the Soviets that the U.S. is close to first strike, an evidence so conclusive as to tempt them to strike first.

In any case, MAD or FTO, why would civilians abandon their homes for absurdly inadequate protection? Why move at all, when official estimates range from 100 million to 150 million casualties, and when the ensuing devastation—always unmentioned—will be harrowing enough to make living dead of the survivors?

The lunacy of "crisis relocation planning" was especially real for Phil. His experience of the devastation of World War II gave him imaginative access to the unimaginable, gave him avenues to compassion in face of the unknown.

"While in Britain in early 1944," he wrote, "I was assigned to pick up supplies for our battalions' move to the continent; and in the process I visited a score of major cities. I viewed the remains of Hitler's battering air war. Later I saw even worse in Normandy and Brittany, in all of northern France, in the Low Countries, and in northern Germany. In Germany, the devastation was almost total. Some major cities still stank with corpses decaying in the rubble. It vaguely seemed to me, even then, that what Hitler did to Britain, we perfected on the continent. I recalled reading in *Yank* Pope Pius XII's condemnation of Allied carpet bombing: '. . . the seeds of the next conflict are already being sown.' "

"My experience with the military violence," Phil freely admits, "left me ridden with scars; left me joyless and bewildered. I could be excused, I suppose, burdened as I was with the twin legacies of Catholicism and Irish Americanism. Both minorities sought acceptance and equality and encouraged fervent support of the war in our WASP-dominated country. Moreover, my older brothers—three of them—were 'serving their country' with distinction, in regular Army service before Pearl Harbor, in overseas duty, in no less than four invasions—Africa, Sicily, Italy, Normandy. But my experience in violence left me covered with scars, uncertain, and bewildered. Well can I comprehend today the hell from which so many Vietnam veterans struggle to extricate themselves.

"Only later did I learn that our airborne, scorched-earth policy stiffened and prolonged both the German and Japanese resistance, and cost millions of lives. Like many, I learned too the extent to which North America itself became Nazi in those days. The Allies, especially the Americans, absorbed Hitler's methods like precocious, criminal children. Saturation bombing led logically to Hiroshima and Nagasaki and to insane nuclear diplomacy. Josef Goebbels, Hitler's minister of propaganda, had been prophetic when he said: 'Even if we lose, we shall win, for our ideals will have penetrated the hearts of our enemies.' "[9]

Dan was one of two Berrigan sons not involved in military service. (Jim's injured back was cause for his exemption.) Probably Dan's health would also have eliminated him, but as a young Jesuit he was granted a clergy deferment. That Dan questioned the war effort even while his brothers' lives augmented it is likely, but he neither censured them nor vented his reservations on them.

With the end of World War II, the time was ripe for Phil to begin anew, to learn, with brothers and whoever would seek with him, what it all meant—for the U.S., for the Church, for humanity. Jerry and Phil were most receptive of Dan's influence in those years, through college and even more through seminary (Jerry and Phil studied together for the priesthood in the Josephite Seminary). As a creative spirit, as an active and critical mind, Dan was light and strength to them and to the whole family. He broke spiritual and intellectual ground for them, counseled them, suggested reading, advised directions for ministry, and always remained comrade and brother.

The growing relationship among the maturing brothers, their study, conversation, prayer, became the ground upon which—without even having a vocabulary for it—they resisted the homogenization of postwar America.

> Again from Phil's journal:
> After ordination to the Josephites in 1955, I was assigned to Our Lady of Perpetual Help Parish in S.E. Washington, D.C. There I did relief work among the black poor; formed groups of lay people who ministered to the spiritual and

---

[9] Mayer, Milton. *They Thought They Were Free: The Germans 1933-45.* University of Chicago Press, 1955. p. 339.

physical needs of others; promoted integration and black civil rights, and learned about my ignorance in depth—ignorance of my people, of the system, of American racism.

For the next twelve years, black people became my mentors; they taught me about my whiteness. Years later the lessons invited this conclusion: In those days I probably served the white plutocracy better than I served my people. While I served them, in true Josephite fashion, seven days a week, I rarely fought for or with them. I rarely defended them except by word. I was too innocent and too docile.

They taught me about their blackness—that the wealth of this country was founded on their blood, sweat, and tears. They taught survival without capitulation, because they lived it.

They taught hope and nobility and the value of suffering under none-too-subtle racism. Other peoples have met extinction under the white Bible, the white gun and whiskey, but blacks survived and multiplied "as a testimony against them."

They taught me most about religion, how the Bible exposes hypocrisy and murderousness, and blesses the power of sanity and resistance.

They taught that this country, this empire, is a malign enemy of human variety. "You'd better watch out," they said to me. "You'll get in the way. You can be a nigger too, even with that white skin. Then they'll stomp on you like a banker stomps on a cockroach in his kitchen."

I heard that morsel of wisdom in 1961 from a black matriarch in New Orleans. And from others, before and since. Not long afterward, I began experimenting with "getting in the way," however feebly and tentatively. I began to understand the call to poverty and what it implies.

## OUT OF ARROGANCE INTO THE MYSTERY OF INTERDEPENDENCE

We reap what we sow. Farmers know this without being told. Steel and concrete, fast-food stores and supermarkets, assembly lines, and mass transit encourage us to forget this truth only to our ruin.

When we were at dinner one evening with friends, the truth returned to haunt us. We had gathered with Monsignor Joe Gallagher of Baltimore, respected poet and brother of Attorney Frank Gallagher, (Frank worked with our legal team at the Harrisburg Trial. He died suddenly during the selection of the jury.) At the Baltimore supper, Joe introduced us to Dr. Hiltgunt Zassenhaus. This remarkable German ministered with great fidelity and tremendous personal courage to Scandinavian prisoners of war. She held an official position as interpreter and representative of the Nazi regime. Under that cover and at great risk, she brought food, medical supplies, and news to the prisoners.

Phil asked Hiltgunt that night: "What would you say to Americans, to those struggling against the American empire and its militarism?" "Nothing measures a person," she responded, "like their *NO* to evil and to death. That is what reveals the value they place on life." After lengthy rumination and sharing, she said, "If you carry Hitlerism far enough, it ends in the bomb!"

By that time, early 1980, it appeared that a slow public awakening had begun—a gathering sense that people and the bomb cannot co-exist. The awakening was due to a deeper grasp some were gaining of the reality of the bomb. When Alamogordo, Hiroshima, Nagasaki, and the lethal aftermath were learned, people grew more thoughtful. The bomb, we discovered, was the empire's monologue. It was a symbol of the state's malign will to place people on borrowed time, mark them as living dead—enslaved and futureless.

Four of us reflected that evening on the thirty-five years since World War II. The bomb had extended its sovereignty and domination like some planetary epidemic. It had become foreign policy for the U.S. and the U.S.S.R.; it had inspired a competition or "vertical proliferation." Meanwhile the nuclear club spread to country after country in what is termed "horizontal proliferation." In this way the bomb catalyzed vicious, sustained local wars and sponsored a flood of conventional arms sales all over the world.

We saw the bomb invade whole cultures, sapping their humanizing and civilizing elements. We saw it dehumanizing religion, destroying true education, making the law an empty caricature, and turning our planet into a frenzied madhouse, a savage powder keg.

But the focus of talk as we gathered that night was an expose that joined Hiltgunt's concern as a physician to ours as antinuclear activists. Americans, she said, could afford to ignore people still dying from the blasts in Hiroshima and Nagasaki, dying from the cancer those tragedies induced. But now North Americans also died of cancer in alarming numbers. We began to tally the evidence, the connection between the bomb and this domestic epidemic of cancer.

Phil cited an incident at Yucca Flats, Arizona, in August 1957. Three thousand G.I.s were charged to wait a few thousand yards from a steel tower holding "Smokey," a forty-four-kiloton atomic bomb. The G.I.s were in fact reduced to specimens; they would answer, in their afflicted bodies, questions asked at council tables about the effects of nuclear weapons in combat situations.

At the Yucca Flats experiment Paul Cooper of the 82nd Airborne turned his back and covered his eyes as commanded. "I could see the bones in my hands like an x-ray when the bomb went off," he said. Cooper has since died of leukemia, as did many of the 450 veterans of Operation Smokey.

That night we were able to list some 183 incidents between 1946 and 1964 in which the U.S. exploded nuclear devices in the atmosphere. Half a million Americans were exposed directly during these tests. Thousands died prematurely or suffered serious illness from contact with these blasts.

Hiltgunt referred to a map put out by the Cancer Institute; it depicted the above-average rates of cancer mortality. The map, covering the years 1950 to 1969, shows, county by county, the elevated cancer-mortality rates that occur near operating nuclear-power plants. Nevada is prominent because of the atmospheric testing done there. The Northeast has the highest concentration of cancer mortality. "Let's take Millstone," Phil added, "Connecticut's nuclear-power plant at Waterford. Between 1970 and 1975, cancer deaths in Waterford rose fifty-eight percent; in New London, forty-four percent; New Haven, twenty-seven percent; Connecticut, twelve percent overall. And around Connecticut's power plants, high levels of Strontium 90 appeared in the milk of goats and cows."

"Then there's West Valley, New York," Liz added. "There a private industry, Nuclear Fuel Services, attempted to reprocess spent nuclear fuel. They had 1,400 part-time workers, mostly teenagers from Buffalo. Often the NFS exposed them to one-fourth of a permissible yearly dose of radiation in fifteen minutes and then fired them. Dr. Irwin Bross, a cancer expert from Buffalo, called this 'the most callous use of human beings since the slave trade.' "

"The limiting factor in reprocessing," Phil continued, "isn't physics. It's human beings. You can't reprocess waste without killing people."[10]

Then someone quoted an estimate of the Environmental Protection Agency. 21,000 people are dying annually from low-level radiation emission; another 13,500 suffer serious sickness from power-plant seepage. "It is generally accepted," said Hiltgunt, "that ninety percent of all cancers are from environmental sources."

Phil began to talk about the bomb, a spiritual as well as physical one, a theme that occupied him more and more. "Maybe we can say that those in whom the bomb has set up unquestioned housekeeping—and here I think of some of our politicians and generals and those who make a cult of nuclear

---

[10] When NFS found that strict regulations concerning waste cut into profits, it closed down, pushed three million cubic yards of low-level waste into a shallow trench, and covered the trench with tons of dirt. Radiation has leaked into the water tables, and Nuclear Fuel Services runs scot-free. Radioactive filth is now the problem of the people in the area.

technology—are victims of a deformity of spirit similar to cancer.

"The prologue of John's Gospel," he went on, "tells us that the Light of God (truth) is the life of people, the life of the human spirit. In the bomb's disciples, a militarism of spirit substitutes for truth. And it resembles the runaway cells, the tumors, the lesions so common in cancer patients."

Similarly, it could be said, those who support the bomb impose a personal death wish and collective suicide wish upon others. Perhaps this is analogous to a despairing attraction for death in some cancer patient or to incidents of euthanasia and suicide as some seek to avoid hopelessness and suffering. In cancer, the body sometimes drags down the spirit; in the bomb the spirit draws the body of humanity toward death.

We didn't know it that night or it would have been part of our sharing, (or it might have terminated a fine evening prematurely). Sr. Rosalie Bertel of Toronto, Canada—an internationally recognized geneticist—has revealed a phenomenon among Marshall Islanders. As a result of atmospheric tests of nuclear weapons, women there are giving birth to what has been termed "jellyfish babies,"[11] hairy masses of flesh with one eye and no limbs who die as soon as the umbilical cord is severed. The women in their shame and guilt bury them surreptitiously, and many subsequently contract deadly vaginal cancer. Because of the stigma attached to bearing such children, it remains impossible to determine either the percentage of such births or their overall number.

With each step we took toward a deeper understanding of the bomb and of resistance to it, the truth became harder and harder to ignore. By one of those strange twists in life by which the Lord keeps beckoning his people, the bomb has become a

---

[11] Spencer, Metta. "Low Level Radiation and Species Death Syndrome." (Interview with Sister Rosalie Bertel.) *Peace Magazine*. May 1985. p.20. Also *Pacific Women Speak*. Edited by Women Working for an Independent and Nuclear Free Pacific. Green Line. Oxford, England. 1987. p. 8.

counter-grace in our lives. Nothing else has driven us so often to our knees. Nothing else has revealed so vividly our need, a need so desperate it finds expression only in the Psalms. The bomb more than anything else produces a poverty of spirit, a need of God that brings us low, low indeed.

The bomb has led us to search for the truth of God's Word, which calls us to abhor falsehood, especially falsehood from state and Church. The bomb, as symbol and agent of the counter-Crucifixion, leads us to accept Christ's Cross as life, justice, salvation. By its very extravagance, the bomb teaches us frugality of life, poverty of spirit.

We inched toward this truth. To believe in God is to live our lives as a gift, and to regard all that happens as a manifestation of that gift. Slowly we came to understand our arrogance—hubris, the Greeks called it. When we go beyond the human measure, reality has a way of bringing us to heel. When we believe ourselves to be Titans and act accordingly, we are shortly reduced to our true helplessness. It is exactly in that helplessness that one lives the first beatitude.

> *Blessed are those who mourn,*
> *for they shall be comforted.*
> Matthew, 5: 4.

## CHAPTER TWO
# THOSE WHO MOURN

Some spiritual writers suggest that the Beatitudes are not eight distinct attitudes, eight keys, so to speak, to our ultimate—and even to our immediate—happiness. Rather, the beatitudes represent a way of maturing in the Christ life. If that is the case, and we believe it is, then through poverty and displacement, mourning becomes part of us. The reality of poverty and need touches our heart. And we know, as some translate this Beatitude, "what sorrow means."

A cherished brother, Dean Hammer, has acted repeatedly and with great personal risk in "The Plowshares 8"[1] in 1980 and the "Griffiss Plowshares 7"[2] in 1983. In a meeting prior to the Griffiss witness, he asked this question: "Where, physically,

---

[1] September 9, 1980, eight people damaged nose cones for the Mark 12A warheads in the first disarmament of nuclear weapons at the G.E. Reentry Plant in King of Prussia, Pennsylvania. See Appendix B, where this and other such actions are documented.

[2] November 23, 1983, seven people, in the sixth disarmament action, hammered on a B-52 bomber and component parts—the B-52 being the carrier-launcher of the air-launched cruise missile.

is conscience located?" As he posed the question, he held his gut and answered himself: "It is here!"

He is right. We feel something is wrong or right, even before we know it. When we grieve, when we anguish, we live in the gap between what is and what ought to be. Often, it is in the grieving itself that conscience is awakened, and urges us to seek God's justice. Comforting, as well as seeking solace, becomes a matter of righting a wrong (which is the source of the discomfort) and rejoicing when we are given the grace to act justly.

In 1976-1977 we learned some unforgettable lessons in mourning. It was a year in which, repeatedly, we experienced anger ripening into anguish. That year we learned from our own pain and hurt and loneliness that tears can transcend barriers as no harshness or anger can; that tears join pain to pain, when no other solidarity is possible.

By June 1976, the community at Jonah House was three years old. Already we had gone through some painful changes, and faced, however feebly, a measure of suffering and conflict. For example, a couple whose young marriage was already in rough water entered the community. They hoped our community would help them. We could not. We learned only after the fact that people were bringing their problems to us with hope that time and again proved vain. New members brought their difficulties with alcohol, with sexuality. Women came, emerging into a sense of themselves as lesbians; men came emerging as homosexuals, with all the dis-ease of that passage.[3] There were triangular relationships of love between men and women. Then there were folks who felt called to communities of resistance but could not cope with the city; they challenged us to found a rural community; and when we did not respond, they went

---

[3] The dis-ease was, we experienced, with themselves coming to terms with an identity they had long denied. We recall one young man announcing to the community that he was gay and telling us that we disapproved of his sexuality. We pointed out to him that he should not be telling us what we thought.

off to find or found such a community themselves—often to grave disappointment.

Often, through this time, we would sit and look at each other and wonder about our own sanity, about our culture, about the seeming futility of it all. But we would wonder too about people so broken who, despite all, still longed to embrace the suffering and brokenness of others, to make some positive difference in the world. Such friends seemed to personify this second beatitude.

By 1976, all this was behind us—lessons learned—or so we thought. Never for long. The community now included a strong core of people who, for the most part, had some wider experience of life, had made certain choices in their lives, and wished to give themselves to the service of others.

Ladon Sheats was one shining example. He had come to Jonah House in 1975 from the military, IBM (as a rising executive), and Koinonia Partners. He brought us a clear Biblical conscience and orientation. Joan Burds also arrived. She came from a family farm and twelve years of religious life. Jay Dudgeon was a gifted poet, musician, artisan, and loving brother. Joan Cavanagh, a native of Baltimore, had been involved most of her life in movement work, a woman of rare courage and clarity.

In 1976 we were joined by John Schuchardt, an ex-Marine officer, a practicing lawyer, and member of The Bruderhof, a rural pacifist community in Rifton, New York. That fall, Ched Myers came from a young community in Berkeley, California, for a stay of three months as part of an exchange experiment among several communities. Ched was one of three community members who were sent east; two were with the Sojourners Community and Ched was with us. The hope was that they would learn how others live in community and would bring that knowledge back to their communities, even as our communities would be enriched by their presence among us.

That year we began the first of a series of summer sessions of reflection and resistance. People were invited to come together for a ten-day period to reflect on the war/peace issues and to determine their response. Our idea was that people learn by doing, that they move from an idea of resistance to action through planning, working with others: whether with press, with police, or courts. (Too often, we thought, concerned people wait for an organization to call them to action or resistance when it is within the power of all to plan and to act.)

Then in October 1976 a tragedy struck us. Liz's twin sister died in Colorado. She took her own life out of a desperation we could only imagine. She left a husband, two young sons and her whole family wrestling with the questions and guilt that are the inevitable legacy of such a death.

This raw pain was still in us when we went to Syracuse for Christmas that year. Phil's mother, Frida, was on her deathbed. Phil and Jerry were with her as she died, and we celebrated her funeral on Christmas Eve. For years we had watched her nearing death's door; but no preparation was adequate for the finality, power, and loss of that moment. Phil's grief was frightening in its depth and intensity.

In her memory and for the sake of the children, Dan, Jerry, Liz, and Phil went to the Pentagon on December 28, the Feast of Holy Innocents, to express our anguish at the barter and slaughter of innocent lives. We were among forty people arrested for shutting workers out of the building for almost an hour and marking both major entrances with our own blood.[4]

---

[4] For Jews, blood was the vessel of the spirit, the vessel of life. For Christians, blood signs the new Covenant of justice and peace. The pact of sisterhood and brotherhood is sealed by Christ's blood. In both traditions, bloodshed (killing) is prohibited. "Thou shalt not kill!"

When resisters use blood as a symbol, poured on the Pentagon, White House, arms factory, or weapon, they assert several fundamental truths. First, this or that place or instrument is one of bloodshed and death. Second, the bloodshed must stop (the war preparations must stop). Third, the resisters will not shed blood, nor will they remain silent before the bloodshed of any government, corporation, institution, or person. Fourth, and implicitly, we must stop killing if we are to survive spiritually and physically on the planet. In brief, blood as a resistance symbol means "Stop the bloodshed. The

One hundred or more people maintained a vigil throughout the freezing day.

Up to that point our resistance to nuclear weaponry had been met by the courts in Alexandria[5] with tolerance, with a kind of fascination even, and with only ten-day sentences. Our presence even seemed a kind of relief to the court after the tedium of traffic and parking violations at the Pentagon. But this time the hammer came down. Judicial response to the Feast of the Innocents witness caught us off guard; we were sentenced to jail or prison for six months and four months, far longer than usual.

A mistake we make again and again, despite all experience, is to assume we can predict the courts' reactions. In cases of conscience, the only predictable response of the courts is their unpredictability, a characteristic shared by the Nazi courts under Hitler.

At any rate, in early January, Liz was sentenced to six months in prison. Phil and eight others, meantime, had traveled to Plains, Georgia. Their intent was to meet with the newly elected Jimmy Carter, to encourage his campaign commitment to a reduction of nuclear weapons, and to discuss with him, if possible, the Biblical and human urgency of that commitment. Their effort got nowhere. They were arrested and put in jail, even as friends in Alexandria were being imprisoned. Our preparation and rhetoric as both parents and community members were tested. Both Liz and Phil knew at gut level the truth of Wendell Berry's poem:

---

blood is yours!"

The use of the symbol of blood in resistance actions has been carefully weighed since the early 1980s because of the fear of transmission of AIDS through blood. While it may still be used on an inanimate object, a great deal more care is taken regarding the source of the blood and the explanation of it.

[5] The Pentagon is just far enough outside the District of Columbia to fall into the jurisdiction of the Northern District of Virginia, in Alexandria.

For parents, the only way
is hard. We who give life
give pain. There is no help.
Yet we who give pain
give love; by pain we learn
the extremity of love.[6]

Early in 1977, Liz wrote from jail:

> Jerome and Frida are not yet two and three years old. I am serving three months (reduced from six months) in jail in Alexandria, Virginia. By state law, no one under sixteen may enter these premises.
> 
> Frida seems to understand a great deal. She has seen others in the community go to jail, has known why they were there, has welcomed them home. But no one has been gone for three months and when a baby has lived short of two or three years, three months is a terrible slice of her life. When I told Frida, before the trial, that I might have to go to jail, she responded: "No! No!" as if her denial could be more stubborn than reality itself. Her denial continued for days, to be replaced by anger. But I can talk to Frida and she can understand.
> 
> Jerry—will he even remember a mother whom he hasn't seen for ninety days? He does not lack understanding. But he is under two. Communication with him is very physical. Since I cannot see him, hug, hold, or kiss him, how can I reassure him that I love him, that I have not abandoned him? Are both children apt to feel deserted, to believe that their mother and father no longer care for them? What is the potential for psychological damage from this separation?
> 
> I am more than a month away from them as I write. Neither child has forgotten. Recently I received word of

---

[6] Berry, Wendell. "The Way of Pain" *A Part*. Northpoint Press, San Francisco. 1980. p. 30.

Jerry crying in his sleep and saying "Mommy's in jail!" When awakened for comforting, he was fine, but once back asleep he repeated the sobbing and calling, several times. It isn't hard to be in jail; it is a different way of being. But being away from the little ones, unable to respond to Jerry's crying in the night, is terrible. Separation from Phil, while not easy, has been part of our life together, part of our contract with one another, the furnace in which our love is purified.

But what of the children? They both were born in a community committed to nonviolent resistance. They have been surrounded by people who love them, people who are, in every sense, extraordinary: committed, self-sacrificing, deeply spiritual women and men. Each of the adults has developed a unique relationship with the children, has shared in their upbringing, has become co-responsible for them. And this without any lack of clarity about, or sacrifice of, a primary relationship with mother and father.

Life has not centered on the children but their needs have been more than amply met, at times over-indulged. The convictions underlying their early education include the firm belief that children are not possessions but a gift of God. Moreover, these little people are symbols for us of all the little people for whom we are responsible. We share the conviction that we are mature only to the extent that we live for the next generation. Frida and Jerome keep that sense of responsibility before us always.

So many experiences have taught us that children need to see commitment lived out by those who love them. We recall the terrible dislocation and alienation of German youth after World War II as they realized that their parents were silent in face of Hitler's crimes in order to "protect" them. And the English children, rushed to the country to protect them from the daily bombings, fared not so well as those who risked death with their families. And on and on. Our resistance is perhaps our only armor against the hard "why" they will ask. It will enable us to invite them to share in the struggle against the forces of death.

The times are not normal, yet as human beings we are always seeking to normalize the times, to normalize our lives, to normalize even the unthinkable. In preparations for war, as in war itself, pain, separation, death, breakup of families is the price. Frida and Jerry have no more a birthright to normality than the orphans of Vietnam, than those starving in Southeast Asia, the Sahel, elsewhere; than the poor and dispossessed in the United States.

On January 7, when the judge said six months, it seemed that the fine base we had developed, evaporated. All I heard, though no one said it, was six months away from my children. I grabbed Frida, held her tight, and cried. I had requested four days to be with my family before beginning to serve my time. Four days to treasure intimacies, to mother them. And the children seemed to understand. Phil was facing two trials later that same month, with sentences inevitable from both—we couldn't guess how much. Then, on January 8, he was arrested in Plains, Georgia.

My six-month sentence was reduced to three months. I went to jail one day, Phil the next for a total of seventy days. The community was decimated. Joan Burds, Ladon Sheats, and John Ragusa were left at home. Though John was new to the house, Joan and Ladon were not. They knew and loved the children; there was little that needed to be said to them.

My first conflict came in recognizing that I was trying to direct the lives of the children from jail. Since the motivation for this was not lack of trust, I was forced to face my possessiveness—as if I and no one else could do right by them. Detachment comes hard, if at all; and I am not detached.

In a recent letter Ladon wrote: "We are discovering a whole new relationship with [the children]." I rejoiced as one rejoices in sharing a treasure, new insights enlarging it. Then his words took a different turn, eating like rot at my insides, and a second conflict was upon me. Didn't it threaten my special relationship with the children? I realized that the struggle against possessiveness of my children would be a long one. It cannot be resolved by willing it. Having seen it, I must wrestle with it and deal with dimensions of the conflict as they arise.

What will it be like to return to them? How will I respect the relations my sisters and brothers have developed? Will I work to further them, as I hope to do, or, however subconsciously, seek to subvert them, to make Frida and Jerry my children?

How do we know, do we ever know, what is best for our children? What is the pretension that we are indispensable in their lives?

At the time of sentencing I requested designation to a federal prison so that I might have contact visits with my children. The sentencing judge concurred and recommended Alderson. This initial recommendation never reached the marshal's office. The marshals refused to transport me, citing a ninety day cut-off point. Friends outside pressured for transfer; those of us in jail fasted and wrote letters. After thirty-two days, marshals came to transport me to Baltimore City Jail. "Your kids can visit you there; that's what you wanted, isn't it?" Through a glass pane, over a telephone, they can visit. But how does one explain to little ones, who are, in such matters, far more rational than their elders, that they cannot touch or hug Mommy? Explain the inexplicable! Orders were reversed during transport and I was returned to Virginia.

At the same time, Phil wrote from his own cell in his journal:

Elizabeth writes me from Alexandria Jail, where she begins a six-month sentence for dousing the Pentagon with blood. The sentence is gross and outrageous—for breaking the national unanimity and silence.

Liz and I have had our marriage interrupted by repeated imprisonment. Now, we have children, Frida (thirty-two months) and Jerry (twenty months), obviously not with us, but, rather, cared for by sisters and brothers in resistance at Jonah House.

Predictably, separation like this—from one another and from the children—is filled with anguish. Especially for Liz, who gave birth to Frida and Jerry with her blood, pain, and joy. The pangs of separation are proportionate to her investment.

Her anguish would also include concern for her mother and family—less well attuned than mine to prison as witness to the Lord. No doubt, too, she thinks of me, still assimilating the death of my mother, and now, perhaps, more temperate about the compensations of imprisonment for conscience.

I try to pray and think the matter through—what about the separation of war, often permanent, always tragic and deadly? What will peace require—how many separations, how much truth to counterbalance the colossal lie that is war? How much justice before the supreme injustice that is war? How many lives to be offered to God against the mad offerings to death, to Mars? To compute an equation is senseless, is faithless, I know. But the questions remain, made more nagging by the probability of nuclear war.

But I pray and think, nonetheless. We love our children and all children—that is why we are in resistance; that is why we are in jail. We cannot abandon the children; cannot trade them to Caesar for our immunity and comfort. And that love for them, and for the God who blessed us with them, will enrich their lives. So runs our hope.

I am as rash and importunate as Peter—*Lo, we have left everything and followed you!* Mark, 10: 28. (Peter had not put aside everything when he asked that question; nor have I.) But the hundredfold is sure for those who try to declare Christ: grace is sure to quiet the pain of our little ones, and to sustain us. His Word is surety to those who risk fidelity to his Lordship.

I have ample evidence of God's fidelity, of God's Spirit which is given to us. I have seen it compensate for my niggardliness repeatedly—in jail and out. And so, our children, while prison separates Liz and me from each other and from them, have the immediate love of the Jonah House community—more favored than most children with their parents at hand. Moreover, for love of children, that community gathers its witness again to speak publicly of truth, sanity, and compassion against a public scarred by a militarist spirit, and a state mad with corruption and blood lust.

Liz and I have pain, inconvenience. But what is it next to the pain of those in the Ukraine or Armenia or Indonesia or El Salvador or wherever the superpowers grind their iron heels? Perhaps, however, the Lord will show us what we must yet suffer.

We were reunited as family and community on Easter Sunday 1977. The children did not forget us. We were not strangers to them. None of our worst fears was realized. But we did commit ourselves to this: in the future, as far as we could control it (knowing that the day might come when such decisions were out of all control) we would arrange our participation in such actions so that at least one of us would always be with the children and available for the work of the community.[7]

From Liz's notes of this time, she recalls that one of the darker insights of such a jail experience as the one we endured in 1977 led to reflection on marriage and family in our culture. In jail, Liz met not one woman, inmate or guard who had a solid marriage or good relationship with a man. Few believed in marriage as an institution. To the women in prison, marriage

---

[7] The Jonah House community supports itself by contract painting. Its work includes that manual labor as well as educating, organizing, and acting for peace.

was a product sold with the laundry detergent on TV commercials, only another cultural myth. Not a few expressed awe that I wrote Phil and our children almost daily, that Phil and I were friends as well as lovers and partners in marriage. Phil's encounters were less stark, but this may have been due to women's tendency to be more attentive when the men they love are in prison than men are to their women when the roles are reversed.

Our jail experience led us to appreciate more deeply the blessing of our marriage, community, and family; it also invited a closer look into what might be called "Public Morality and the Family." The appraisal of psychologists and sociologists, that the bell tolls for the family, was starkly verified for us by sister and fellow prisoners.

The statistics are staggering in themselves. In the decade prior to 1977, divorce rates doubled in North America; birth rates declined. There was growing suspicion of marriage as a commitment, especially as a permanent commitment. The causes these facts point to are legion, and they go back to the last century.

During the early stages of the Industrial Revolution, production moved out of the home into factories; there, initially, men were subjected to tight supervision, an aspect of social control over activities hitherto left to individuals, families, and small communities. Home and family became a haven where the wife ministered spiritually to her husband, repairing the damage he endured in the market place. In the home, wives and mothers sheltered the children from the corrupting influence of the world. Then, accompanying and following industrialization, social control reached into the home itself and the private lives of people. Doctors, psychiatrists, teachers, child guidance experts, juvenile courts and other specialists began to supervise the raising of children. Later, TV further homogenized family life, undermining the family's capacity for self-direction and self-control.

In face of these despairing "givens" of sociology and psychology, we at Jonah House agonized about radical hope for marriage and family today.

Hope worthy of the name is rooted in shared memories and nourished on God's promises; so we sought our hope in the Scriptures.

The Gospels give little direct attention to the family. Christ, however, speaks repeatedly about God as sovereign parent of us all. Christ, Lord and brother, prepares the family to accept the entire human family. By symbol and definition, the one is microcosm of the other. This was our essential, by no means new, realization. From it flowed our longing and labor for the good of sisters and brothers, and our standing against the nuclear evil that threatens all.

Thus the family, in the light of the Gospel, sees itself as a community that embodies sisterhood and brotherhood. From this base, a rhythm of communion becomes possible with other people, with other families and, inevitably, with other nations.

The Lordship of Christ prepares family people for fidelity. Fidelity in the family includes, but goes far beyond, the sexual trust of wife and husband—the two in one flesh. The marriage, we realize, is in Christ; so is the fidelity. Then the suffering and sorrowing of all families become implicit in our family; their flesh is included in the flesh of husband and wife.

The Gospel does not permit abstraction when it speaks of terror, suffering, lonely death. It rather asks, "What will you do to protect God's daughters and sons? Where did you stand on that shameful war? What did you do to resist it nonviolently, and to stop it? Where do you stand on the bomb, on your country's militarism? What will you expend for your children and the children of the world, that they might have a chance to live?"

Christ summed up his expansive understanding the night before he died. He prayed that they all might become one in the Parent; even as he was one with his Parent, so that all people might believe that Jesus was sent by God. (A paraphrase of John, 17: 21.) What, we are led to wonder, can be the spirit of a marriage, its vision or purpose, if it is devoid of a sense of God, or divorced from suffering humanity.

The violence done against marriage and family through the Industrial Revolution reaches its climax in the violence wrought by the state today; and this despite all official rhetoric concerning the sacredness of the family. This was brought home to us in a vignette a couple of months after our term of prison in 1977.

Reading an issue of *The Bulletin of Atomic Scientists,* Phil came across an ad seeking parents of children aged three and under to become parties to a class-action suit against the U.S. government for violating our children's basic and primary right to life. Given the probability of nuclear war by the 1990s, scientists calculated that children three and under have five chances in a thousand of reaching maturity (and that apart from all other threats against the lives of children).

We discussed it and wrote immediately, eager to be part of such a suit. Within two weeks we got a response that dismissed us with gratitude, for lawyers had advised against filing such a suit. The incident gave us a new perspective on the government's usurpation of our children's most basic right. Under the propaganda of defense and deterrence, North Americans have been tricked into paying for their own destruction, the destruction of their own children.

Through our community study of Scripture, which we undertake twice each week, we began to make connections between the malaise that haunts the American family, and the primary source of that malaise, the state. Indeed, the Book of Revelation marks the state as the adversary of God's kingdom. For the state, power is more important than life; life is reduced to a means to power.

In the United States, the state has usurped the role of the Church as guardian of public morality. Its morality is that of pragmatism and expediency; the question dominating American imperial morality goes something like this: What means will maintain our status as number one military and commercial power, as number one consumer of the world's energy, food, raw materials, and services (although we number only six percent of the world's people)?

Individuals, families must break out of the death offered by the culture—a death springing from the abstraction which says in effect, "I can accept any horror as long as it doesn't touch me or my family." To be a spectator as the world lurches to self-destruction is to accept madness. Such a spectator role simply rationalizes collective insanity.

As families we keep the key commandments, love of God and love of sisters and brothers, only if God is sovereign in our lives. This implies a continuous dethronement of false gods.

Nor can we honor the fifth commandment—*You shall not kill.* Exodus, 20:13.—unless we give unequivocal rejection to the false gods of ego, government, money, security, irresponsible sex, the bomb. The prohibition against killing is also an essential application of the first commandment. We are forbidden to take human life, and governments are likewise forbidden to use capital punishment and war. The question therefore is an urgent one: how would government and the military conduct themselves if citizens honored the fifth commandment?

A common interpretation of the Sermon on the Mount speaks of "doing good" and "avoiding evil." The interpretation is ambivalent and deceptive. Good must be done, surely; but evil must be engaged and resisted. If evil is merely "avoided," it triumphs, spreading a deadly pall over everything, polluting and subverting the good. Warmakers welcome nothing so much as do-gooders intent upon avoiding evil. U.S. militarism, and the insane momentum toward nuclear holocaust, would never be possible without millions of do-gooders who avoid evil, and yet continue to pay their taxes, maintain public silence, vote with the ballot alone (instead of with their feet, bodies, lives) and place their hopes in the promises of self-serving politicians.

Our times, and our predicament and opportunity evoke the choice presented by God: *I call heaven and earth today to witness against you this day, that I have set before you life and death, blessing and curse; therefore choose life, that you and your descendants may live. . . .* Deuteronomy, 30:19.

Insights into the role of family in today's world prepared our community to welcome married people and families. So, perhaps, did our willingness to share our own pain, to make audible the suffering of separation from one another and children that are a significant part of parenting and peacemaking. We were giving marriage and family significant focus in lectures, writing, speaking. Whatever the movements of the Spirit in those days, in the period between 1978 and 1980 a number of young couples came to Jonah House. None of them remained. The reasons are obscure; but, however limited our own insights, they require some attempt at analysis.

We had evolved a procedure for those who were interested in joining our community. After some initial sharing, we'd invite them to "come and see" (usually for three months). At the end of that time, we would together decide whether the stay should be prolonged.

In 1978, two couples joined us. Each couple remained until 1979; then they departed to form a community in D.C. This new venture, in turn, lasted about a year. Both couples were gifted people who brought music, theater, and fun into our lives. One is tempted to wonder if the outcome would have been different if the circumstances of that year had been different:

Carl Kabat[8], an O.M.I. priest who joined the community in 1977, was given a year's sentence as a result of the Feast of the Innocents witness. He was in prison from December 1977, until October 1978. In April 1978, Phil, Ladon, John Schuchardt, and Ed Clark[9] were sentenced to six months each. The five became a small community in the Federal Corrections Institute, Allenwood, Pennsylvania. It was one of a number of times when our Baltimore community was devastated by prison.

---

[8] Carl was jailed repeatedly for his nuclear resistance and is now serving an **eighteen-year** sentence for his participation with the Silo Pruning Hooks (four people who disarmed a Minuteman Silo in Missouri in 1984).

[9] Ed was a younger resister who came to the community in 1977.

Liz was at home with three other adults and the children; two of the adults were the couple that had come to us in January. We were joined soon after by others, some coming for a limited stay, others with hopes to remain. We began as individuals and, inspirited by our brothers in prison, we quickly became a community. There was so much that was special in those days, deprived of those in prison on whom we had depended so much, we learned to depend on each other and to work well together.

Two people left after three months. The rest of us welcomed the brothers home from prison in October. But the two communities (older and newer) never became one. The newer folk regarded the returnees as "movement heavies." They became more silent, more withdrawn, sharing their counsel with one another rather than the whole community. The issue was one of experience, but it was also one of numbers; we have learned that our limit as community hovers around eight or nine adults. Physically the house cannot hold more without robbing people of the personal space which is so essential to the contemplative aspect of our life. A sit-down meal, for example, is not possible with more than that; and for us meals have become sacred times.

We came to learn that our community functions best with eight or nine members. If those numbers are exceeded, community suffers. Meetings become endless and more burdensome than need be; some members grow silent; those who speak with ease carry the day and the decisions. These decisions are not then community decisions, and some withdraw energy and will. It ceases to be a community breathing together at its greatest level of intensity. We knew all that. We had even shared that "wisdom" in retreats with others, but for some reason we chose not to heed our own advice.

The dis-ease grew around and within us. It came to a head on the day the first child was born to one of the couples. The birth was imminent; Phil and Liz left to lead a retreat in Massachusetts. We missed the baby's birth and the celebration that surrounded it. Our absence was resented, labeled as indifference to our community life, a "duty-first attitude." When we returned, it was as to a strange place; relationships were never the same. A decision had been made to begin a new community in D.C. after the new year.

An embarrassing memory of the time is the anger that ate at Liz. She had known a deeper intimacy with these folks and so felt the alienation more keenly. She felt rejected, not so much by their decision to begin anew elsewhere as by the process in which the decision was made. (Liz thought the decision should have been discussed thoroughly by the whole community.) Her anger drove the hurt deeper, increased the alienation. A chasm yawned between rhetoric and reality, between what is and what ought to be. She knew it, and recalled with pain her own "wisdom" written the previous year from jail:

## HOW COMMUNITY SHAPES OTHER COMMITMENTS

"What life have you if not life together?
There is no life that is not in community..." (T.S. Eliot)

A woman came to visit one day, a woman I'd very much like to know better. She had phoned me after my sentencing and offered to help with the children. She had recently left a community in D.C. because she found it authoritarian and confining. Her personal response to my sentence—a call to offer help with caring for Frida and Jerry—was put under criticism by her community. She had, they said, acted unilaterally.

Our commitments shape our communities. A community is conceived in a shared commitment; its vision holds it together; the "task" or "work" of the community flows from the vision, gives the community vitality, and serves, if all are patient and prayerful, to heal the wounds that flow from the variety of its members.

(In fact, her community misread the delicate balance between community conscience and individual conscience, dogmatizing the first and suppressing the second. In some areas, this led to autocracy, inflexibility, and the stunting of dedicated and generous Christians.)

Community becomes more and more consuming. Like others, I have family, friends, concerns other than those of the community. There is never enough time. I find that I must constantly choose. So many people to be with, so many interests to cultivate, so much to see, try, taste, touch, hear. To take a road with sisters and brothers, to feel our way as we go, to try to share, even to create some good news amid all that is bad, excludes a host of "might have beens."

I am convinced that for community to be itself, each member needs to do more than an allotted share. A non-calculating attitude marks real community. "I've done my part!" is its death knell. There is a real danger here to which a community such as Jonah House is exposed. One aspect of our struggle is to provide, assure, protect space and time for individual spiritual life. Community spirit, as we have come to know, is impoverished if the individuals are over-burdened.

With individual commitments, the poles appear to be accountability and unilateral action. Growth in love and willingness to be accountable within community constitute a thermometer of its spirit. Conversely, unilateral action ought to be rare. It arises from thoughtlessness, perhaps even from lack of trust in the ability of sisters and brothers to hear or understand us and our needs. It would be ideal if individuals go forth into other commitments as people sent, given a mission by the community, even blessed by sisters and brothers.

The new community that developed out of Jonah House in D.C. may or may not have been a good experiment for those involved; we don't know. But we sensed that it had little hope for longevity—an insight, given the circumstances, we chose not to share. Community must be formed on hope and vision; it needs members who undertake a common work. "Freedom from" or "freedom for?" In any case, there was too much emphasis in this new endeavor on the "from" and inadequate thought and planning.

It was a long time before anger was translated into anguish, before it was possible to heal the pain of those weeks. The Scriptures do not tell us how to live through such times: they promise that when we do, we will be comforted. It seemed poor consolation, our hope that friends would learn something better (or that we would learn something better) from an experiment gone sour. We knew what sorrow meant, not just for ourselves but for our friends as well, and for the struggle for justice that joined our lives for a time, a struggle that was marred by our own egos.

In 1980, in the midst of "The Year of Election—1980,"[10] Jonah House was embraced by two young couples, the first arriving in June. In reflecting on their impact on our lives in the year they were with us, we are hard put to express a perception and experience that was ours alone. We and the new arrivals clashed repeatedly. Overall it is an embarrassing and painful memory. But it may be useful to crack open that memory a bit, so we and others might learn from it. Because as we confront the sources of violence and power, we need to open our hearts more deeply to a mysterious truth: confrontation involves self-confrontation. The evil we would confront has its best accomplice in our own hearts.

Our friends taught us, as a starter, that we are hard people to live with. Phil and Liz had the initial discipline of growing up in large families; and after that of living in religious life. We expect a lot of ourselves, of one another, and of the people with whom we live. Having sacrificed a great deal for what we believe, we cannot take our faith lightly. One way of living is

---

[10] A year-long presence at the Pentagon sponsored by Jonah House during which groups from all over the country came to D.C. to strengthen community and resistance. Each working day of the year resisters were at the Pentagon; civil disobedience took place almost weekly.

by no means as acceptable as another. This attitude limits the support, the encouragement we can give, authentically, to the experiments others choose. In some cases, we should add, we too have tested and abandoned similar experiments for what we deem are good reasons. Combining a resistance focus with ongoing service to the poor is not as easy as many of our friends would like to believe. So we tend to be focused and single-minded—some would say narrow-minded or obsessed.

We have come to a conviction: our kind of community can be chosen only by people who have tried other options and found them wanting. For those still exploring options for their lives, perhaps ours is a place to stop, to test, to spend some time, to move on, and perhaps return.

The first approach of our new friends came through Phil. They visited us while Liz was in D.C. jail serving a month for a witness at the White House the previous Holy Week.[11] The circumstances framed the irony; within three months Liz and they were the only members of the community remaining at home. Phil, John, and Carl were in the Norristown, Pennsylvania, jail for the next four and a half months.[12] And Liz was

---

[11] This was an altogether easier time than 1977. The children were older. Their dad was with them at home. The time was limited and they understood time. Also they were able to visit—albeit through the glass dimly—weekly.

[12] In early 1980, John Schuchardt—later Phil Berrigan and Carl Kabat—considered two possibilities with the Brandywine Peace Community: first, that General Electric's Plant No. 9 in King of Prussia, Pennsylvania, could be disarmed. Second, that the imperative for disarmament would come from Isaiah 2:4 *They shall beat their swords into plowshares and their spears into pruning hooks.*

Since September 9, 1980, and the disarming of two Mark 12A's, twenty-six other Plowshares actions have taken place—mostly in the U.S., with two in West Germany—all of which have symbolically (and really) disarmed First Strike weaponry or its components. In addition, four disarmament actions (not necessarily inspired by Isaiah 2) have taken place.

Plowshares witnesses invariably use hammers and blood—to convey a simple reminder: we must disarm, we must stop killing one another, we must outlaw war as institution and politics. And we must eliminate the moral, social, and political causes of war.

ill-equipped to be the resource needed by our friends. Part of her energy was consumed trying to maintain the spirit of openness to the consequences of the "Plowshares 8" action, as it came to be called. She was also occupied in maintaining the Year of Election Presence. But more to the point here, she had grown careful about intimacies with people, slow to form judgments, and slower to give the kind of affirmation that this couple needed. Conflicts multiplied.

Conflicts, as we discovered, are as endemic to community as to family, and they multiply geometrically with families in community. The issue is the way they are resolved. Initially we worked hard at the resolution; but as time went on and conflicts multiplied, the will to resolve them weakened, and personality conflicts became the focus. After his return home and trial, Phil clashed with the young man; resentments with Liz went very deep and the couple left us. There has been no mutual examination of our time together; there has been no healing of the grief in their leave-taking.

The second couple arrived in October 1980: Barb Kass and Mike Miles. (We feel we can name them since a different kind of relationship, and a continuing one, grew between us.) Young as they were, they were acquainted with poverty and accustomed to hard work, to a simple life style, and to sharing space and processing ideas with others. An easy intimacy and a valued friendship grew among us.

They were a wonderful addition to our community. Their first child was born in our midst during the trial of "The Plowshares 8;" eight months later they ministered to the birth of our third child, Katy Berrigan. Phil wrapped the still unwashed newborn in a receiving blanket and brought her upstairs to meet the community assembled there waiting. And so Katy greeted them, her first gesture singling out Ollie Jo Miles, a child not much older than herself.

Shortly thereafter Mike went to jail for six months in D.C. Barb had the separation and Ollie to deal with; she did so in wonderful spirit. She was able to talk about weakness and strength, able to cry. We were able to cry with her.

Barb taught us much about the importance of family, about handmade gifts, about a thousand ways of being thoughtful, about things we had not stressed adequately. But it was their family and a couple of personal considerations that led them to leave us. Their relatives lived in the Midwest and there was a mutual longing to be closer to one another.

A second factor was the longing Barb and Mike felt to be closer to the land, to farm, to live a more ecocentric life. The inner city and our postage-stamp yard were inimical to those pursuits. A third factor was the emphasis growing within the community on the Plowshares-type witness. Mike felt this was given too much emphasis, to the neglect of community life and growth.

They opted to rent a house nearby; the property included a half-acre of land, enough to develop a good garden and still continue work with our community. They did a beautiful job but we felt bereft without them. After a year they moved to the Midwest, to be closer to their families. There they continue their efforts to form a community that will share a commitment to both the land and to resistance. If such can be done, they can do it. We treasure their friendship and all we share and have shared.

Perhaps the greatest gifts such friends have given us is their criticism of us. By being able to step back from encounters with them and attend to the criticism they levy at us, we may be able to increase our capacity to mourn. And mourning—grieving—is the beginning of the capacity to engage in real criticism, for grief is the visceral announcement that things are not going well. Sensing the troubles, we gain a larger insight into our personal lives, into our corporate and national life.

As Walter Brueggeman rightly observed, "The ultimate criticism we have to levy at our culture and the makers of culture is not one of triumphant indignation but one of compassion. Passion and compassion completely and irresistibly undermine the world of competence and competition. The contrast is sharp and total: the passionate one set in the midst of numbed Jerusalem. And only the passion could finally penetrate the numbness."[13]

---

[13] Brueggemann, Walter. *Prophetic Imagination.* Fortress Press. Philadelphia, Pennsylvania. 1978. p. 91.

*Blessed are the meek,
for they shall inherit the earth.*
Matthew, 5: 5.

## CHAPTER THREE
# THE MEEK

Christians are not asked to overcome the world. That was Christ's work, a work he claimed to have accomplished: *But be of good cheer, I have overcome the world.* John, 16: 33. We are asked to become human. The divine definition of being human is given from the Mount of the Beatitudes, and it stands contrary to every cultural and imperial definition.

Presidents of our country in this century have talked invariably of "strength," by which they meant military might. Maybe the translation accounts, in part, for their electability. Certainly this preoccupation with strength exposes how lonely and foolish is the cry for lowliness or gentleness, which, in some translations, is called meekness. The world goes its way. Sometimes the best that one can summon is the refusal to go along.

Often we think of gentleness as a quality of children. This can be accurate, though any of us who have spent much time with children know how obdurate and selfish, how aggressive and spiteful they can be. Our own children are no exceptions. They can and often do provoke their parents to most ungentle forms of behavior.

In holding up the child for imitation, Christ is holding up the better qualities of children—their openness, their relentless pursuit of truth, their trust—qualities we as adults need to relearn. Like all learning worthy of the name, gentleness comes from pain visited and revisited. The passage from anger to anguish, endured repeatedly, can bring us to a gentle spirit, can grind down the harshest, most abrasive edges of our souls.

Nor is this process peculiar to humans. It appears in all of nature. Wendell Berry, in his poem "1975," reflects on a valley near his home, carved by the moving waters of the river ". . . in violence so long and slow it was gentle."[1] A similar image comes from the seas, pounding hard rock to sand. Both mirror the cutting to size, the cutting to shape of heart, of flesh that time and pain can do within us if we let them. When pain and loneliness, mourning and suffering are accepted, not fought against or run from, even we can be made gentle.

The gentleness Christ holds up to us is a long patience; the word not accidentally shares the same Latin root as passion— *'pati'*—which is to say, suffering. Like patience, gentleness is the disposition to see difficulties through. It implies attentiveness to the present moment, overcoming fear of controversies, welcoming criticism, searching for forgiveness. It implies that one is willing to be influenced by people and events, even when the requirement is severe; willing to relinquish control, enter uncharted waters.

## GENTLENESS IS STAYING WITH IT

On the tenth anniversary of Jonah House, June 1983, we had a birthday party at St. Stephen and the Incarnation Church in D.C. The day after the party the celebrators took themselves and the celebration to the Pentagon—a celebration of resistance, a redefinition of strength.

---

[1] Berry, Wendell. "1975." *A Part.* Northpoint Press, San Francisco, 1980. p. 80. (The line of the poem reads: ". . . the valley keeps the shape of the escape of water. Moving water carved it in violence so long and slow it was gentle.")

# The Time's Discipline 53

One group of people blocked the doors at the River Entrance, putting their bodies in the way of the work being done within. The men and women pleaded with employees not to walk on or over them, to see that the reality of their jobs, given our times, was treading on the bodies of sisters and brothers throughout the world. Among those blocking were Jean and Martin Holladay, mother and son. Both are small of stature but great of spirit. Their witness was a meditation on the power of gentleness. The biggest, most powerful cops, it seemed, were on duty that day. They had opted, or been ordered, not to make arrests, but to keep the doors clear.

We watched as repeatedly the police seized Jean and Martin and tossed them aside. Repeatedly the Holladays regained their posts, walking, crawling or squiggling back. Neither registered any reaction to the man-handling they were enduring. They looked into the face of each employee that passed under, over, or through them; they pleaded with all to reflect on their work, the weaponry, the waste. We were awed at the resilience that enabled Jean and Martin to return to the fray without any trace of anger; all were moved by their constant plea for the future of our world. What changed was the attitude of the cops. They'd smile as they picked up a Holladay one more time; they'd set mother or son down to the side rather than toss them; they'd shake their heads in disbelief when they turned and found Jean and Martin back in place.

This action came on the heels of a question Ladon had put to the community. He was recently freed from a year in prison, most of it passed in segregation because of his refusal to work. So he was transported from one prison to another, from one segregation unit to another, as prison authorities sought to break his resistance. Ladon was not broken, but he was exhausted and drained. "How," he asked, "do we prepare ourselves to go back and back again into the ugliness, the darkness, the deprivation, and violence of prison? How do we live so as to be able to risk yet another long sentence?"

It is one thing to act once and endure the consequences of that action. But once one is familiar with those consequences, it is a different thing to act again. To be willing to do it repeatedly, that's the rub. How, without becoming cynical or cold, arrogant or jaded?

Phil faced this question during one of his re-entries into the din and darkness of prison:

> *Let the children come to me, do not hinder them; for to such belongs the Kingdom of God.* And He called a little child over and stood the child in their midst and said: *Truly, I say to you, whoever does not accept the kingdom of God like a child shall not enter it.* Mark, 10:14,15.

This is a mysterious and subtle passage, especially for those of us whose spirits are hardened with the task of mere survival in this ghastly society.

People, even the most sour and broken, will rarely fail to receive a child with joy and relief. I recall vividly the transformation effected by our little children, Frida and Jerry, at the geriatric hospital where my mother died. Old folks forgot pain, self-pity, lethargy. They smiled, revived, stretched withered hands to touch the tiny ones. They "accepted" the little children.

To accept God's reign as we would accept little children, to accept God's reign as little children accept it—both require us to become like children: to make ourselves lowly and trusting.

Who do the "children" stand for? Who are they? They are metaphor and symbol, best depicted by the "Blessed" of the Beatitudes, by those perpetually youthful, gifted with purity and courage. Those "happy" or "blessed" relive Christ—Christ, the poor person, Christ the meek, Christ the peacemaker, Christ persecuted for doing what God requires, Christ the prophet—slandered, rejected, murdered. They are the "little children" who accept God's reign, who welcome the freedom of Christ's Lordship.

This Scripture requires that I relearn the lowliness of a child so that I might accept Christ's Lordship. The lesson is threatening to my ego and false image; it cannot be learned easily or quickly. In fact, I resist Christ's Lordship, I harden my forehead against it, to use Old Testament language. Instead of welcoming it with joy and gratitude, I find there is more often suspicion, repugnance, rebellion.

Jail is always an antidote, hewing one down to proper dimension and capacity—a powerless prisoner among powerless prisoners. (Caesar has locked one up; Caesar alone will decide to let one free.) The illusion of being a champion of something or other in the witness, or in the courtroom, fades quickly in the squalor and violence of lockup. In such circumstances, one tends to see the self for what it is—the bomb ticking away.

Become like a child then; accept Christ's reign. *Fiat!*

Liz also could feel Ladon's question echoing in her while in prison, and shortly thereafter. Enduring one's situation, that can be done. One focuses on where one is, on those around; love and caring, doing and growing become possible. Then once one is home, the horrors come like flashbacks from a nightmare. "How did I survive that!" The women who shared the Alderson prison experience had a number of discussions on this subject, but they couldn't be conclusive; we were all still in prison at the time.

The parole board examiners asked Liz if she would again break the law. She responded that it was her deepest hope that as long as our government, or any government, continued with research, development, deployment, and planned use of devastating weapons, she would continue to resist them. "But that," she said, "is a matter of fidelity. I can't guarantee that I'll be faithful. I hope so!" They cleared that unfamiliar knot of truth from their throats and said, "Well, you're honest about it, anyhow!"

Liz could say no more, no less. Fidelity does not depend on the native capabilities of our hearts but rather on the gifts that God grants to us. That truth humbles us; it makes us prayerful as well. Slowly our pride and arrogance are ground down; slowly we learn to identify with the poor, the sorrowful, the prisoners;

slowly, too, we see the abundance with which we have been blessed.

Under the impact of Ladon's question and our own ruminations, a few things grow clear. We know what sustains us through rough experiences such as prison. If we were to list them, the list would begin, be punctuated by, and end with *prayer*. Prayer takes more forms that we can name or know. In prison, more than anywhere else we know, prayer teaches us that our deepest freedom rests not in being able to do what we want, but in becoming the people God will have us be. We pray not to find the energy to go back to the real stuff of daily life, but to be transformed by God. We pray so that the worldly myths and fictions of our lives might fall like loosened handcuffs from our wrists, like broken shackles from our feet.

Then, right with prayer, we would cite relationships, friendships, friends whose fidelity is a source of strength. Friends who let us be what we are, broken human beings filled with frailty and foibles. Friends who refuse to make of us heroes or martyrs. Friends who continue to challenge us. Friends who keep alive the seeds of hope and resistance, who share in the struggle for justice and peace.

It may be true, as Merton repeatedly observed, that a good spiritual director is hard to find. But, he said, and we know it's true, our real spiritual directors are the friends who burden us and lighten the burden. By our love and our need for love, we become for each other midwives of the future. We become the people God wills us to be. In our response to the outstretched hand of a friend, we touch the infinite.

Prayer and friendships are sustaining and challenging. They put us in touch with better reasons than we can know, better reasons for re-entry into risk and prison. If we aren't changed, if our reasons aren't better than they were, if they aren't more deeply etched into our conscience, body and soul, none of us would risk returning to prison. Or, if we did, it would be as certifiably insane people.

As we write, Ladon is back in prison, probably for another year, probably in solitary confinement. Aside from the prayer and relationships cited above, his preparation to return involved drinking deeply of the beauties of nature. He spent a month in Snowmass, Colorado, a valley thousands of feet high in the Rockies. The scenes are etched behind his eyelids, retrievable at will. They remind him of the beauty we must preserve for our children, the world we've literally borrowed from them and from their grandchildren's children.

Gentleness is in stark contrast with forcing life, forging it to our will. Much as we long for God's Kingdom, it will not arrive from our efforts, though indeed we hope that our deeds may be used by God. That is our prayer.

Early in the story of Jonah House, Ezechiel 33 became large for us all, a summons and a challenge. Often it has been the bread and butter of our searching, a metaphor of our work and witness, a reminder of the modesty to which we are summoned.

> The word of God came to Ezechiel telling him to inform the people that God was bringing war upon the land. The people were to choose one of their number as a sentry. The mission of the sentry was to watch for war coming upon the land and sound the warning. Any who heard the warning and did not listen, were themselves responsible for their deaths. But if the sentry failed to sound the warning, the sentry would be held responsible for the death of the people. (A paraphrase of Ezechiel, 33:1-6.)

From a Judaic view, the prophetic vocation is essentially to become a sentry who communicates God's warning of "sword" to the people. The overall metaphor is that of war ("When I bring the sword against a country"); but the context discloses that "wickedness" inspires war. The sentry's warning to the people is therefore against wickedness and its lethal companion, the sword. The warning is against war—its roots, its paraphernalia, its consequences.

Christ's view of the Good Shepherd clarifies the divine charge laid upon the Jewish sentry. The shepherds are those who lay down their lives for the sheep; they are the protectors against thieves and vandals, in contrast to the hirelings who catch sight of the wolf coming and run away. (A paraphrase of John, 10:1-18.)

It would be unimaginable for the true sentry or shepherd to remain silent at the sight of war or wolf, to hire out or run away. Nor does the apparent exclusiveness of the sentry, or of the shepherd (*You did not choose me, but I chose you and appointed you that you should go and bear fruit.* John, 15:16), provide for Jews and Christians an escape hatch from responsibility toward the helpless, from a faithful vigilance on behalf of the powerless (sheep). Indeed, the Biblical summons to protect life makes it emphatically clear that exclusiveness or aloofness lies not with God, but with the "hireling" who poses as a believer but shuns involvement. Many prefer silence, selling themselves, running away. Most refuse to leave the majority, the rank and file, the flock or herd, to become a sentry or shepherd.

Whatever the case, the sentry or shepherd resists the taproot of war; the sentry resists wickedness and violence, death and its assault upon life and the law of life: love of God, of neighbor, of enemy, of self, of nature. The shepherd is the servant of life. Such a one stands in resistance to war and its roots and by-products, whether psychic, physical, interpersonal, official, international.

The texts from Ezechiel and John lay solemn emphasis on a loving, gentle resistance against wickedness and violence. But if the sentry sees war coming and fails to sound a warning, so that the people are killed, God will hold the sentry responsible for their deaths.

*I am the Good Shepherd; I know my own and my own know me . . . and I lay down my life for the sheep.* John, 10:14-15.

Those summoned to God's revelation are sentries and shepherds. We see war or wolf and cry out against the peril, even with our lives. For the threatened spirit and flesh are our own. When innocent blood is shed, we remain innocent only when we strive against its shedding. God will hold the sentry responsible for the deaths of those killed in war. The good shepherd *lays life down his life for the sheep.*

There remains the vision of Ezechiel and John. Fidelity to God and to Christ requires, first, that the sentry or shepherd speak truthfully about the Beast—unmask its bomb, nukes, lies, exploitations, enticements, conspiracies, buying and selling of lives, distractions, image makers, and recuperative powers.

Second, the sentry or shepherd must accept the Beast's punishment, its wrath upon those whom it ravages spiritually and physically, and upon those who reject its mark, its anti-baptism, its chains, its death. The only model we have is the sinless Christ, who, for the sake of all, submitted before the Beast's rage.

Third, the sentry or shepherd must take the truth to the Beast's redoubts, to its White Houses, Kremlins, Pentagons, military nests and nuclear stations. There the sentry or shepherd must give warning by breaking its laws, confronting its courts, receiving its sentences, experiencing its prisons, enduring its contempt and humiliations, even risking its assassins.

> *And you, Son of Man, say to the house of Israel, Thus have you said:* "*Our transgressions and our sins are upon us, and we waste away because of them; how then can we live?*" *Say to them, As I live, says . . . God, I have no pleasure in the death of the wicked, but that the wicked . . . turn back, turn back from your evil ways.* Ezechiel, 33:10-11.
>
> *Truly, truly, I say to you, I am the door of the sheep. All who came before me are thieves and robbers; but the sheep did not heed them. I am the door . . . any one enters by me . . . will be saved, and will go in and out and find pasture.* John, 10: 7-10.

Toward the end of the film, *Paul Jacobs and the Nuclear Gang*, a film we often find useful, a reporter asks Paul how he goes on in his struggle, suffering as he is from terminal cancer. (Jacobs died of cancer before the film was completed.) Paul answers with a quote from the Bhagavad-Gita, "It is not our task to finish the work, but neither are we free to avoid responsibility for the part given to us."

We can grow into gentleness, into nonviolence, as long as that kind of modesty remains: to give warning, to fulfill one's part, to be care-filled about means, to leave the results in God's hands. It is when we become obsessed with results, with measuring effectiveness, with building organization, that the temptation to fight violence with violence looms so large.

## BUT WHAT OF ANGER?

Our own struggle toward gentleness and nonviolence is thrown into consternation, however, as the evidence mounts of official treachery, violence, and hypocrisy. Our children probably learn most of their foul language as we watch the evening news together. Rage gets a foothold. At times we'd like to scream and smash the tube like the ancient kings who murdered the messengers bearing bad news. The only words that feel appropriate at such times are the words of Jesus or the prophets when they confronted the leadership of their day.

Jesus sounds a special note in his encounters with the Pharisees and Sadducees; it gives us words for our feelings. It also dismays us. Can the relationship between Jesus and the Pharisees be called nonviolent? Is it imitable? With them, Jesus takes the offensive, reveals anger, is scathing even. In these interactions, and they are many, his gentleness and compassion seem to recede. He calls them . . . *hypocrites* . . . *blind guides* . . . *blind fools* . . . *white-washed tombs* . . . *full of dead* . . . *bones* . . . *serpents* . . . *a brood of vipers.* . . . Matthew, 23. With such invective he crowns the woes he pronounced upon them. He polarizes the scene. Or better, he exposes the polarization between his ministry and theirs.

For two years, in our weekly gathering for scripture reflection and Eucharist, the community at Jonah House studied The Book of Revelation. We found it a mysterious and highly political book—as well as a suppressed book. Among other things, it articulated our reality, our anger, our fears.

The Book of Revelation abounds with military metaphors, none more strikingly revealing than those of the ninth chapter:

> *In appearance the locusts were like horses arrayed for battle; on their heads were what looked like crowns of gold; their faces were like human faces, their hair like women's hair, and their teeth like lions' teeth; they had scales like iron breastplates, and the noise of their wings was like the noise of many chariots with horses rushing into battle. They have tails like scorpions, and stings, and their power of hurting . . . for five months lies in their tails. They have as king over them the angel of the bottomless pit; his name in Hebrew is Abaddon, and in Greek he is called Apollyon.* Revelation, 9: 7-11.

Note the violent implications of "horses ready for battle;" "teeth like lions' teeth;" "iron breastplates;" "chariots rushing into battle;" "tails like scorpions and stings;" and "their power of hurting people."

Revelation exposes five fundamental characteristics of war. First, war begins in the spirit: *The rest . . . who were not killed by these plagues, did not repent of the works of their hands nor give up worshiping demons and idols of gold and silver and bronze and stone and wood, which cannot either see or hear or walk; nor did they repent of their murders or their sorcery, their immorality or their thefts.* Revelation, 9: 20-21. The literary figures of Revelation unerringly suggest the militarist spirit of the idolator: one picks up the sword (or the bomb) to defend demons and false gods. St. James makes the same point in other words: *What causes wars, and what causes fightings among you? Is it not your passions that are at war in your members?* James, 4:1.

Second, war is demonic. As peacemaking identifies Christ's Kingdom, war identifies Satan's counter-kingdom. *They* [the locusts] *have as king over them the angel of the bottomless pit; his name in Hebrew is Abaddon, and in Greek he is called Apollyon* (meaning The Destroyer). Revelation, 9:11. War is the immediate and temporary triumph of satanism. Can anyone doubt this of nuclear war? Political ideology, religious purity, nation-state diversity, and financial profit are all shamelessly sold to citizens by the state as the supreme justifications for war. War is thus the prime tool of the anti-Christ: the summit of human malice, degradation, and failure.

Third, war is a plague, and the worst of plagues. The locust is an inspired metaphor to describe the militaristic spirit. In the Middle East, the locust is the symbol of destruction. Hebrew names the locust *gazam* the shearer; *arbel* the swarmer; *hasil* the finisher; *solam* the annihilator; *hargol* the galloper; *tzelatzel* the creaker.[2] The locusts travel in a column a hundred feet wide and as much as four miles deep. Reportedly, Algiers was struck with a plague of locusts in 1866; 200,000 people perished of famine as a consequence.[3]

A more recent example in Indochina. The Vietnam War as plague raped and deformed an entire peninsula. It was total war, and it had total destructive effect upon the Indochinese. It destroyed an ancient, agrarian culture, supplanting it with a perversion of our own. The war caused widespread malnutrition and starvation; it coerced urbanization to reduce insurgency in the interior of the country. It prostituted local leaders, enticing them to betray their own people; it attacked the unborn through the indiscriminate use of toxic chemicals, and it killed and crippled millions,[4] perhaps ninety percent of them civilians. And it produced a spiritual plague for the American people, the beginning of decline and collapse for the American empire.

The epitome of war as plague is nuclear war. Take the worst of Nazi scorched earth in Southern Russia, or the worst of North American scorched earth in Indochina, universalize one or the other, and the example still fails to measure a nuclear cataclysm. Nuclear war is unimaginable; it is unthinkable. Language fails, nightmare fails, even the inspired metaphors of Revelation fail.

---

[2] Barclay, William. *The Revelation of John. Volume 2.* Westminster Press. Philadelphia. 1959. p. 61.

[3] Barclay, William. *The Revelation of John. Volume 2.* Westminster Press. Philadelphia. 1959. p. 60.

[4] Herman, Edward S. *"Atrocities"* in Vietnam: Myths and Realities. Pilgrim Press. Boston. 1970. Herman estimates South Vietnam suffered over a million civilians dead and over two million wounded. Figures predate the end of the war by seven years.

To force either mind or imagination to engage its hellish dimensions is to tempt madness.

Fourth, war enlists everything in its service. Notice the aspects, levels, and realities of life represented in the Revelation passage: "horses" for the animal world; "gold crowns" to suggest premiers, presidents, leaders, the politician as war chieftain; "faces" for men; and "women's hair" for women; "breastplates" for military accouterments, ever more complex and expensive (for example, a pilot and his multimillion-dollar fighter-bomber); "wings" and "noise" for technical modernity (can anyone forget the sight or sound of the helicopter swarms in Indochina?); "tails" and "stings" and "hurt" depicting the appalling range of human suffering in war: the butchery on the battlefield and the butcher's trade in the first-aid tents; the fear and hatred and guilt; the anguished bereavement of families, of widows, mothers, and fatherless children; the terror of civilians: the elderly, women and children, all considered as combatants, as enemy, as objects of total destruction; the spiritual, emotional, and psychological crippling of veterans; the psychic numbing of whole populations, the feelings of powerlessness, of betrayal, of being a cog in a machine of systemized death.

And all for what? War cannot even be considered as educator, as exposure to salutary suffering from which might emerge a grasp of its uselessness, waste, horror, and criminality. Have the Russians learned from twenty million dead in World War II? If they have, what are their options? Have we learned from Korea, from Indochina, from the Cuban Missile Crisis? If we have, what are our options? What we learn from the history of war is that no one learns from the history of war. Rather, war has seized the education establishment everywhere and at all levels: with patriotic propaganda at lower levels, with technical and scientific "grants" at the university level, until the whole education establishment resembles another arm of the armed services.

War is total mobilizer, enlisting, enticing, impelling, conscripting, draining, deranging every element of life. It is system, a way of life; it is culture; religion; enthronement of technique, best epitomized by the bomb; it is economics: the Pentagon and other war ministries are economic overlords and coordinators of America and indeed of the world.

Fifth, war has become "natural" to the political process and to politicians. When politicians possess the bomb, the bomb pollutes every political decision. But politicians are persons. And war is not natural or inherent to human life. Just like peace, war must be learned to be lived. Politicians choose and accept "power," which is to say, the means of domination. Whatever good will and naivete are brought to "public service," a huge misnomer, the means are warlike: police, courts, bureaucracy, economic patronage in the local milieu; nationalism, ideology, imperialism, propaganda, the whole administration and legalization of supremacy and privilege internationally. These invariably erupt in outright war.

The problem, the high-wire act for politicians, is simply this: how does one administer a scale of violence acceptable to the majority? To suggest the futility of such a trick is useless. The perquisites are too enticing.

To the French poet Charles Peguy, the politician is a parasite. (The Biblical image of "locust" is more precise.) But Peguy strikingly addresses the politicians' abuse of means:

The politicians get even with us, or they think they get even

—by saying that at least they are practical and that we are not.
In this they deceive themselves and they deceive others.
We will not grant them this much.
It is the mystics who are practical and the politicians who are not.
It is we who are practical, who do something
and it is they who are not, who do nothing.
It is we who gather up, and they who pillage.
It is we who build, it is we who nourish others
and they who live as parasites.

It is we who create works and community, people and races.

And they who ruin all.[5]

To Christ, politicians were "hypocrites." Certainly, he was keenly aware of their priestly and teaching functions; they were the Pharisees and Teachers of the Law. But they were also "rulers" of the people who plotted his death and finally murdered him. . . . *So the chief priests and the Pharisees gathered the council, and said, "What are we to do? For this man performs many signs. If we let him go on thus, every one will believe in him, and the Romans will come and destroy both our holy place and our nation."* John, 11: 47-48. Then, of course, Caiaphas, who as High Priest was also political pharaoh and puppet under the Romans, offered his classic wisdom, a Machiavellian abuse of means, that it was better for one person to die for the people than for the whole nation to go under.

The Lord's condemnation of these base sellouts was fierce and uncompromising. They are "hypocrites" who lock the doors of the Kingdom, who devour the substance of widows under the show of long prayer. He calls them "blind guides" who have destroyed the meaning of justice, mercy and honesty. Terribly, he calls them "whitewashed tombs," which look splendid on the outside, but are full of dead men's bones. He accuses them of having murdered the prophets, an accusation absolutely verified in his own case. He calls them *"snakes and sons of snakes,"* who killed the innocent just as their ancestors did. . . . *upon you may come all the righteous blood shed on earth, from the blood of innocent Abel to the blood of Zechariah the son of Barachiah whom you murdered between the sanctuary and the altar. Truly, I say to you, all this will come upon this generation.* Matthew, 23: 35-36.

This way of Jesus draws us, even as it gives us pause. Did he stand so against the Pharisees because, like us, he was human—all too human? Was it because, being God, he could read their hearts? Was it because he knew that such was the only way he could speak to them? That he spoke the truth goes without

---

[5] Peguy, Charles. *Basic Verities.* (French-English Edition by Ann and Julian Green.) Pantheon Books. New York. 1943. p. 109.

saying. "There are things that hurt more than the truth," someone once said, "but I can't think of them at the moment." Truth is the two-edged sword that cuts into the marrow of bone and spirit. It can heal our spirits when it is spoken in love. In the joining of truth and love is the power of nonviolence. Spoken without love, truth is violent; love devoid of truth is sentimentality.

At Jonah House we work hard on loving our political leaders, loving those who cannot or will not hear the cry of the poor, the oppressed, the victims. Before each peace witness we stand in prayer and remind each other, after the example of Thich Nhat Hanh—"Remember, people are not the enemy!"[6] The prayer inspires reconciliation, reminds us of the need in our heart if we are to be ministers of God's Word.

We work hard on our anger, knowing it can be inimical to the mandate toward meekness or gentleness when anger is directed against people made in God's image. And while we've grown to the point where, much of the time, we do avoid hatred, we cannot stop hating what some people do and the justifications through which they defend and deface their deeds. The rational distinctions do not always filter through to the emotional realm, and we know and express raw anger. We need to confess that. We need to beg pardon of friends whom that anger has alienated, friends who because of our anger could no longer walk and search and be in community with us.

Lee Griffiths is one such brother. He is a seminary graduate who came to Jonah House from CCNV in 1975 because he sought a deeper commitment to resistance from a Biblical perspective. Lee is a gentle-man and a student of the Scriptures. Raised in the Church of the Brethren, he took the Sermon on the Mount literally and focused on the translation, *Anyone who is angry with a brother is liable to judgment.* Matthew, 5:22.[7] His

---

[6] Hanh, Thich Nhat. "Alone Again." The Cry of Vietnam. Unicorn Press. Greensboro, North Carolina. 1968.

[7] *New American Bible.* Catholic Book Publishing Company. New York. 1970.

reaction to expressions of anger initiated a series of meetings among us to discuss anger, to share the things that provoked us to anger, our responses to provocation, how sisters and brothers could help us through it. These were probing questions and power-filled meetings as we recall them. The process itself might be a good exercise for every family and community to engage in frequently. But they were of no help to Lee. He did not get angry; we should not get angry. At least that is the best sense we could make of his reaction and words.

Lee was unable to remain with our community at Jonah House. Certainly there were other factors, but inability to accept anger as allowed to Christians was predominant. He became part of a group that began a new community in Baltimore, "Advaita House." (Advaita means "the way of love.")

The anger of Jesus became anguish when he wept over the city of Jerusalem. His tears revealed how close these emotions are to each other. Significantly, Matthew places this sorrow a short four verses from his invective against the Pharisees: *How often would I have gathered your children together as a hen gathers her brood under her wings, and you would not!* Matthew, 23:37.

In us, the tension is unresolved. We are often angry. We call our leaders bad names and justify it. Jails and prisons add color to the basic Biblical vocabulary. We sometimes anguish, but our sorrow is mingled with anger. At times we can be gentle as a fruit of anguish, and so can return to witness, to prison, and to pain, albeit screaming and kicking against the goad.

With all our hearts we long for the fruit of the promise: the meek inheriting the earth. But we remember and remind one another that, like all the Biblical promises, it is not fulfilled in a vacuum but is tied to our faithfulness: in this instance, to our willingness to become more gentle, tolerant, patient, trusting in God who uses all our efforts in mysterious ways toward the establishment of justice. Our problem remains one of wanting results, and wanting them yesterday, and wanting to change others who, to our mind, inhibit the realization of God's Kingdom.

In his *Prophetic Imagination,* Walter Bruggemann spoke to our hearts:

> "The riddle and insight of Biblical faith is the awareness that only anguish leads to life, only grieving leads to joy and only endings embraced lead to new beginnings."[8]

## GENTLENESS AND STRENGTH

Brueggeman highlights what has long been a focus for us. How to avoid the benumbing of our own hearts? How to overcome the benumbed spirit of our postnuclear age? One massive effort in that direction was mounted in "The Year of Election—1980."

Throughout 1980, members of Jonah House and friends sponsored a year-long presence at the Pentagon. People kept vigil there every working day of the year to say "NO" as well as to seek to build the kind of society of which they dream.

The idea for this sustained witness came from a fine and gentle brother, a Mennonite, Al Zook. The idea came as he reflected on the Jericho event. We can not claim that walls crumbled in that year, but we live in faith that the end is not yet.

More than 900 people participated in an unbroken vigil that scrutinized the Pentagon throughout the year, shedding some light on its works of darkness. From as far away as Washington state and Alaska, day after day, week after week, month after month, people came to express their concerns, share their dreams, vent their anger, deepen their commitments, and strengthen their communities. By midsummer more than 600 had come to cast a most unusual vote in an election year. They came to speak with their lives. They came to offer themselves as a living hope that all is not lost. They said in many ways that hope is subversive, that it is expressed in forms not necessarily

---

[8] Brueggemann, Walter. *Prophetic Imagination.* Fortress Press. Philadelphia, Pennsylvania. 1978. p. 91.

explanatory or argumentative, that hope is often lyrical, touching lives at many different points.

There were groups as large as fifty who filled the concourse with song, theater, and dance. There were groups as small as two or three, who remained all but invisible in the bustle of people going to and fro. There were those who broke the law by trying to block the entrances to the building as people came scurrying to work in the morning; those also who poured blood and ashes, symbols of our future, the devastation left as a legacy for children. There were those who offered flowers, freshly baked bread and cookies as a symbol of hope and reconciliation. There were children who held live bunnies in their arms, and offered them, asking that employees commit themselves to protecting life. At different times people screamed in anger, cried in sadness and despair, made jest of the absurdities of militarism through theater. Once, out of frustration, a resister wrapped a heckler in a banner.

Each of the more than forty-eight groups brought with them a wealth of originality and newness. Chicken Little arrived on April Fools' Day with chickens and the warning that the sky was indeed falling. People from Oregon brought with them thousands of small bags of ash from the eruption of Mount St. Helens, offering them with the question: "Is this a vision of a nuclear hell?" A young man from Montana disrobed in the concourse with hopes of urging others to stand naked before God, to put down guns, bayonets, neutrons, and megatons. They spoke of NORAD, Rocky Flats, the Trident submarine, the cruise missile, the MX and all of the horrid clutter the Pentagon has put in their back yards. They spoke of militarism and how its roots are found in the oppression of women, the poor, the homeless, the black, the Hispanic. They were arrested for trespassing, littering, excessive noise, creating a nuisance. They were convicted on these charges as well as on trumped-up charges of assault and, at times, other more bizarre charges—anything, in fact, the government thought might gain conviction. People went from the Pentagon to the courts to the jails and then home again to seek out new ways of carrying on the struggle.

Apart from these activities, the pilgrims searched out new meanings of community. They lived in cramped quarters, dealt with periodic robberies and assaults, invariably urging themselves and each other onward. There is nothing that tests meekness and gentleness and nonviolence like community lived in this way. At times they came to new truth and clarity; at other times they ran from the truth and clarity they had discovered.

To do justice to the people who made this year possible, to portray clearly the many experiences, events, and changes that occurred seems literally impossible. What can be said with certainty, though, is that people attempted to dull the cutting edge of our nuclear arsenal and undo some of the wrong imposed on us since Hiroshima.

In so doing, we believe that all who joined in made an important difference to the work that goes on at the Pentagon. True, the Pentagon is still open for business twenty-four hours a day, seven days a week. True, injustice is still being mass-produced and exported there daily. Still, something extremely important remains; people offered a new direction, a new hope, a new way. Those going daily to work saw and heard injustice labeled injustice; killing labeled killing; lies labeled lies. Employees were offered a suggestion: there might be a better and more honest way for them to make a living. Those who arrested resisters were reminded that they arrested good people, that the law they protect is the law that keeps us all oppressed. Seeds were planted; good seed; though the harvest may be a long time coming, it is certain to occur. We have God's Word for it.

St. Stephen and the Incarnation Church opened its doors to our effort and acted as host throughout the year. The people there offered us several rooms and helped to defray the cost of turning the rooms into a living space.

On New Year's Eve 1979, as we looked to hopeful beginnings, a young woman was raped at knifepoint in the church itself. It was the first of many efforts to stop the resistance at its source.

In consequence we worked together with the church council, developing a response that would be human and nonviolent.

As the year went on it became clear, through information from an F.B.I. employee, that such incidents were generated by the bureau to scare us off and make it appear that the "crimes" were racially motivated. Without hard evidence, which we were unable to acquire, we were not able to verify the charge.

More than 900 people returned for the culmination of the Year of Election. They were housed and fed in nine different locations in the D.C. area. On December 29, all walked to the Pentagon and held a silent vigil with banners and signs at various entrances. There was an evening meditation with Daniel Berrigan, and planning for the 30th. On the 30th, there was a rally on the parade ground of the Pentagon, followed by an encircling of the building with children in the lead. Then people joined hands around the building and amid shouts, released balloons. We regrouped on the parade ground to conclude the rally. Many then gathered in the concourse for a liturgy led by Maryknollers in honor of the four women killed earlier that month in El Salvador.

On December 31, each small community concluded the year with its own act of hope. The day included the blockading of major entrances and a die-in by the Vietnam Veterans in which the bodies of "the dead" were put in body bags and hauled off. Others marked the building with blood and ash. There were also theater presentations in the concourse. Thirty-one persons were arrested and each served from five to thirty days in jail. Forty others risked arrest but were not taken. One group continued its blockade of the River entrance from 7:30 a.m. until 4:30 p.m. About 150 people returned to the Pentagon from 10:00 p.m. until midnight for a candlelight vigil.

900 people, or even 9,000 people, if that were possible, calling the Pentagon to sanity and disarmament would still be helpless before such awesome power. David and an army of Goliaths are evenly matched in contrast. But the power of the Pentagon is an illusion, if only we understood.

In the midst of the Year of Election, Pentagon officials confided to Jack Woodard, pastor of our host church, that the quality of demonstrators was changing. "They are people like us. They make sense. What does it all mean?"

What does it mean indeed? From the standpoint of the third beatitude, it is not only useless to look for direct effect, but it is also the road to violence, it is faithless. Overcoming, changing the world is God's work. Ours is the work of witness to the light and against the crimes that we see. Glimmers of meaning get to us now and then—just enough light to go on. And we don't need more than that, much as we might want much more.

*Blessed are those who hunger and thirst for righteousness,*
*for they shall be satisfied.*
Matthew, 5: 6.

## CHAPTER FOUR
# THOSE WHO HUNGER AND THIRST FOR JUSTICE

Gentleness, meekness, lowliness are not passive. On the contrary, they lead us to act for justice. In *Being and The Messiah*, a book we read and reread, studied and discussed, Jose Miranda says that the only intervention of God in human history occurs when a cry for justice rises. Do justice! Seek justice! Hunger and thirst for justice! This imperative occasions the sole manifestation of God in history. People who call to us in their need impel us to godly acts of justice.

As we grow in gentleness, we are better prepared to appreciate and reverence the uniqueness of suffering people. We are better prepared to see their needs, to hear their summons in our lives, to let our hearts embrace their situations. As we internalize the pain of others, we begin to announce it, to act against the injustice that causes such pain. The passion for justice becomes a yearning as deep as physical hunger and thirst.

The fourth beatitude calls us to struggle for justice as though we felt a physical and spiritual need, to bypass no injustice, to plot, to plan, to conspire for justice in the midst of blatant injustice. This passion for justice impels us to note and interfere with injustice. The fourth beatitude thus calls us to an aggressive resistance against injustice, against the misconception that one resists only if evil knocks on one's own door.

## FOR WHAT DO WE LONG?

Our longing for justice, our hunger and thirst are for God's Kingdom, for God's promise to be fulfilled in our midst. We plea, we strive, we pray, and ultimately we wait for the gift of an entirely new situation for our world: the arrival of the Kingdom, the promise of which punctuates the pages of Scripture.

Indeed, if we are *alive* to our world, we cannot but be flayed by the sense of being abandoned by God. We cannot but be torn apart by the delay of God's promises, by the delay of the Kingdom, by the seeming hopelessness of life itself.

Delay, mischance, catastrophe. Yet we believe that history is no mere series of throws of the dice. We know that history has known only one absolutely unique event, the incarnation of God in Jesus. The independent, surprising, unlooked-for factor, which introduces initiative and the possibility of a fresh start, which overthrows and changes the rules of life, is the intervention into our dreary world of the Word of God. The Wholly Other cuts across history, and the course of history is altered. All things become new.

Yet the Kingdom is not solely an act of God. The return of Jesus and the establishment of his Kingdom are absolutely linked to our acts of hope. Biblical hope thus arises when those apparently abandoned by God press their demand that God be God and intervene. It is then, when we impress our hope upon God, that we assume our true authority, the authority of God's daughters and sons.

As long as all the tears are not wiped away, as long as suffering follows suffering, and guilt is piled upon guilt, for just this long there will be no ease, no satisfaction. In this crepuscular meantime, we abide by what is written, namely *the promise*. We value hope more than reality. None puts our longing so clearly as the prophet:

> *For behold, I create new heavens and a new earth; and the former things shall not be remembered or come into mind. But be glad and rejoice for ever in that which I create; for behold, I create Jerusalem a rejoicing, and her people a joy. I will rejoice in Jerusalem and be glad in my people; no more shall be heard in it the sound of weeping, and the cry of distress, No more shall there be in it an infant that lives but a few days . . .*
> *They shall build houses and inhabit them; they shall plant vineyards and eat their fruit. They shall not labor in vain, or bear children for calamity; for they shall be the offspring of the blessed of the Lord, and their children with them.* Isaiah, 65:17-23.

## THE SEASON OF LONGING—THE CENTRALITY OF ADVENT

The above passage from Isaiah belongs to the Advent season. It is a text filled with the passion of longing, yearning for God's Kingdom. This being true, it is shocking to sense the neglect that greets such sublime expressions of the Advent spirit. Many Christian churches and homes display an Advent wreath, light the candles weekly; some have an Advent calendar; a few read the "Oh! Antiphons." But despite these efforts at entering the spirit of Advent, for most the focus is Christmas and the attendant preparations for celebration, gift-giving, and a mostly materialistic binge.

In religious communities we celebrated Advent as spiritual preparation for Christmas; at Jonah House we discovered in Advent a season for our times. It began with our first Christmas at Jonah House. With friends from CCNV we went to the White House on Christmas morning and enacted a medieval morality drama of Herod's massacre of the Innocents called "Herod and the Kings." For the first time we made the connection publicly between the Massacre of the Innocents (December 28th in the Catholic Calendar) and the contemporary response of political rulers. On Christmas morning 1973, we left broken and bloodied dolls on Nixon's front lawn, gruesome reminders of the Vietnamese victims of our war. They spoke there as image, an image parallel to the photo poster of the ditch at My Lai: *Question: And babies? Answer: And babies!* Since that Christmas day, the Feast of the Innocents has become a day for us to give public witness to the peace of Christmas, and against the policies that victimize and murder children.

Each year, as that feast nears, we have tried to understand better the import of Advent, the feasts of Christmas and the Innocents. This process was helped in 1976 by our friend Ched Myers. Ched, a Biblical scholar and resister, took the bare bones of our insight and wrote an article called "The Hope and Cost of Advent."[1] He concludes that piece in telling fashion:

> ... Advent is not a time for losing our problems in the euphoria of feigned religious good will. It is rather an event which *is set for the fall and rising of many in Israel, and for a sign that is spoken against ... that thoughts out of many hearts may be revealed...* Luke, 2: 34-35. It is a time to test allegiances and scrutinize political realities in the light of God's truth.
>
> What is the cost of Advent today? What shall we who profess Christ say to those in power who would seek the child that they might "worship" him and who do seek, if not the approval, then the silence of God's people concerning their current contingency plans to reduce the world to radioactive ash? What do we say to the starving innocents in our world who continue to die of malnutrition while we obediently pay our taxes for the construction of cruise missiles, Trident submarines, and military satellites? When will we face reality in our day and acknowledge that

---

[1] Printed in *Year One. Vol. III. No. 5. Year One* is a quarterly publication from Jonah House. Orbis Press, Maryknoll, New York, has recently published Ched's work on the Gospel of Mark—*On Binding the Strong Man.*

there is nowhere for the Peace Child to be born in our midst, that our hearts and minds are deserts as we continue to exist in harmony with depthless sufferings and monstrous evil?

Until we understand that the prophecies of Micah and Jeremiah are one prophecy, until we recognize the child in swaddling clothes together with the child at the end of the royal sword, until we remember in the same season the infant child and the infanticide, we will not understand the cost of Advent. If we cannot understand the cost, then how will we know the cost of birthing Christ into the world?

These ideas found root in good soil in many places; before long there were Christian communities across the United States coming together to witness on December 28th to these connections.

In 1978, for the first time, we encouraged the participation of children in the Feast-of-the-Innocents witness. Aware of our potential for using our children (and thus abusing them) we prepared carefully, and asked other parents to show the same care. Our initial idea was to prepare an Advent booklet for the children and ask parents to read, reflect and pray with their children each day of the season. Then we came to realize that such a work would require a depth of understanding that we lacked. So we prepared a reflection booklet for adults and a packet of material to use with the children. For the next couple of years, we refined the booklet to include new insights into the pressing relevance of Advent to our reality in nuclear America. By 1981, we wrote in the introduction to the booklet:

> All who are even marginally alive to events today, begin Advent with a keen sense of promise and foreboding. We are faced with pressing tasks to which we are summoned . . . by the presence of human misery (the solution to which cannot be put off until tomorrow). As we enter the season of hope, a distinction has to be made between hope and the thing hoped for. We are living in a world in which we

think there is no way out—it is hopeless. We find ourselves saying we can only hope that people will wake up and resist so the holocaust might be averted. Hope is too often identified with that state of affairs, with the little absurd and childish leap into the irrational assumption of happy outcomes....

What Advent and Biblical Hope invite us to is something totally different. Biblical Hope is the passion for the impossible. But it is connected with the promises of God. Because there is a promise, there is a history (or a possibility of history). Hence there is a possibility of action and a commitment to make this history, to "implement" it at all costs. Our Advent hope wants us to write another history, that of the impossible life, of the true life, which the minds of men and women never conceived but which God has promised.

Advent puts us face to face with a God who intervenes in history, who makes his own decisions and acts as sovereign, creating the world he wants through his Word....

Our obedience to the fourth beatitude and our work of hope call us to entreat God: "Come and reveal Yourself!" In Advent we see ourselves as poor once again; as actual beggars for the Spirit of God, since it seems, at times, that the Spirit has abandoned our world.

We began to understand what the Church has taught for centuries: that there are really two advents (comings) of Christ. In the first, he entered the world. That is the Advent that leads to Christmas. But Christmas also leads beyond itself: to the second coming, the Great Return. He will come to us once more, to lift up and point out those who have received his love, and those who rejected that love. In the first Advent, he comes to seek and to save; in the second he comes to take us to himself. The first is promise, the second is fulfillment.

The "coming and a half," as Dan called it,[2] might be understood as Christ present in our lives and in our world, here and

---

[2] Berrigan, Daniel. *The Book of Uncommon Prayer*. Seabury Press, New York. 1978. p. 107.

now. It depends on us, on our willingness to open our lives to the message of Christ and to spread that word abroad by our hunger and thirst for justice.

Six years were to pass before the hope of producing a daily Advent meditation for children was realized. In 1984, Liz was in prison in Alderson, West Virginia, serving three years for her part in "The Griffiss Seven Plowshares" at Griffiss AFB in Rome, New York. From there she prepared and sent these graphics, scripture readings, and reflections to the children.[3] Each day of Advent, Phil and the community at Jonah House read a reflection with the children and hung it on an improvised Advent Tree. We share the images here in the hope that the practice will be adopted by other parents or individuals who live or work with children.

Such rituals with our children have proven fruitful. Through prayer together, we share with them our dreams and hopes. Where there is no dream and no hope, there is nothing for which to long. Yet, we are told, there is. There is the promise of God, far from realized in our midst. "You would not seek me, if you had not already found me," Augustine wrote of God. The converse is also true, as Merton wrote:

"We cannot arrive at the perfect possession of God in this life, and that is why we are traveling and in darkness. But we already possess him by grace, and therefore in that sense we have arrived, and are dwelling in the light. But oh! How far I have to go to find you in whom I have already arrived!"[4]

## THE IMPACT OF BIBLICAL LONGING

Our efforts to offer a contemporary translation of the spirit of Advent intensified yet another change in our community. Our preparations changed; so did the character of our actions. And finally, we described our work in a new way. For a long time

---

[3] The graphics and daily meditations are found in Appendix A.

[4] Merton, Thomas. *The Seven Storey Mountain.* Harcourt, Brace and Company, New York. 1948. p. 419.

we believed the term "civil disobedience" was an apt description of our acts of resistance. While we continue to use it occasionally, less and less does it describe our actions.

Civil disobedience implies a basic faith in a system. One acknowledges what one recognizes, even negatively. A person who disobeys the laws of an institution or system gives credence to that very institution or system that might require changes in certain areas. So the civilly disobedient activist presses for those changes, on the twin levels of personal conscience and the civil law. The civilly disobedient activist then appeals to constitutional rights for protection. There is an inherent contradiction here, as we came to see.

In our day, it becomes obvious that the Pentagon, in league with gigantic multinational corporations, industry, academia, and labor, forms the clandestine government of our country. These powers, in turn, are protected by a massive intelligence-gathering apparatus. In concert, these are the powers that shape our world into rich industrial centers on one hand and continents of misery and exploitation on the other. The constitutional fabric that, as many citizens wrongly believe, once valued humanity and human rights has been undone.[5] In any real sense, our country is no longer (if ever it was) governed by a constitutional system.

In such circumstances, to employ ordinary civil disobedience is dangerous and misleading, for it feeds an illusion. Our constitution speaks of government and citizens as if they make up the whole calculus; but the real powers are ignored. The struggle, therefore, is deeper than civil disobedience can express. It is a spiritual struggle. As Paul stated. *For we are not contending against flesh and blood, but against the principalities, against the powers,*

---

[5] One need read but one of the many books on the American Indians to know that their rights and their humanity were never respected by the North American government. We suggest *Bury My Heart at Wounded Knee* by Dee Brown. Holt, Rinehart & Winston. New York, Chicago, San Francisco. 1970.

*against the world rulers of this present darkness, against the spiritual hosts of wickedness in the heavenly places.* Ephesians, 6: 12.

On another and more important level, we began talking about our resistance in terms of advocacy for the poor and those without a voice, or as *acts of witness*. The change was more than a change in vocabulary. It reflected a deepening of a Biblical perspective and of faith. We remembered the words of Jesus, *You shall be my witnesses.* Acts, 1: 8. He was not recommending a course of action; he was not giving advice; he was conferring a vocation on his apostles and disciples. Witnessing, we understood, is something granted to a person, rather than something undertaken arbitrarily.

The early chapters of John's Gospel show Christ as a witness. The term is applied to him well over 100 times in this Gospel. Christ was a witness to what he knew of God; what God is and does. His mode of answering questions regarding his identity was to tell where he came from and where he was going: the Parent sent him! (A paraphrase of John, 5:23.) the will of the Parent sent him. (A paraphrase of John, 5: 30.) He was going to the Parent. (A paraphrase of John, 16: 28.) This defines Christ, his way of being authentically human: to have a mission and a sense of mission. Christ was and will be sent. The question for the Christian becomes: "What is my sense of mission; in sum, the meaning of my life?"

Throughout history, the message of Jesus has often been obscured: so has been a true sense of Jesus himself. In our own time: Jesus Christ Superstar! Thus the passivity, the waiting, the failure to create a climate, an opportunity, for speaking and hearing the truth. In the Gospels, though, the mission creates its own climate. Christ did not wait for people to "be ready." The mission of the Christian is one of witness to Christ in the here and now.

The witness listens to God and to the world. Christ in our being implies a contact, a transmission, a relation, the joining of God with humanity. So Christ prayed . . . *As thou didst send me into the world, so I have sent them into the world.* John, 17: 18.

All of us, if we would be truly ourselves, would speak such words, witness to such truth.

To be a witness is to be in a position to tell a truth. The witness has the authority and the *duty* to speak on the matter in question. To be a witness is to risk one's very self. We had seen how risky it is to be called as a witness. The grand jury that brought down the indictment in Harrisburg, Pennsylvania, in 1971, continued to sit on the case well beyond the indictment, and subpoenaed many of our friends as witnesses. Many resisted, refused to testify against friends, refused to cooperate with the "search and destroy" mission the government was mounting in that and in other grand jury proceedings at that time. Many were imprisoned for their refusal to testify. They witnessed for truth, refusing to cooperate as "witness to the state's lies."

Often we have wished for an easier way to live with our longing for God's Kingdom; yet, in our better moments, we sense that any other way would mean turning our backs on clues as to what constitutes a decent and meaningful life. The search, the struggle would die of neglect along with a real part of us. Maybe our souls.

For we have heard a call to live in a condition that is not yet real: the Kingdom of God. In an unjust world we have been set free to practice justice; in an oppressed world, to speak for and with the oppressed, to show forth God's love and mercy and justice until these come to be. Thy Kingdom come!—even through us.

What has happened to us, what have we seen that we must tell?

First, we've read and reread the Gospels and heard Christ's injunction: *Follow me!* Luke, 9: 59. *Remember me!* Luke, 22: 19. To us it sounded as if we were called to undergo a radical change in our lives and values.

What have we seen that we are compelled to tell?

That, hand in hand with the destruction of our environment, has come the destruction of human life. The evidence is overwhelming. Those who march lock step with society's definitions of life, peace, freedom, justice, the enemy, become walking dead. Meantime, the humiliation and degradation of human life is endemic.

And at root is the bomb. After the bombing of Hiroshima in 1945, Dorothy Day, founder of the Catholic Worker Movement, pointed to a truth that we began to grasp only in the late 1970s: the Lordship of Christ has been replaced by the lordship of the bomb. By the time this truth became apparent to us, the bomb controlled national life, attitudes, psychologies, the economy, diplomacy, international relations, the total human environment.

To be a witness demands a constant spirit of watchfulness: *Watch therefore, for you know neither the day nor the hour.* Matthew, 25: 13. Such mindfulness demands a constant effort to dispel ignorance, to control fear. The summons is two-fold: on the one hand to listen, to hear—in prayer and in reality—what is of God and what is destructive of human life; on the other hand to speak, of God and God's plan, of what we know of Christ, of what we know of the world.

Watchfulness is being alert for opportunities for truth speaking, thus creating a new climate for learning compassion. Where such a spirit reigns, the Kingdom already is. The Holy Spirit is both the agent and servant of watchfulness, the essential request of any prayer. Prophecy and witness are watchfulness in action, another way of speaking of the dynamic of resistance and contemplation.

How do Christians witness to Christ as Lord in face of the lordship of the bomb? This is our consuming question. Once the question is seriously posed, a serious truth emerges: the imperial apparatus is incapable of change, self-control, or reform. Obsessed with itself and with its organization of privilege, it blunders along like a blind colossus, spreading its delusions as truth, threatening, and destroying. And the last to see the truth are the functionaries of the Big Lie.

According to the present arrangements in most states throughout the world, everything is war: cold war, hot war, war against poverty, war against cancer, war against drugs. Project follows project, always into sourness and futility. Scandal follows scandal; corruption intensifies. Politicians and government bureaucrats run like caged mice on their wheels, faster and faster, staying exactly in the same place. Each political election has the vitality and meaning of a puppet show. The bureaucracy runs of its own mad momentum, tolerating only a change in the palace guard. A self-propelling, self-addicted, self-serving bureaucracy ensures its survival at all costs.

Knowing all this frees us from false hope; now we may discover a basis for true hope. By exposing the wellspring of death, we invite people—whoever will hear—to reassert the Lordship of Christ, to exorcise the demon from both national and personal life. That means transcending the assumed rationality of it all, facing the total irrationality of public life and structures, the madness of those in authority. That in turn implies an appeal to realities deeper than reason, to powerful symbols and actions: the use of blood poured on temples to name them "blood-drenched;" ashes spilled to reveal the residue of "the fire next time" threat of nuclear war; the earth dug to expose the grave we dig for ourselves by our silence.

Rationality! One indication of national fragmentation is the widespread illusion that rationality is at work. Irrationality, in fact, is everywhere. So we have recourse to symbols.

In more civilized times, symbols tend to belong to everyone. In times like ours, driven and captivated as they are, people misunderstand symbols and fear them. Restoring symbols and purifying them through suffering and public exposure is part of the renewal of a community of sanity; in fact, a definition of the Church.

Biblical stories speak of the hope that is placed in God, a hope that, even in the midst of nothingness, puts its faith in the power of one who created the world out of nothing. God's creative act takes place in that which is without form, void, in the darkness above an abyss.

Even where the forces of evil seek to end all possibilities of people and of nature, we place our hope in God; for God is the power of a future that proves itself creative despite the threat of total nothingness. What is, in the beginning, created out of nothing, is, in the end *life from the dead,* Romans, 11:15. In this way is God's Kingdom proclaimed. Therefore our hope is kindled by the God of Genesis and the God of Exodus and the God of resurrection of the crucified. We place our hope in the future (the Kingdom) by grasping in obedience and anticipation the open possibilities of humanity redeemed in this world. While we do whatever prepares the future, our hope must be prepared to suffer through dark nights in which, it seems, no one can be effective. Doing whatever prepares the way, we reach out to the God of Abraham and the Parent of Christ Jesus and to his promise in the midst of our own history. We recall a promise yet unfulfilled; more, we demand, yes demand, its fulfillment. We hunger and thirst for justice.

## A NEW INSIGHT INTO CHRISTMAS

During Advent 1980, Jonah House prepared for the largest witness for peace it had yet mounted, the culmination of "The Year of Election—1980" at the Pentagon. Meanwhile Phil, Carl Kabat, Elmer Maas, and John Schuchardt were in jail in Norristown, Pennsylvania. They had been there since "The Plowshares 8" action in King of Prussia, Pennsylvania, awaiting trial, inevitable conviction, and sentencing. Sentences of twenty-five to forty-five years hung over them and over all of us.

Would Liz ever see Phil outside prison again? The question was real and made itself felt over and over. The temptation that she and many felt in that pretrial time was to play the "what-if" game, to seek to second-guess the outcome, to create a "known" to replace the awful uncertainty of the "unknown." Liz fought this tendency even as she was drawn into it. Frida and Jerry felt their father's absence deeply. Often at bedtime they'd ask: "When will Daddy be home?" "We don't know," Liz would answer and sit with them and talk about it. As Christmas neared, the questions became: "Will Daddy be home for Christmas?" and "What can we give him for Christmas?" and

"What is Christmas like in jail?" These questions became a source of anguish that Advent season.

The fact was we couldn't give Phil a gift for Christmas. Liz even became maudlin over that realization. Under the guise of concern for Phil, there lay a measure of self-pity. And no way out; until she turned over the coin of the Christmas gift. On the other side was the truth that Phil (and co-defendants) had given us the gift of all gifts for Christmas! Consequently, Christmas would be a season of joy to the extent that she, the children, and friends opened themselves to receive that gift in a spirit of gratitude.

During the family visit in the tiny visiting room of the Montgomery County, Pennsylvania, Jail just before Christmas, Jerry became the spokesperson for this insight:

"We want to thank you, Dad," he said. "You've given us the greatest Christmas gift anyone could." "What's that, Jer?" Phil asked. "Your action," Jerry answered. "You were making peace, just as Jesus was in coming to us at Christmas!"

That half-hour visit allowed us a joyous celebration of the gift.

Liz was to give the homily Christmas Day at Unity Kitchen, the Catholic Worker house of hospitality, in Syracuse. As she and the children drove north Christmas Eve through a heavy winter storm, she determined that her homily would speak of this journey from sorrow to joy.

Then she addressed the depression that attends Christmas for so many. People find that the magic they've been taught to expect eludes them. It will continue to elude us, she said, until we determine to flesh out, in deeds, the peace Christ came to give. Without that, the magic of Christmas is worse than elusive; it is illusion. The more we perpetuate the illusion, as adults, by heaping gifts upon our children, looking for the magic reflected in their eyes, the more prone we will be to depression and letdown. In that process, we hurt our children, teaching them greed instead of gratitude. They soon become crabby, as the gifts they really wanted are not given; and those given are fought over and broken. Making peace, on the contrary, opens us to the gift of each other and to gratitude.

## A SEASON OF CONTRASTS: DARKNESS AND LIGHT

The trial of "The Plowshares 8" began February 22, 1981. The defendants met together the day before at the home of the Bauerleins in Ambler, Pennsylvania. That evening and each evening of the trial, there was a meal together, followed by a Festival of Hope at Gwenyd Mercy College. If the defendants were disallowed from speaking their hope in the courtroom, they would speak it in the context of these evening forums. Expert witnesses, whose testimony was suppressed by the court, also spoke at Gwenyd Mercy. And there was music, theater, art, the strengthening of community.

On the first night, Liz was asked to speak. She reflected on this passage from Paul's letter to the Ephesians:

> ... *Now you are light* ... *walk as children of light (for the fruit of light is found in all that is good and right and true), and try to learn what is pleasing* ... *Take no part in the unfruitful works of darkness, but instead expose them. For it is a shame even to speak of the things that they do in secret; but when anything is exposed by the light it becomes visible, for anything that becomes visible is light. Therefore it is said, "Awake, O sleeper, and arise from the dead, and Christ shall give you light." Look carefully then how you walk, not as unwise* ... *but as wise, making the most of the time, because the days are evil. Therefore do not be foolish, but understand* ... Ephesians, 5: 8-17.

Four points emerge for reflection, Liz said. First, Paul tells us that light produces good fruit in our lives. It produces benevolence, generosity of spirit, righteousness, and truth. Truth in the New Testament is not simply an intellectual attitude to be grasped. Truth is described as moral truth; it is something to be done, to be lived. The "Plowshares 8," for example, when they acted to disarm Mark 12A warheads, did the truth with a generosity of spirit on behalf of all. In a truer sense, however, their act on our behalf was a summons to us to act in truth, to act for life. Knowledge of the light, knowledge of the truth, Paul implies, makes each of us strong to do what we know is true.

Second, the Light enables us to discriminate between that which is just and that which is not good. In the Middle East, where people shop in little covered enclosures with no windows, they take the piece of goods they wish to purchase out into the streets and hold it up to the sun so that the light might reveal any flaws. They purchase the merchandise only if it stands the test of light. Paul summons us to expose every action, every decision, and every motive to the light, and to make our judgments on the basis of what the light reveals to us.

Is it not our task to expose (bring to light) the true work of the military-industrial complex? To reveal the bomb makers for the charlatans and murderers they really are? The "Plowshares 8," for example, exposed the works of General Electric, self-described as bringing "good things to life," as, in truth, preparing to put good things to death. Furthermore, what is the truth about the work of many major North American corporations? For example: Monsanto ("Without chemicals life itself would be impossible") manufactures explosive detonators for the bomb; Du Pont ("The leading edge") supplies tritium gas for the bomb; Rockwell International ("Where science gets down to business") fabricates plutonium and beryllium components for the bomb; Union Carbide ("Today something we do will touch your life") contributes uranium, deuterium, and lithium to the bomb; Bendix ("We speak technology") makes the paper honeycomb shield and polystyrene foam that help focus radiation pressure on the hydrogen bomb's fusion tamper; Western Electric, a subsidiary of American Telephone and Telegraph ("The system is the solution") does general engineering for the H-bomb in its laboratories. And these are but a very few of the companies involved in making the bomb.

The light would reveal that the motive of these bomb makers is greed. G.E. and all the others who profit from nuclear research, production, and deployment are less concerned about being murderers than they are about this year's, and next year's, and the next ten years' profits. But the end result for humanity is the same: nuclear destruction.

Third, Paul tells us that the light exposes that which is evil. Over and over again the message rings out: the best way to rid the world of any evil is to drag it out into the light. So long as the evil is being done in secret, it continues; but when it is dragged out into the light of day, it dies. Paul also tells us that the surest way to cleanse the depths of our own hearts and to cleanse the practices of our society is to expose them to the light of God's truth.

Friends in Hawaii recently published a book aptly titled, *The Dark Side of Paradise: Hawaii in a Nuclear World.*[6] The book and the ongoing resistance work of "Catholic Action of Hawaii" have gone far to reveal that it is not only ignorance that makes us oblivious to the local and global implications of nuclear matters. Conscious deception by the military is involved. The military goes to great lengths to keep the ordinary citizen in the dark about the armed forces' top-secret operations.

In contrast, investigating and exposing nuclear weapons in our own communities is not that difficult. The process of locating the bomb plants and bases, of learning more about them, of sifting through that information, and finally acting to expose them to the light of day, of truth, are processes we can all learn and in which we can all engage. Maybe they are processes in which we must engage if there is to be continued life on this planet.[7]

---

[6] Albertini, Jim. *The Dark Side of Paradise: Hawaii in a Nuclear World.* A Project of Catholic Action of Hawaii. Peace Education Project. 1980.

[7] The resistance groups listed in the Appendix of *The Dark Side of Paradise* as well as those listed in *Swords into Plowshares* can provide people with the tools needed to discern their community's involvement in the nuclear complex. We bring these lists up to date in Appendix C.

Fourth, Paul tells us that everything which is brought into the light is made light; that the light is not merely condemning, not merely judging, but that it is healing and transforming as well. *Make the most of the time, because the days are evil.* Ephesians, 5: 16. This is the hardest word of all for us. "Your lives should redeem this age!" reminds us of all the cliches that we have heard. For example: "That for evil to continue in the world it is enough for good people to do nothing." What is painfully clear is that nuclear weapons possess the ascendency they have because all of us, to one degree or another, have for so long either accepted the justifications given for them, or have remained silent in face of them, or have refused to have our lives interrupted by them. But the horrible truth is that our lives will not merely be interrupted by them—all life will be ended by them if we refuse to heed the summons.

It is helpful to remember Job who confessed: *My days have passed far otherwise than I had planned. And every fiber in my heart is broken. Night, they say, makes room for day and light is near at hand to chase the darkness.* (A paraphrase of Job, 17:11-12.) We can always be near at hand as sisters and brothers in and of the light, willing to commit our lives to the light, to make room for day, to chase the darkness.

Seeking the light, being eager to use the light: this is yet another way of stating the beatitude: we must hunger and thirst for justice.

> *Blessed are the merciful,
> for they shall obtain mercy.*
> Matthew, 5: 7.

## CHAPTER FIVE
# THE MERCIFUL

Can it be that mercy is gentleness at a deeper level of our souls? The journey into the Beatitudes may suggest that it is. It may suggest, too, that we not deify gentleness—it isn't an end, after all—but that we allow ourselves to be carried by the requirements of gentleness into the struggle, into the hunger and thirst for justice. There the Lord holds us to mercy in order to counteract our enmity against those who confound, thwart, or betray the search for justice. He reminds us that we will be treated mercifully if we are merciful.

There are many understandings and meanings of mercy; but we are more interested in chronicling and sharing our own journey toward merciful action than any exhaustive treatise on mercy (or any other attitude). We concentrate on three aspects of mercy: mercy as pity or compassion; mercy as mitzvot or good deeds; mercy as patience or forbearance. We have wrestled with these attitudes and, in all probability, will have to wrestle continuously with them until our dying gasp.

## MERCY AS PITY, COMPASSION

Every day from July 21 until August 9, 1975, we brought "Little Boy" and "Fat Man," mock-ups of the bombs used against

Hiroshima and Nagasaki, to the steps of the Capitol in D.C. We estimate that in those three weeks, some 25,000 people viewed those horrid symbols of national failure, which directly or indirectly killed nearly 400,000 Japanese. Graphics around the bombs clarified the gap between American rhetoric and practice. For example, paraphrasing from 1 John, 3: 15, Anyone who hates sister or brother is a murderer, and murderers cannot have eternal life. Below the text was this commentary: "Our choice of death—we continue to enlarge nuclear arsenals at the rate of three hydrogen bombs per day. We have over 9,000 bombs and warheads, each with over three times the explosive yield of the Hiroshima bomb."

The graphics also spoke of "broken arrows" (nuclear accidents), some of which, except for a vigilant Providence, could have devastated whole states, or could have triggered what informed people consider "the last war." For example, in January 1961, a B-52 on a training mission over North Carolina had to jettison a 24-megaton bomb. Five of six interlocking safety devices were tripped by the fall. A single switch prevented an explosion that would have obliterated the state of North Carolina.

For a touch of drama, a person dressed as a death specter fondled the horrid symbols and exhorted tourists to continue paying with their silence and taxes—factors that made research, stockpiling, and threatened use possible. Another person, taking the role of life-defender, reviewed Schlesinger's recent refusal to "rule out" limited (tactical) nuclear war, or in circumstances of international face-off, a first strike against "enemy" nuclear silos employing the new American maneuverable re-entry vehicle (MARV). Frequently, demonstrators reminded the vacationers that every weapon created and produced in history has shed blood. Hiroshima and Nagasaki are evidence of that. The bomb will inevitably turn against those who trust in it. In a word, if the arms lunacy prevails, North Americans who created and who alone used the Bomb will themselves taste its cataclysmic violence and poison.

It seems fair to say that most vacationers passed the demonstration vaguely apprehensive and uncomprehending. Some lingered, understood, and hurried away frightened. Some others stopped to argue heatedly, often evincing a fervid anti-Communism. A few screamed epithets at us, furious at our desecration of a national shrine. Only a handful from day to day lingered quietly, reading our literature, or talking thoughtfully among themselves. Virtually no one came forward to ask "What can we do back home?" or "Can we join you here?" or "How do we awaken North Americans (and others) to this peril?"

Such inertia we found most unnerving and shocking. Experience had prepared us for the confused and numb ninety-nine percent. But the tiny number of thoughtful people—that none of them would acknowledge our common and deadly peril; that none of them would offer to lift a hand! We remember leaving Washington daily with a millstone hung from our spirits. Does God and His Redemption mean nothing? Does the sanctity of life mean nothing? Have Americans sold out totally to Caesar?

That millstone saps our spirits. There is about us, and at times within us, so much indifference, so much coldness, so much untruth that we become overwhelmed and hopeless. To resist these feelings we have had to try to fathom the causes. What has afflicted us so? On a base of understanding, we hoped to build the compassion that would enable us to be instruments, ministers of healing. We hoped to learn the mercy that would open the doors to solidarity and to hope.

Thomas Merton helped a great deal in this search. The world, understood in its most negative light, he explained, is the place that fosters our deepest lies about ourselves.

> The mother of all lies is the lie we persist in telling ourselves about ourselves. And since we aren't brazen enough liars to make ourselves believe our own lies, individually, we pool our lies together and believe them because they

have become the big lie uttered by the vox populi and that kind of lie we accept as ultimate truth.[1]

By now the collective lies—told and retold—have assumed the stature of myth, the most important form of collective thinking. Myths are the foundation of social life and culture; they are thought to express the absolute truth because they tell a history that is both real and sacred. Myths are exemplary, repeatable. So they serve as models, justifications, patterns for human behavior.

Mircea Eliade, in his *Myths, Dreams and Mysteries,* expounds the thesis that the modern world is destitute of myths.[2] We believe he is correct. What has replaced myths might be called anti-myths. These exert tremendous force in American political life. Many of our crises and much of our dis-ease spring from our being dominated by these anti-myths, rooted in lies. Unlike real myths that bring into play life-giving symbols, that enable people to draw upon fresh spiritual resources and to renew their creative powers, our anti-myths enslave the imagination and spirit.

Our thinking went something like this: if the root of our incapacity to respond humanly lies in our enslavement to these anti-myths, maybe it would be useful to expose them to the light of truth. *The truth will make you free,* Jesus said. John, 8: 32.[3] So we set out to research these anti-myths and, in seminars, retreats, talks, and writings to expose them, to unmask them for the lies that they are. We understand this as an aspect of Christian ministry and a work of mercy. Through it we came to see that indeed there were sisters and brothers who would walk with us toward personal and social liberation.

---

[1] Merton, Thomas. *Conjectures of a Guilty Bystander.* Doubleday & Co., New York. 1966. p. 71.

[2] Eliade, Mircea. *Myths, Dreams and Mysteries.* Harper and Row. New York. 1957.

[3] Flannery O'Connor had an adaptation of the quote that may be more apropos to our experience: "The truth will make you odd."

Undergirding the whole rush to destruction, we discovered, is a series of anti-myths about security, ideas that possess us profoundly now and can kill us later. The lies are not that difficult to expose, even though such exposes are all too rare.

## THE ANTI-MYTHS (LIES)

1. *Peace requires preparation for war.* North America must be strong; it must be stronger; it has to be strongest. Its strength and, symbiotically, its security lie in its military arsenal. An aspect of that strength, which is hauled out for dusting at regular intervals, is the economic vitality that is generated through the research, development, and deployment of nuclear weaponry.

So Reagan and other post-World War II presidents identify themselves as peacemakers. MX missiles are named "Peacekeepers." The Strategic Air Command (SAC) abandons its World War II motto of "Death from Above" in favor of "Peace is our Profession." This motto is written billboard-large at each SAC base. It is emblazoned on much of its hardware and all of its stationery. Against this lie, we have sought to broadcast the integrity of ends and means: "There is no way to peace; peace is the way."

Both sides of the arms race are confronted by the dilemma of steadily increasing military power and steadily decreasing national security. It is the considered judgment of professionals that this dilemma has no technical solution. If the great powers continue to look for solutions in the area of science and technology, the result will be to worsen their situation. The arms race can thus be seen only as a steady spiral into oblivion. Our leaders fail to admit this. They operate, plan, proceed with the ultimate certainty that there is no problem that cannot be solved by a little more power, by a new round of weapons. This is best illustrated by Robert McNamara's revelation that his problem, as secretary of war, never was to get sufficient dollars for defense, but rather, to avoid buying weapons that weren't needed. The United States military, for example, didn't plan to have the numerical advantage it did in 1966 or 1967 vis a vis the

Soviets. It was not needed. The reason the military had it was this range of uncertainty that one must guard against, and there's no better way to guard against it than by, in a sense, assuming the worst and acting accordingly. Then, when the worst doesn't happen, you've got more than you need, and that's bad enough. But worse than that is that the Soviets see you have it and they react, and then you have got to do it again. That's what causes the escalation: that's what makes it so dangerous.[4]

The means-ends relationship needs to be studied more deeply. There is a mysterious connection between what people believe and prepare for, and what occurs in consequence. If we, as Americans and world citizens, cannot begin to envision a world without these deadly weapons, then we cannot do anything to bring such a world into being. Vision is first; faith in that vision follows, and with faith, the deeds follow that will give flesh to the vision and lead to a different future.

The "double-speak" of Orwell's *1984* is not fantasy. It is in use among us here and now in the claim and name of "Peacemaker," "Peacekeeper." A few years ago, double-speak went to the extreme of naming a fast-attack, nuclear submarine "Corpus Christi" or "The Body of Christ." A good friend stared death in the face in a fast against such blasphemy; he won a victory of sorts. The name "City of Corpus Christi" was eventually applied to the weapon.

The bomb cannot provide security. President Kennedy in a 1961 proposal to the United Nations calling for general and complete disarmament pictured nuclear terror, "spread by wind and water and fear," and asserted that "humankind must put an end to war, or war will put an end to humankind." He continued, "The risks inherent in disarmament pale in comparison to the risks inherent in an unlimited arms race."[5]

---

[4] McNamara, Robert S. "The Military Role of Nuclear Weapons: Perceptions and Misperceptions." *Foreign Affairs.* Volume 62. Fall 1983. p. 79.

[5] Kennedy, John F. September 25, 1961 address to the United Nations. Quoted in *To Turn the Tide.* John Gardner. Harper and Brothers. 1962. pp. 207-223.

One could, with some cynicism, claim that the statement, given Kennedy's performance, lends more credit to his speechwriter than to the president. Nonetheless, the statement is a solid one, morally and politically, because it springs from an unassailable axiom: we have no right to such weapons. No one does!

"America is strong and growing stronger every day," Mr. Reagan said in his State of the Union address on February 4,1986. He could not have lived in, he could not have seen the same country we saw in 1986 and still see today. Poverty, hunger, homelessness, joblessness plague our people. Schools, prisons, hospitals, shelters are oversubscribed and underequipped, qualitatively and quantitatively. Strength? Daily, air, land, vegetation, and water are poisoned. Medical care is out of sight for millions. Senator Hollins remarked that Reagan's address was "good theater but bad arithmetic." How can theater be good that is devoid of truth? Such theatrics are an instrument of propaganda; they feed the anti-myth. And Reagan's performance, like that of most politicians, was geared to maintain the status quo and to enslave citizens to the machinery of militarism.

2. *Our real enemies,* the anti-myth goes, *are godless communists who seek nothing less than world domination.* This lie has evolved into a catch phrase; it is wheeled out on every occasion: "The Russians are coming. . . ." Through the bomber gap, the shelter gap, the missile gap, the window of vulnerability, the space-warfare gap, our leaders have sought to seduce us; we must at all costs increase military spending once again, get on top of the arms race once again. Forty years of propaganda have pushed the same line; protecting us from communist aggression is our nuclear arsenal, and our willingness to use it.

More than any of the other lies, this one approximates the mythic. It has the mythic precedent of the "evil force seeking mastery over the world." But as it works in our culture, it had to become rooted in "collective thinking," by fair means or foul. The enemy, fear of the enemy, had to be carefully contrived, sold, imposed on our people. Finally, as this anti-myth operates, there is no need of a "hero of freedom" to accept the godly task of standing against the enemy and winning freedom for all. The weapons replace the hero. The bombs become the master symbol; henceforth they guide the policy.

Still our history is a different matter. The United States time and again has refused to enter serious disarmament talks with the U.S.S.R. The deception of our people in this regard, the rewriting of history to suit the policies of our leadership, is crass and shameless. A National Security Council Memorandum No. 68,[6] (1950 vintage, declassified twenty-five years later), revealed that disarmament negotiations are a mere subterfuge for "building strength;" for rearmament, not disarmament. Salt I and Salt II, Vladivostok and the rounds and rounds of talks in Geneva have been a cruel hoax on both North American and Soviet peoples, according to Sidney Lens, author of *The Day Before Doomsday*.[7] NSC No. 68 and documents like it reveal that more than 6,000 sets of disarmament talks were clearly intended to: (1) permit an increase of American arms, (2) confuse and divide public opinion and (3) neutralize any opposition, especially any opposition arising from the North American Peace Movement.

In 1988 much was made of the Soviet-American treaty to eliminate intermediate-range nuclear missiles (INF Treaty). Before the treaty was signed, each of the branches of the military had more than compensated for the "loss" to the U.S. arsenal of those weapons. The result was an escalation that produced at least three times more missiles than existed before the treaty.

We don't adduce these matters as a way of blessing the Soviet Union, whose nuclear irresponsibility is, in our judgment, only slightly less lethal than our own. Still, it is worth recalling that the Russians suffered perhaps twenty million fatalities in World War II. Perhaps four or five million more Russians died—no

---

[6] Lens, Sidney. "The Doomsday Strategy." *The Progressive*. February 1976. p. 19.

[7] Lens, Sidney. *The Day before Doomsday*. Doubleday and Company. New York. 1977.

one knows, but Russians remember—as a result of Stalinist and later purges. In consequence they know more about war than we do. And they act accordingly. When the Atmospheric Test Ban was negotiated in the early 1960s, the U.S.S.R. wanted all tests stopped. We refused. In 1977 the Warsaw Pact Nations, led by Moscow, sent a letter to President Carter urging both sides to sign a joint declaration that neither would use nuclear weapons first. Carter refused. Since Gorbachev's ascent to power in the U.S.S.R., his repeated disarmament efforts have been spurned, most notably the eighteen-month test ban and the Reykjavik proposals.

The real enemy is not the other, of whatever stripe or color, but the grasping heart that gives us no peace. The real enemy is the fear that controls and drives us. It drives some of us into isolation, away from others, especially from those who differ politically, racially, ethnically from us. The same fear drives others to make common cause with those we judge very like ourselves, so that together we might keep those who are different at safe distances, in places like prisons, mental hospitals, refugee camps, even concentration camps. As native Americans, black Americans, and each of the immigrant groups learned in its turn, it is hard to be different in America. When they can't be bought off, those who are "different" are excluded and nullified.

3. According to another powerful anti-myth, *our leaders are too disciplined and balanced to start or to fight a nuclear war.* This fiction would have us believe that the more terrible the weapons, the more sensitive and responsible our leaders become. It fails to take into account that the arms race is maintained by a self-propelling bureaucracy to which our leaders, even the best of them, are subservient, are victims. It fails to take into account our history, especially the ten to twenty unilateral nuclear threats made by American presidents since 1945.[8] It fails to take into account the reality and the pathology of power. Some

---

[8] Betts, Richard K. *Nuclear Blackmail and Nuclear Balance.* The Brookings Institution. Washington, D.C. 1987.

among the organization of Physicians for Social Responsibility, we think of Dr. Caldicott, have claimed that leaders of the nuclear nations are their first patients, that is, those most in need of medical help, of psychiatric help.[9]

4. Another anti-myth professes that *the bomb has kept the peace* for forty years, making the price of its development and deployment a small one. The argument is both absurd and destructive. The fact is the bomb has critically distorted the nature of peace and justice at its foundation; it has exacerbated militarism, instead of furthering the truth that war is now obsolescent. The bomb has indirectly caused some forty wars on the planet; through testing it has poisoned air, soil, and water globally, and perhaps irreparably. And it has brought humanity close to nuclear midnight.

Whatever the restraints practiced by Superpower leadership, they have eroded and worn thin, deeply vulnerable to some of the following factors:

1). Having achieved rough parity with U.S. military power, the U.S.S.R. national security managers are much more likely to think like their U.S. counterparts and conclude: "We can't afford to back down and look like helpless giants."

2). As presidents become weaker—between Eisenhower and Reagan, we had no other two-term president—they are likely to find it impossible to resist unanimous military advice, especially if the country is full of hawkish ideas and the peace movement is too weak to offer resistance.

3). World power relationships are changing faster than we can comprehend, and the arms race has become an entirely new game, no longer the simple arithmetic involving two nations, the U.S. and U.S.S.R.

4). Most arms-control and disarmament experts agree that the spread of nuclear weapons increases the likelihood of World War III. In "Nuclear War by 1999?" (The Arms Control Seminar of Harvard and M.I.T.), the faculty confessed that nuclear

---

[9] Caldicott, Helen. Quoted in a public address given in Baltimore, Maryland, in October 1980.

war in some form was likely before the end of this century. "It would probably occur as the direct result of the proliferation of 'nuclear powers' and weaponry. The more people who have such weapons, the more probable their use."

The world today is on the verge of a vast and rapid development of nuclear weapons by countries that at the moment are non-nuclear states. It is well established that Israel, Pakistan, and South Africa now have nuclear weapons. Soon the nuclear club will include Argentina, Canada, West Germany, Italy, Japan, Sweden, and Taiwan. Within five years Australia, Belgium, Czechoslovakia, East Germany, the Netherlands, Spain, Switzerland will join. Within ten years Austria, Brazil, Bulgaria, Chile, Cuba, Denmark, Egypt, Finland, Hungary, Indonesia, Iran, South Korea, Libya, Mexico, Norway, the Phillipines, Poland, Romania, Thailand, Turkey, Venezuela, Yugoslavia. Forty-six nations are likely to possess nuclear weapons by 1999.[10] This horizontal proliferation goes on, aided by the nuclear power industry and the insatiable appetite of arms profiteers for new markets for weapons.

The design and manufacture of a crude explosive is no longer a difficult task technically. If the essential nuclear materials are at hand, it is possible to make an atomic bomb, using available information:

> On October 27, 1970, the city of Orlando, Florida, received a note demanding $1 million and safe escort out of the country as the price for not blowing up the city with a hydrogen bomb. Ransom instruction, a workable bomb diagram, and a note arrived saying the fissionable material had been stolen from Atomic Energy Commission shipments. The AEC could not give absolute assurance the materials had not been stolen. The ransom was assembled and would have been paid, but the blackmailer was caught. He was a fourteen-year-old honor student. Suppose he had

---

[10] Epstein, W. *The Last Chance: Nuclear Proliferation and Arms Control.* The Peace Press, N.Y. 1976.

been a twenty-five-year-old terrorist, or a forty-five-year-old Mafioso?[11]

Acquisition of special nuclear materials remains the only substantial problem facing any group desiring such weapons. Already special nuclear materials are being stolen in alarming quantities from nuclear power plants. Non-governmental proliferation, as it is called, is a reality.

Today technology itself as well as the policies of "limited nuclear war" and "first strike capability" make nuclear exchange ever more proximate, more probable.

5. *The anti-myth of deterrence and of limited nuclear war.* Henry Kissinger first aired the lie that a nuclear war can be limited, fought, and won. Few were able to point out the contradictory anti-myth: that the primary purpose of our nuclear arsenal is as a deterrent. And on the anti-myth of deterrence, most North Americans have been nurtured for years.

Policy makers argue that the U.S. has no choice: it is under intensive and long-term siege by a gruesome enemy; so it needs this massive nuclear stockpile to "deter" the enemy. The deception begins with the word "deter." The comforting conviction that the goal of our government is not to initiate aggression but to sustain a stalemate has been buttressed by the rhetoric of our national leaders:

> Eisenhower: "This world-in-arms is not spending money alone. It is spending the sweat of its laborers, the genius of its scientists, the hopes of its children. . . . This is not a way of life at all, in any true sense. Under the cloud of threatening war, it is humanity hanging from a cross of iron."[12]

---

[11] Dumas, Lloyd J.. "National Insecurity in the Nuclear Age." *Bulletin of Atomic Scientists.* Volume 32. May 1976. p. 31.

[12] Eisenhower, Dwight D. April 16, 1953, before the American Society of Newspaper Editors.

MacArthur: "War has become a Frankenstein to destroy both sides."[13]

Kennedy: "The primary purpose of our arms is peace, not war—to make certain that they will never be used, to deter all wars."[14]

North Americans are reassured that thermonuclear exchange is no longer a practical possibility. The "assurance" is confirmed by the fact that no bombs have been used since 1945. Still, the truth is another matter. Deterrence is no longer part of the useful rhetoric of our nuclear policy, though it is lodged fast in the hearts of North Americans. The two contradictory lies work side by side to lull any who would question military wisdom. One or the other is drawn out, depending, it seems, on the knowledge of the questioner.

The government cannot defend its people. More to the point, it exacts payment for a profound imperilment, payment for the prospect of mass suicide. The gravest failure of the Pentagon is its total impotence to deliver on its promises (defense and deterrence). The failure began in calling the Pentagon the Department of Defense. It was more honestly called the Department of War through World War II. Today the more insistently we label it for what it is, the more clarity and freedom we create for ourselves and others. For the truth is, there is no defense, there is no protection, no warding off a nuclear attack.

We have been told[15] that 140 million North Americans would be killed in a nuclear attack. This is a conservative estimate. When the next $1.8 trillion is spent on weapons, we will be no closer to defense than we are now. Against the anti-myth that "America must be No. 1," that the survival of the U.S. as a

---

[13] Lens, Sidney. "The Doomsday Strategy." *The Progressive.* February 1976. p. 13.
[14] *Ibid.,* p. 14.
[15] Barnet, Richard. "Ultimate Terrorism." *The Progressive.* February 1979. p. 14.

sovereign actor in the world justifies mass murder, poisoning of the earth, and even the hideous mutation of the human species, we must be willing to envision a more modest place or a different posture for our country. The vision comes first. What we envision, we can then work for.

Many of our people do not know "the truth." We have all, at least for segments of our lives, believed a lie, because the printing presses said "such and such" was true. Once the lie is exposed, people can help one another erase the effects these lies have had on all our lives. The anti-myths have reduced most of us, at least for a time, to a state of ignorance, dependence, and confusion. Rather than enabling us to transcend the present and gain a glimpse of the eternal, as myths do, these anti-myths have driven us to childish pursuits, distractions, and diversions. Rather than inspiring life-giving symbols, as myths do, these anti-myths have driven us to believing all that our leaders say, almost without question. How else can we explain Americans' acceptance of the invasion of Grenada in 1983, of the bombing of Libya in 1986, of the shooting down of the Iranian passenger liner in 1988?

But, for many, the problem is not just not knowing.

North American experience of the last few decades has made us shock-proof. We have become so insensitive to even the most incredible events—Dachau, Auschwitz, Hiroshima, Nagasaki, Camp Desert Rock, the elimination of rain forests, the choking smog of over-industrialization, the contamination of the oceans, rivers, lakes, drinking water, human caused climatic changes—that we are no longer capable of being aroused or stunned. We take what comes, incapable of reacting thoughtfully, intelligently, and reasonably. This plague of conscience is best described as "spiritual death." The expression contains and sums up all obstacles to sanity, peace, and continued life on earth.

Why indeed is the Marxist prophecy of perpetual war best exemplified by the U.S.? Why, in a cold-war context, was this nation responsible for genocide in Indochina? Why did North American leadership, fresh from defeat in Indochina, confidently bluster about first strike and "winning" a nuclear war? Why are the harrowing lessons of Indochina avoided or ignored? Why is North American arms traffic now approaching $25 billion in sales annually? Why the hypocritical, unending concern with "horizontal proliferation," even while continuing a mad "vertical proliferation" competing with the U.S.S.R.? Why the reliance on newer and more costly forms of weapons production? Why the constant interference in the internal affairs of other countries, smaller and weaker than ourselves?

A clue is offered: what the Bible calls invasion by the Dragon (Satan) and his Beast (the state). Revelation, 13: 1-2. Under the Beast image the bomb is seen as Lord and Peacemaker, Supplanter of God and his Christ. Implied too is our submission to a state that contaminates the world with its culture, and arms the "Free World," mostly against itself. The same state has used nuclear weapons twice and threatened their use repeatedly since. And it plans, a la Herman Kahn, to dig out from under a nuclear convulsion, prepared once more to build and dominate.[16]

Can one not speak Biblically here of "possession by the bomb," a people deprived of understanding, of our need of exorcism? Surely we have here the spiritual counterpart of Freud's death wish, the longing to "end it all" through mass murder, mass suicide.

Such has been our speaking, writing, sharing, aimed at unmasking the anti-mythic pretensions of our culture, at ending the injustice perpetrated in our name. Acting, we hope, in a spirit of mercy, we have also tried to build a community of conscience that would undertake to live in an alternative way, faithfully, justly, modestly, mercifully.

## MERCY AS MITZVOT OR GOOD DEEDS

Of seminars, lectures, articles, there has been no end among us. Our efforts to teach and learn continue to be important.

---

[16] This is evident in the number of governmental departments and major corporations that have created underground headquarters to keep important records safe against nuclear attack.

Important, but not enough. Since spiritual death is the mystery we face, in ourselves and in others, we concluded that awakening and enlivening our spirits was our deepest need.

Words, words, words. We are a people so inured to vacuous speech, vain hopes, and passive acceptance that turning to the Word of God seems a fantastic undertaking, literally radical beyond words. Take, for example, these verses of Isaiah:

> *For as the rain and the snow come down from heaven, and return not thither but water the earth, making it bring forth and sprout, giving seed to the sower and bread to the eater, so shall my word be that goes forth from my mouth; it shall not return to me empty, but it shall accomplish that which I purpose, and prosper in the thing for which I sent it.* Isaiah, 55: 10,11.

The text offers a hint of the integrity in God, between word and deed, between hope and the thing hoped for. We need recall only the first chapters of Genesis; when God speaks a word, the word creates.

As God's people, we are drawn into that integrity. We are invited to turn words to deeds, hopes to reality, the impossible to the possible. We are drawn into the godly task of making peace, which is the work given to humanity in Genesis. The Creator told our parents that our mission was to exercise dominion over creation—dominion (or the restoration of harmony) in a world where domination (or the urge to control) is the major disrupter of that harmony.

Our mission of restoring harmony, of peacemaking, is inseparable from the works of peace. To say, as we so often do, "we can create a world without war" is to commit ourselves to building that world stone by stone, deed by deed.

Mitzvot are understood as Messianic good works, works or acts through which it is possible to see and recognize the Messiah. It is the deeds, the good deeds, the Mitzvot of God that scripture celebrates. It is the good deeds, the Mitzvot of Christ, that brought conflict with the authorities of his day, and so the

Cross. We who would follow Jesus are commanded to act even as he acted.

This Biblical insight helped us understand the urgent role of symbolic action. Much of our time and wit has been invested exploring symbolic action, in both concept and practice. We concluded tentatively that the purpose of symbolic action is not to convey information but to touch and disclose previously unknown depths of awareness lying unplumbed at the center of being. Merton wrote:

> Traditionally the value of symbol is precisely in its apparent uselessness as a means of simple communication. Because it is not efficient as a mode of communicating information, the symbol can achieve a higher purpose of going beyond practicality and purpose, beyond cause and effect. Instead of establishing a new contact by a meeting of minds in the sharing of news, the symbol tells us nothing new: it revives an awareness of what we already know and deepens that awareness.... The symbol awakens awareness and restores it.[17]

There is, we learned, a radical difference between the use of symbols and true symbolic action. A group of religious Jews, during the Vietnam War, did a "symbolic" destruction at the Pentagon of a golden calf, a toy bomber, and other trinkets. Dan Berrigan, hearing about this action, referred to it as taking salt from a dead pillar to pour into the wounds of the living. Dan said: "I am called to create new events in the spirit of the older ones." The Golden Calf—militarism—rages in the world. Real bombers fly while the toy breaks up. Real symbolic action, such as that of the "Catonsville 9,"[18] draws on symbols to break

---

[17] Merton, Thomas. "Symbolism: Communication or Communion." *The Monastic Exchange.* Summer 1970. p. 6.

[18] May 17, 1967, nine Christians took the 1A draft files from the Catonsville, Maryland, Draft Board and burned them with home-made napalm in the parking lot. All were arrested, tried, and convicted. All but Dave Darst, who was killed in an automobile accident before the appeals ran their course, served time in federal prison for their action.

real laws. Jesus broke the temple laws and the laws of the land; his criminality is not to be doubted.

We are all called to create new events, open new possibilities, in the spirit of the traditional symbols. We are called to break into this world, as Christ broke into the temple, in nonviolent rampage against those who rattle the missile keys and level the megaton guns. Such events, it goes without saying, are not created by isolated individuals. They arise, if at all, from community.

Phil wrote of an experience in Arlington County Jail, Virginia, that also illustrated the difference between the use of symbols and symbolic action:

> A seminary student came to jail today to teach us about the Book of Daniel. He brought us information on the captivity in Babylon, that is, the geography of the imperial city and historical and cultural settings. Then he turned to the text itself (Daniel, 1-3) retelling the old story of how King Nebuchadnezzar of Babylon destroyed Jerusalem and took the Jews into slavery. Notice the imperial sequence supplied by the text. Nebuchadnezzar, fresh from mass murder, moves immediately to consolidate his conquests. Warfare does not cease but continues in a different, less abhorrent form. He takes slaves, plunders the temple of its vessels, and brings them to his own temple treasury. The vessels are symbolic loot suggesting his enslavement of religion. Nebuchadnezzar's own priests, as it develops, become court appendages and clowns, diviners and soothsayers. His object is to reduce the Jews to similar levels of trivia and subservience. Next step: he colonizes the Jewish hearts and minds even as we North Americans did in Indochina. He culls out a young Jewish elite for steeping in Chaldean language and culture. And then he offers the Jews patronage, come-ons, privileges. Chaldean names come next, attacking both Jewish and human identity. If the king could destroy their past, their grasp of themselves, their memory, then their colonization would become com-

plete. He would thus succeed in devouring their souls, in owning them. Like Black "Oreo cookies" consumed in the white supremacist's dream—the husk would be Jewish, the core Chaldean!

During the summer of 1974, Vietnam's General Thieu and his cabinet visited Washington, D.C., in order to lobby the Congress, the White House, the State Department, for, you guessed it, more money for their fading government. While in D.C., they visited veterans' hospitals to present gifts properly inscribed "With gratitude from the people of South Vietnam." The gifts were Zippo lighters, which, like defoliants and 500-pound bombs, were symbols of U.S. scorched-earth policy. The Vietnamese, I believe, were utterly oblivious to the true meaning of their gesture. What had destroyed them? What had made them such total, vacuous marionettes jerking from American strings? Why, the same education as offered by Nebuchadnezzar, of course.

Imagine the "image," the cohesion, the "justice" of an empire managed by the colonized. Nebuchadnezzar brought the conquered into the imperial court, and after acculturation, sent them to manage the provinces. We do the same—the military heads of fascist regimes all over the world were all initially trained by our military.

Our seminary student made all the connections except the most obvious Biblical/political ones. In his mind Nebuchadnezzar has no counterpart today. Neither Nixon, Carter, nor Reagan apply. For him the American empire has no record of slavery (least of all enslaving its own people); no record of absorbing religion (religion is truly "separate" from the state); no privileges for which food and wine are metaphor; no record of forcing its insane culture upon every corner of the world. . . .

Much discernment has gone into our efforts to offer symbols and symbolic actions that are, if not adequate to the horror humanity faces, at least evocative of such horror. . .

Such was the effort of "The Baltimore 4" in 1967 when Phil, with Tom Lewis, Dave Eberhardt, and Jim Mengel, poured blood on 1A draft files at the Customs House in Baltimore. This action was followed in 1968 by the burning of draft files at Catonsville. These files are not innocuous papers, the actors said in deed and word; they are licenses for hunters whose prey is members of the human family.

These acts caught the imagination of many; roughly 200 direct actions against draft boards took place in America from 1967-1971.

Bob Aldridge was an engineer at Lockheed in 1967 and 1968, designing missiles for greater and greater accuracy. He reached the point of saying, "This accuracy means only one thing. We're designing for a disarming first strike." He could not continue such work. He confessed that the turning point came for him when he learned of the Customs House action of 1967. It stayed with him hauntingly, until he could discover the freedom to act on its inspiration in his own way.

In the early stages of our resistance to nuclear weapons, we learned of a Pentagon plan to use abandoned mines as fallout shelters in the event of a nuclear exchange. "They'd be mass graves," someone protested. Subsequently we performed a series of actions under the slogan "Disarm or Dig Graves!" an attempt to give public expression to the horrid government plan. The first action took place on the lawn of the White House; the grave diggers were "Specters of Death," people robed in black with skeletal faces, accompanied and encouraged by an "Uncle Sam" figure.

We continue to use the symbol of blood spilled on the portals, porticos, floors, walls, and porches of the "sacred" temples of our government, as well as at corporations that make the weapons and at bases that store them. If only the horror with which people respond to the blood as symbol can be transferred to the reality of shedding blood! Then the blood symbol will approximate the horrors that hover above us.

Friends whose work has focused on Latin America and the terrible sufferings of millions under tyranny there, have staged "torture tableaux" in public places. We have also used the "die-in" many times. The question is always in the air; how remind ourselves and others of the unthinkable? How depict those who might survive an initial nuclear blast, and yet be vulnerable to shock and radioactive poison? These questions are illumined harrowingly by the "die-in;" performed with intelligence and restraint, it can somewhat approximate the real horror of nuclear war.

In some settings we have found the "die-in" can serve not only as useful theater, but also as an act of resistance. For example, a "die-in" may block the concourse of the War Department. Creative theater, simple and real, has aided us to voice the pain in many hearts. The enactment speaks, in metaphor and truth, of the death that gnaws within us all.

Furthermore, we have searched our own history for the Biblical images and symbols that are the content of our collective memory. The symbols of Exodus, Covenant, of the Incarnation, Passion, and Resurrection of Jesus form an exemplary pattern and the basis of our hope and our struggle toward new life. The liturgical calendar has formed a kind of time table; each event invites a contemporary dramaturgy.

But the most profound symbol of all, we believe, is the community itself. On what ground do we enter an Exodus, a Covenant, a life of displacement, loss, risk, hope? Surely we cannot count on ourselves or our own resources to live so deep a commitment. Rather we begin with the person of God holding empty hands before the abundance of gifts that the Lord bestows upon us. The greatest gift, as we have come to know, is a loving unity, a sign of God's presence and a source of the new creation God wills to bring into being through us.

Community remains a beacon and a burden to us. We seem incapable of living in community and incapable of living without it. Perhaps our double mind stems from a dread of trusting God and one another. We try to build a *faithful* community. Only by beginning with the absolute fidelity who is God can other fidelities (such as in community or in marriage) become possible for us.

We have tried not to elevate perplexity to a divine call. So a few conclusions, necessarily tentative, seem better than none:

—Community starts with a vision. People can come together out of confusion and isolation, and bind to one another in hope. In so doing, they consent to a rigorous displacement.

—Community finds its authority in Christ's mandate: *Remember me!* Luke, 22:1 9, and *For where two or three are gathered in my name, there am I in the midst of them.* Matthew, 18: 20, and in his often repeated: *Follow me.*

—Community grows through the willingness of its members to conspire or "breathe together" on behalf of life. This is the proper work of community formed by the spirit of God.

—Community lives in covenant with God and with the neighbor brought near. Living the ancient covenant, or the Christian covenant, makes visible the power of God in our world.

"With my mouth," God says, "I kiss my own chosen creation. I uniquely, lovingly embrace every image I have made out of the earth's clay. With a fiery spirit I transform it into a body to serve all the world."[19] No lonely task this, but one that involves us with our world and with one another.

The daily newspapers and newscasts give us a ceaseless litany of human agony. Yet mere information does not lead us to deeper solidarity or greater compassion if we hear the daily dosage of the bad news as small, powerless, isolated people. When there is no community to mediate between the world and personal response, such news is a crushing burden. In community, on the other hand, we keep eyes and ears open, without being numbed by overstimulation or angered by powerlessness. In community we weep, laugh, suffer, and rejoice— no longer a mass of helpless individuals, but one people of God.

Can such communities quicken conscience and concern? Can they bring life out of our world of death? The question is not whether saving lives, saving the world and the world's children,

---

[19] Hildegard of Bingen. Quoted in *Original Blessing.* By Matthew Fox. Bear and Company Press. 1983. p. 184.

whether such high designs are certain or even probable of outcome. The question is obedience to God: fidelity to God and to one another. We are in fact seeking to express a future that almost no one thinks is imaginable. We know it is the future to which God summons us, a hope and yearning so long denied the human heart. It will take time, and more time, and so we live in the meantime. We seek to live in *the shadow of God's wings*. Psalm 63: 7, in fervent cherishing of the life God has created and surely cherishes.

## MERCY AS LENIENCY, PATIENCE, FORBEARANCE

Revealing the anti-myths that obscure and frustrate the spirit is an act of mercy.

Uncovering, discovering the symbols that vitalize the spirit is a further act of mercy. With these we struggle.

But what, we ask our souls, are we to do with the anger that wells into dumb rage against those who perpetuate deception, violence, fear; who deepen the pits of darkness? Mercy summons us to patience, humaneness, forbearance, reconciliation! There, we must confess, the road before us is a long one. We bluster at our leaders. We know outrage and rage at them. Unloving, even hateful, feelings well up. We can be snide, abrasive, judgmental, arrogant. Our criticism becomes carping, in face of the real need: the simple assertion that their power is illegitimate; their promises are false.

In our better moments, we understand that Jesus (whose very name means *to save*) takes sides. We know he sides with the victims of violence and injustice. We know too that, ever faithful to himself and his name, he wills to save the victimizers from themselves and from victimizing. We understand, at least in remote corners of our souls, that Jesus challenges and spurs us to abandon our own hostilities, however righteous they may seem. He calls us to be patient with our impatience (and true as well, to be impatient with our patience). He wills that anger be a flame that drives us to good deeds, rather than a fire that consumes.

Liz and Phil each spent many active years in religious life. The discipline of those years taught us the difference between our better moments, and those other, less praiseworthy ones. The difference was marked by prayer. The difference between our ability to be loving, toward friend or enemy, and our lovelessness, is a difference created by prayer. We know that all our strength, hope, courage, and confidence come from that holy Source, the Lord whom we meet in prayer.

As lovers, as parents, as members of a community that often seems like the interior of an accordion, squeezed and stretched as we are by the comings and goings in such a house as ours, making time for prayer is a challenge and a discipline. Finding ways, places, times for daily prayer takes real creativity. We learn to grab quiet moments, to treasure drives alone, to read a passage of Scripture, to reflect on it as we go through the day, to find God's face in the neighbor who comes importunately to the door.

In our weekly Eucharist, prayer finds its most profound expression. The community gathers. One of our members has prepared a reflection on the next section of the Scripture we are studying. She or he presents it and together we reflect on it, trying to apply it to our life together. After about an hour and a half of this sharing, we pray those prayers that are in our hearts, bless and break the bread, share the cup, then greet one another with the sign of Christ's peace.

There is midweek community prayer and weekly study of Scripture with the children. Phil began this when the children were about five years old. He reads a passage of one of the gospels and spends about an hour with them, talking it through, applying it to their lives, to our life together. "I learn more from these sessions than from sessions on the Scripture with many adults," he confessed. The children do not have the burden of so many years of hearing the Good News neutralized.

Each trip is begun and punctuated with Scripture and prayer. Our little one, expectant of this ritual, asked on one trip: "Isn't anybody going to read some Scripture?"

Often we pray for our leaders; but, we add to our humiliation, not often enough, not as we ought. If our prayer were adequate to their need (and our vocation), we would know that it is not possible to pray for them and to harbor ill feelings toward them.

Our best prayer for them is an event of reconciliation. We invite them to our own hearts, that they and we might be touched by the healing Spirit of God. It is out of such prayer as this, now and then granted us, that our best actions[20] come, actions through which God's love touches the heart of humanity.

Such actions are truly free. They strive to remove the greed, fear, suspicion, and competition that are the root of the arms race. They are actions that lead us to listen, to speak truthfully, to heal and be healed. Moreover, they are actions that violate unjust laws, laws that legalize an utterly wasteful and insane violence. The laws enforce the waste (now nearly $1 billion a day for the U.S.); enforce the approaching catastrophe (four or five minutes to nuclear midnight); enforce the hostage-taking of every living person, every unborn person, every potential person of every future generation. The laws legitimate the war crimes of leaders of the nuclear nations; enforce the non-future to which children are condemned, enforce the prospect of global suicide—the Second Crucifixion of Christ.

Let it be shouted around the world—from every parliament, pulpit, classroom, farm, factory, street, and home—the nuclear state is a criminal state whose law is criminal. That law must be broken; that law is not law but lawlessness legitimated.

In 1979, Pope Paul, writing to the United Nations, expressed the moral outrage that should possess every responsible person: "The arms race is a danger, an injustice, a form of theft from the poor, a folly, a machine gone mad." He continued, "Even

---

[20] Actions, as we frequently refer to them, mean public acts of resistance or peace witness. They may or may not include divine obedience; they may be small or large.

when they are not used, by their cost alone, armaments kill the poor by causing them to starve. Let these shameful weapons be banned ... let this terrible art, which consists in manufacturing, multiplying and storing bombs to terrorize the people ... be outlawed."[21]

We know too that our anti-nuclear actions must be offered as acts of mercy. Such was the spirit of "The Plowshares 8"— "We are filled with hope!" they wrote, "for our world and for our children as we join in this act of resistance." The eight acted knowing that if the arms race is to be stopped, it must be stopped by people, by us. They acted knowing that security, even the security that supposedly protects these weapons plants, is illusory.

Such was the spirit of Peter de Mott, who decommissioned a Trident submarine in Groton, Connecticut, and served a year in jail for his action. "I saw the Trident," Peter said, "knowing that it was a weapon made especially for a first-strike, nuclear war ... I judged that the Trident has no right to exist ... I acted to dismantle the Trident, because not to have done so would have been to make myself complicit in the mass death for which it was designed."

Such was the spirit of the six who assembled in Amarillo, Texas, for an act of witness at the final assembly point for all this country's nuclear weapons. They scaled the outer fence, to the astonishment of the security people, and prayed and held a banner that read: "Security ... in the Bomb or God?" They refused cooperation with the jails or courts, attempting to speak clearly and simply about the evil of Pantex, described as the "heart of darkness."[22]

Such was the spirit of the four who entered the Lockheed plant in Santa Clara, California, and happened on the room

---

[21] Pope John Paul II. "The Dignity of the Human Person is the Basis of Justice and Peace." 1979 Address to the United Nations. *The Pope Speaks, 24.* p. 310.

[22] The article, "The Heart of Darkness," appeared in *World Press Review. Volume 34.* March 1987. p. 51.

where components of the Trident missiles were stored. They poured blood on the missile, on the blueprints for making it, and on naval order forms for the missile.

Such has been the spirit of each of the small groups of people, moved by the plowshares concept to act, with hammers and blood, with hearts and lives. They and their actions were neither to be admired nor venerated. Rather they hoped to challenge the complacency of an imperiled humanity, and complicity in nuclear death dealing. So the actions proceeded, in as loving a spirit as the resisters could muster. And the actions were, in each case, above all, prayers. Conceived in prayer; developed in an atmosphere of prayer and Scripture study; and enacted as prayer. Prayer that the Spirit might use the action as a means of unleashing within and among us the spirit of disarmament. They were admittedly and deliberately provocative; the evil of nuclear weapons is so blatant that only prayerful, strong, unambiguous action will do. As Dan wrote:

> We are malign enough, twisted enough, to bring creation to a smoking ruin. We have the instruments, we have the myths, we even have the blueprints stashed away in some war room in some hollowed-out mountain. Who will confront this crime, this seizure of creation by demonic tooth and claw? I think it is only resisting people . . . and I believe they will prevail. I believe this because I believe in God. The two sentences in fact merge in my soul: they are one. They will prevail because in them (in you and me) very nearly all our hope rests. Because in them goods of mind and heart, neglected squandered human goods, coalesce and survive, and shine forth.[23]

Blessed are prayerful resisters—their actions are works of mercy; blessed are the merciful, they shall receive mercy.

---

[23] Berrigan, Daniel. *The Book of Uncommon Prayer.* Seabury Press. New York. 1978. p. 108.

> *Blessed are the pure in heart,*
> *for they shall see God.*
> Matthew, 5: 8.

## CHAPTER SIX
# THE PURE OF HEART

Too often the imperatives of a given beatitude are lost in the language. We can regain them if we split the word: be-atitude, emphasis on the be: become, do it! Be an attitude. *Have this mind among yourselves, which is yours in Christ Jesus.* Philippians, 2: 5. Thus the Beatitudes are seen for what they are: the imperatives of Christian life.

Another way of understanding this sixth beatitude is to read it as "We will be happy if we are single-minded in God's service." We are called to eliminate the inconsistencies between faith and life. Jesus starkly stated the consistency faith requires: You cannot give yourself to God and money. (A paraphrase of Matthew, 6: 24.)

If our practice of mercy is authentic, it frees our hearts from selfish pursuits and endeavors. In the beatitude urging purity of heart, God commandeers our hearts into service. It is from the heart that thoughts, plans, memories, affections flow. So the summons unites us, heart and soul, in the search for God, for the good, for the truth, for all that the name and person of God evokes in us. It is a summons not so much to renounce our own good, but to grow in the awareness of how intertwined is our own good with the good of all; the good named godly.

Through each of the Beatitudes we have sat with friends, sometimes in silence, always in affection, listening, remembering. The Beatitudes give the very shape to our lives and ministry! One shape and the same. Our spirit has not been one of self-congratulation. We long only to share the insights we have gained on our way, a way made easier by others making similar (or different) journeys. We admit to our discomfiture that under each beatitude yawns a chasm: how we are called to live and how we, in fact, do live. The obvious gap may or may not be bridged in later life. If it is, it will be because of the generosity of God's Spirit, who gently assaults our perverse desire to control our lives and to limit that Spirit's access to our hearts.

Jesus puts before us in this beatitude a restatement of the commandment given through Moses:

*I am . . . your God, who brought you out of the land of Egypt, out of the house of bondage. You shall not have other gods before me. You shall not make for yourself a graven image, or any likeness of anything that is in heaven above, or that is on the earth beneath, or that is in the water under the earth; you shall not bow down to them or serve them.* Deuteronomy, 5: 6-9.

Thus the essence of the beatitude. The language of Jesus simply brings into focus the blessing, the happiness that are the consequence of obedience to this, the first commandment.

The beatitude enjoining purity of heart forces us to look long and hard at contemporary idolatry, the false gods who have a throttling hold on our personal and national life.

## SINGLE-MINDED OR NARROW-MINDED?

Who can claim to be single-minded in God's service? And if one did, who could trust that claim? And further, if such a one existed, and the claim were verifiable, who could live with such a person? These questions stir memories of stories of the saints, some true, some legend. Stories of saints who gave away all their own possessions and then claimed for the poor the possessions of family and friends. Stories of saints who brought into their homes the blind and the lame and the sick, and then charged their family and friends to care for the guests.

The hardships of such singleness are suggested in these words of Charles Peguy, words which are dear to both Phil and Liz:

> I believe that one can find a number of persons who suddenly perceive the truth and seize it. Or persons who seek and find the truth and in so doing deliberately break with their interests, break deliberately with their political friendships, even with their most cherished friendships. I do not think that there are many who make this first sacrifice, and have the second courage to sacrifice their second interests, their second friendships. They are willing for the sake of the truth to fall out with half the world, all the more so because in so acting and paying, they usually make partisans of the second half of the world, partisans who ask nothing more than to be antagonists of the first half. And if for love of the truth, one falls out with the second half, who will become his partisan? So the life of an honest person is an apostasy and perpetual desertion. Such a one is a perpetual renegade. The one who wishes to be faithful to the truth must be continually unfaithful to continual successive indefatigable errors. And the one who wishes to be faithful to justice must be continually unfaithful to inexhaustibly triumphant injustice.[1]

When Liz was in Alexandria City Jail in 1977, a friend wrote her and asked, "What is the relationship between Christianity and your lifestyle?" And a second question: "What are your hopes and goals for the future?" The letter Liz wrote in re-

---

[1] Peguy, Charles. *Basic Verities.* (French-English Edition by Ann and Julian Green.) Pantheon Books. New York. 1943. pp. 48-49.

sponse highlights our aspirations for faithful living; and more; the gaps in our hope.

I am not a Christian woman. Ours is far from a Christian community. Our lifestyle is shamefully middle-class, American—even in jail. We know warmth and comfort, the power that comes from good education and our "infamy;" we have access to the best materials for reading and writing, good and cherished friends, good and ample food, even cash crops. We are not poor, not meek, not in touch with what sorrow means. Our struggle for righteousness and justice is still compromised, far from the single-mindedness to which we are summoned.

We grow weary though we have endured but a little. We resist even the call to *Awake and strengthen what remains and is on the point of death.* Revelation, 3: 2. The struggle is constant, against egoism and the individualism in which we were raised, toward a spirit of love, of patience with human variety. Throughout, we have come to recognize that the community we work to build can come only as a gift and not as a consequence of our own effort.

Have we graduated into adulthood in these years? I doubt it. I can only confess that though from the outset my orientation was moral and Biblical, I have begun to realize that I am an infant in Biblical faith. It is as though I am opening the Book for the first time and feeling its judgment: a two-edged sword in my soul. As we face the Pentagon and the power of nuclear death that possesses (literally) all of us, the best in us despairs of confronting it, the worst in us acts in complicity with it. It becomes at once impossible and essential to act there: we must perform an act of faith in Christ, whose death and resurrection have already defeated this power; we must issue a summons to this authority (the state) to fulfill its vocation to serve rather than to destroy humanity; we must live out a testament for anyone with eyes to see, that the choice between God and money needs to be made each day in each heart.

> Community is a gift. Our goal, our hope, is to grow to be less unworthy of the gift, the blessing that is community, to become citizens in the Kingdom of Christ. To worship God in truth and truly to resist the false gods we have put before him. (The chief god today, according to Merton, is the self.) To do this with resilience; to be a part of the community that confounds, rebukes, and undoes every regime until that moment when humanity is accounted over the nations and principalities in the last judgment of the Word of God.[2]

In another jail letter from the time, Liz traced the threads in her life that had brought her to this point of consciousness and commitment.

> I have become one of the endless stream that passes in and out of prison gates. It is good that I do. It is right that we should know how to suffer; that I am forced to the level of the most miserable of people before I judge; and that I experience in my heart again and again the sufferings of the dispossessed.
>
> So many of the women who come through here are on drugs and have committed "crimes" to support their habit. I don't know whether it was a compliment but one woman studied me and said: "You don't belong here! You should be a wife and mother." "I am," I said, "but as long as you are here, I belong here too."
>
> The argument is not heredity vs. environment; both play a role in human development. I was raised white, middle-class, suburban, Irish-Catholic, one of seven children, a twin. My upbringing was geared to prepare me for that style of life, but I came out differently. A few elements stand out in my own pilgrimage which, in retrospect, weave

---

[2] Cf. Stringfellow, William. *Conscience and Obedience: The Politics of Romans 13 and Revelation 13 in Light of the Second Coming.* Word Books. Waco, Texas. 1978.

a thread somewhere close to the center of my being. Throughout childhood I knew an urge to have my life serve people more directly than seemed possible in the wife-mother models about me. Was it more than childhood fantasy? Is childhood fantasy too often ignored in adult life? Religious life as I perceived it in my teachers did not answer the longing I felt. And there were no models for me. It was a time before Peace Corps, Vista, Jesuit Volunteers; I knew nothing of the Catholic Worker. Service to the poor seemed proper to the Salvation Army, but was strange to me.

Interestingly, as I reflect on it, mine was a life devoid of heroines. I was not attracted by movie stars—their indulgence was contrary to what I sought. There were no women politicians to whom I could look as any kind of model. Something was calling, though, and after both searching for and running from it, I entered into the silence and prayer-life of the novitiate of the Religious of the Sacred Heart of Mary. To what service was I called? That was still an unanswered question as I went into religious community with only a love of the Scriptures and an open heart.

The change in that time had been subtle. A vague, even naive sense that citizenship in the Kingdom could not be reconciled with citizenship in the Great Society, that rationalizations about containment of communism could not justify widespread killings in war, that Christ and not the presidency (even in its Camelot years—1962-1963) was the Way, the Truth and the Life. I was reading the bad news but with my other eye on the Good News. For several years, it was all personal, interior. "Of course the war in Indochina is irreconcilable with the Gospels!" I told my art-criticism students at Marymount College in our attempts to comprehend the critical theory of "Symbolic Form" in art (Suzanne Langer). And they were horrified that I thought David Miller's act of burning his draft card to be not only fine symbolic form but also a just and good action. I did not understand all the political implications, but I knew in my soul that war was wrong. Though very inexperienced, I knew the justifications for our Vietnam involvement to be congested with falsehood, euphemism, deception, if not straightforward lies.

The floodgates opened as the Marymount community heard of my position (already labeled "pacifist").[3] Reproaches, rebukes, denunciations, efforts came from many sides to educate me to the real facts of real life. There was only silence and avoidance from other quarters. And from a few unexpected ones came rejoicing, nurturing, supporting. A small community within that community was already groping, like a few elsewhere, to be responsible to the Gospel in a time of war.

There were a few in the anti-war movement in those days whose roots and perceptions were Christian or Biblical. Innocent, even childlike, we could not comprehend the length and height and breadth of the violence we were seeking to confront. As the revelation came upon us, slowly, by degrees, each of us had to face personal fear, doubt, despair. Many dropped out, many were plucked off along the way. Those who remained were forced to dig more deeply into motivation, nonviolence, Scripture, each other. Phil and I shared those years. They seemed hard then—then we hardly knew what 'hard' meant—and yet so joyful.

Young men resisted the draft and went to jail. What of us? How do we move from dissent to resistance? I recall being bewildered by the question. Peacemaking for me was still part time, an extra-curricular activity. Phil took the

---

[3] "Pacifism" describes those who abhor war and violence. It has many levels or meaning. Tolstoy as a religious anarchist found all government to be coercive and involved in criminal conspiracy against the governed. In place of government he stressed the primacy of voluntary associations, collective in nature and based on nonviolence. In place of violence he called for moral revolution and, when necessary, passive resistance.

lead in the transition in October 1967, when with three brothers he poured blood on files that made murderers of young men. The action, called "The Baltimore Four," became a precedent for four years of work with small groups who wanted to live what they believed. Some 200 or more draft-board actions occurred; there were innumerable encounters with courts and judges and jails.

Were the actions symbolic or effective? Through them we became enemies of the state, a threat to its political hegemony. Intimidation, defamation, harassment followed. We were subject to a massive prosecution with big guns aimed to cut off our credibility if not our future. Harrisburg, 1971-1972, the celebrated indictment for conspiracy to kidnap Henry Kissinger and blow up the underground heating tunnels in D.C., the long trial on revised and broadened charges, was a time of evaluation, reflection, redirection.

The war continued unabated, being met more and more by public silence, acceptance, weariness. For resistance to flourish, we faced the need to begin again, to rebuild, reform. We needed to see to it in our rebuilding that we and our friends (to the extent that we could urge it) planted roots deeply enough to sustain the long-haul effort. It would require our whole life, perhaps that of our children. We needed to see that in our rebuilding, people were making their own decisions. We needed to weed out coerciveness as much as we could, while keeping alive a sense of urgency, to sustain the positive dimension of strong community for the sake of growth and nonviolent resistance. We needed to work so that community might become strong, real, Christian.

There is a thread of difference here (and the thread is unbreakable, and so makes all the difference) between the single-minded and the narrow-minded; between fixing eye and heart on justice, and becoming fixated; between fervent peacemaking, and obsession, being out of touch with the real world. We hang by that thread, aware at times and unaware often of our purity or impurity of heart. Even when we do not lose our balance, we are at least perceived as having done so. Like it or not, such labels as "fanatic"[4] or "dreamer" are often placed on us. We don't expect the labels to change. We try to retain good humor, and our sense of ourselves, no matter what the labels.

## CONTEMPORARY IDOLATRY

"Happy are those who are single-hearted *in God's service.*" ". . . in God's service." What does that mean to us as Christians, or to Americans in general? As Americans we make much of the concept of freedom. We want not service but freedom. It is a knotty situation. There is so much misunderstanding of freedom, in concept and in practice. As people we can not choose freedom; we are not independent. There are only two states of being open to us: submission to God and the works of justice, or the refusal to submit to anything beyond our will, a refusal that enslaves us to the forces of evil.

Like the Jews of Christ's time, Americans think that to be an American is to be free; they see freedom as if it were a possession. And this notion is largely unexamined, merely taken for granted. But any deeper sense of freedom, and certainly any Christian perspective of freedom, is one with the concept of service and with the question: "What god does one serve?"

As Scripture assumed a more central role in our lives and in the life of our community, so did its language. Scriptural language helped us both to understand and to articulate the meaning of our times and our country, as well as the meaning of to be "in God's service." Others helped to mold that Biblical awareness.

It is difficult by now to recall when we first began to understand our nation's preoccupation with militarism as an aspect

---

[4] "A fanatic is a person who passionately believes in something you don't understand." This definition is part of the oral wisdom of the Reverend Maurice McCracken, a good friend.

of idolatry, or when we first began to use such language publicly. To many it may still sound strange. Idolatry is a phenomenon presumed long gone, vanished in the sophistication of modern life and technology. But for us the insight has emerged in ever starker relief. Certainly Bill Stringfellow, his friendship, his person encouraged us. His *An Ethic for Christians and Other Aliens in a Strange Land*[5] gave form to our feelings long before we could verbalize them. He challenged us in mind and heart to connect our Biblical story with our contemporary story. Bill was a man of the Good Book. It was, he told us, the only book he read. We believe his testimony as we cherish his person, even as we miss his mind and spirit among us.[6]

The view of life offered by the Bible is inimitably radical because its inspiration comes from God, the Author, Sustainer, and Redeemer of life. The radical response to questions is contained for us in the word of God: about creation, about life, about people. The Psalmist says that individuals, like nations, can choose their gods, whether real or illusory. The Psalmist warns that the choice of false gods (idols) narrows, even destroys, freedom. The idol transforms the idolator into its own image, an image of death. The text is precise and incisive.

*The idols of the nations are silver and gold,*
*the work of human hands.*
*They have mouths but they cannot speak;*
*eyes but they cannot see.*
*They have ears but cannot hear;*
*nor is there breath on their lips.*
*Their makers will come to be like them,*
*and so will all who trust in them.* Psalm 135: 15-18.

The Psalmist charges that the false gods of nations are silver and gold; it is a stark foreshadowing of Christ's stark alternative:

---

[5] Stringfellow, William. *An Ethic for Christians and Other Aliens in a Strange Land.* Word Books. Waco, Texas. 1973.
[6] Bill Stringfellow died March 2, 1985, after a long illness.

"Choose God or money." The idols are the handiwork of people, radically opposed to the handiwork of God, opposed to God's creation. The false gods are dumb, blind, deaf, and lifeless. *Nor is there breath on their lips,* the Psalm has it. The idol gains control of the idolator, changing her or him into itself: numb, blind, deaf, lifeless.

The idols, the Psalmist reminds, kill us, make us dead like themselves. In a deeper sense, they lie to us, secure for themselves an expanding credibility, sap and drain off our life in a lingering murder. Christ warned of this in one of the most neglected texts of the New Testament, calling Satan a liar and the parent of lies. (A paraphrase of John, 8: 44.) False gods are the Devil's instruments, his deadening artifices, his killers.

It goes without saying that unless we discern the idols and muster a resounding "NO!" to their lethal influence, we cannot say a "YES!" to life; we cannot live, we cannot be truly free. We were struck by Paul's magnificent insight in 2 Corinthians, 1: 29, that Jesus is the "Yes of God" and wondered how one could become a Yes of God and live with a false sovereignty crippling one's life, denying one's freedom? Freedom is freedom from death and death-dealing or it is nothing. Freedom is the choice of life that we derive from God and from his Christ. Freedom is the refusal to dominate anyone, and the refusal to let anyone be dominated. Freedom is the reign of the true God in us, saying "Lord!" with meaning and unequivocation. Freedom is the struggle to give God's life entrance and mastery.

We have our own American idols; we live amid the slavery and death these idols produce. They are visible in the numbness that has become endemic, a phenomenon we have already addressed. The next question is: "What have these idols done to our people?" Most citizens cannot speak of the realities of life and death, nor see, nor hear. Many are simply lifeless. To most, Christ's revolution of the spirit means nothing. To most North Americans even the grandiose rhetorical aspirations of the eighteenth-century American reformers (they cannot be considered revolutionaries) mean nothing. When we remind our people that there is no hiding from nuclear weapons, they attempt to run and hide anyway, an habitual reaction. The common plight of leaders and led reminds us of the precision of the 135th Psalm. Or, of the words of Christ in the ninth chapter of John: *"For judgment I came into this world, that those who do not see may see, and that those who see may become blind." Some of the Pharisees . . . said to him, "Are we also blind?" Jesus said to them, "If you were blind, you would have no guilt; but now that you say, 'We see,' your guilt remains."* John, 9: 39-41.

Perhaps there is the nub of the problem: most North Americans, leaders and people, say "We see!" They see with the sight of idols. A child can tell us that idols are blind; idols are deaf; idols are dead.

The proposition that gradually imposed itself upon our consciences is that our "self" is our chief personal idol; the state is our chief social idol; and war is the chief liturgy of the state. Occasionally we catalogue North American idols using our favorite "isms," such as materialism, consumerism, nationalism, sexism, racism, even neuroticism. Without exception, they evince a desire to exploit property that belongs to all, or to dominate others who are made tools for our comfort or control. The appetites require a structure (the state) to legitimate the domination, to give it the trappings of morality. Hence the alliance of Church and state: to legislate and arbitrate the rules to protect good property holders; to elevate property to the status of idol, to the status satisfactory to corporate appetites. On an imperial scale, therefore, the state must finally assume God's sovereignty, especially his power over life and death.

There come to mind two modest examples of the state's tendency to assume supreme power over the lives of millions. Some time back, *Harper's Magazine* published an article called "The Most Embarrassing List in Washington." It concerned sanctuary and protection in case of nuclear attack. Most politicians refused comment when asked if they had "made the list." One lackluster gentleman, though, noted equally for his verbosity and ambivalence, recalled the security offered him when he held the office of vice president. Only a senator when the list was published, he was incensed that congresspeople were reportedly excluded from salvation. He blustered that it was impossible to maintain confidence in government if the people's representatives were not protected.[7] What a monumental irony! People might die by tens of millions, yet the issue for him was confidence in government (and his own safety).

A second example is of the loss of the true lessons of Indochina. North American presidents have exhorted the country to "avoid recriminations" against parties and presidents over that long war; and the people, exhausted and fragmented by the moral repercussions of genocide, obey. Actually, the intellectuals of Church, media, and campus bear special culpability for the vacuum of reflection and evaluation of that war. One can only imagine the tragic consequences of learning virtually nothing from three decades of bloody intervention in Indochina. War crimes? The moral consequences of genocide? The nature of crimes against international peace? The capacity of criminal power? Its potential to strike again? These are questions that may forever rest untouched in North America even as, for all practical purposes, the holocaust of the 1940s remains untouched a generation later in Germany and Eastern Europe.

But to return to the state and its nearly unchallenged position as the new god. Its decalogue is reduced to the one commandment of self-interest, and its gospel is the gospel of war. Peruse the Beatitudes again and notice the antithetical nature of cultural, social, and political values as our North American society interprets them. According to our culture, we are blessed if we are rich in spirit. Most North Americans in fact consider themselves rich in spirit in the sense of moral superiority and rectitude. We are blessed if we are unmerciful and if we escape persecution. The state is the patron of such values. More than that, its gospel of war has resulted in a singular propaganda

---

[7] Collier, Barney. "The Most Embarrassing List in Washington: Who Gets Saved When the Balloon Goes Up?" *Harper's Magazine*. Volume 250. May 1975. pp. 18-28.

victory, the public acceptance of the qualitative similarity of conventional and nuclear war.

In effect, North Americans have ceded to the state, by and large, the moral responsibility for war, conventional or nuclear. They have submitted to the civic gospel in its main outlines: the economy cannot endure without war; doomsday weaponry is necessary as long as our enemies agitate; 100 million casualties are morally acceptable. Conceded also is the practice of triage, the choice of who is to live and who to die.[8] Conceded also is the state's constant and exacting appeal for faith, trust, confidence, and support.

In a word, the state plays god in Satan's manner—it lies and it murders. The prevaricating and bloody years under Nixon prove this amply. But whatever the management, whether Truman or Reagan, Lincoln or Wilson, or Roosevelt, the ruthless disregard of life differs only by degree.

Where does the Christian minister stand vis a vis the pathology of the times, as the times reflect the presumptuous claims and sanctions of the state? Today, as in the past, the minister of the Gospel confronts a sick world and its violence through nonviolent living, and through communities of resistance. We have Christ's own insistence on the mystery of sin, and its infidelity to God's sovereignty and power.

Nonviolent Christians believe Christ's revelation as light of the world, as way, truth and life. The disciple unequivocally dedicates him/herself to light over darkness, to truth over falsehood, to life over death. In a world haunted by violence, the believer sees that nonviolence is the only antidote, the only path to social and international sanity, the only means to attain the God who is truth.

---

[8] Triage is a system of assigning priorities of medical treatment to battlefield casualties on the basis of urgency or chance of survival or availability of medical supplies. Translated to the political arena (where it has no right to be) it has become an acceptable means of determining those worthy to receive monies, education, rights, and ultimately life itself.

The minister of Christ is communitarian, capable of building a community of resistance, eager to struggle in one as well. Christ called the disciples to community as his first public act. After Pentecost the disciples left Jerusalem for the most part, to build the Church, to build communities of nonviolent resistance. Their resources did not exceed ours—the same Gospel, the same Baptism, the same Spirit. But their vision differed. Paul told the Corinthians that the ways of God were completely different from human ways. Cf. 1 Corinthians, 1: 25-29.

In preparing for the disarmament action at Griffiss Air Force Base, Thanksgiving 1983, the community of the Griffiss Plowshares devoted substantial time to the inevitable trial. A defense of "necessity," a defense of "international law" had precedents; and we would, we agreed, prepare to make those defenses.

But a question arose. Why not go to court with our deepest motivation for such an action? Why not allow our effort to be single-minded in God's service speak for itself? Legally stated, that would be a "freedom of religion" stance. If we recall correctly, it was Karl Smith (one of the seven) who first put the idea, and who was most firmly behind it. We agreed to try to formulate the statement. Initial versions were done even before the action; but before these could be translated into an argument in court, a great deal more work was required. Elmer Maas and Ramsey Clark were "resources extraordinaire" in the process. The argument we presented orally in our pretrial hearing went as follows:

## ON FREEDOM OF RELIGION AND CONTEMPORARY IDOLATRY
**(An argument to the Court)**[9]
Syracuse, New York, March 19,1984

Judge Munson,[10] the government has responded to our written motion by declaring it totally without merit; that we made no

---

[9] Liz presented the argument in court on behalf of the seven Griffiss Plowshares. The seven are the "we" throughout this argument.

[10] Judge Howard Munson, Federal Court Judge, Northern District of New York.

showing that nuclear weapons constitute a religion in any generally accepted sense. We are not surprised by this response because we are dealing with a phenomenon that has grown among us and remains largely unanalyzed. We believe it is finally time that the issue be heard. There is a great debate abroad on this issue; may it be heard in this court where it has long needed to be heard.

We speak today for ourselves and many in our own and in other religious traditions. We think especially of Native Americans who, for generations, held as sacred, land that is now being mined for uranium; whose faith and religious values are trampled by such actions. We think, too, of Buddhists for whom honoring all life and the spirit of compassion are foundations for sanity and happiness and who, because of their religious faith, must constantly resist the nuclear threat.

Hear us a bit; we are, above all, trying to find our voice here, trying to articulate feelings that have long disturbed us, looking for this articulation. I will be as brief as possible; but still it may take a few more words than you or I would like to hear or speak.

We are dealing with serious constitutional issues—namely, the issue of a national religion having been established in our country in violation of the First Amendment. The religion of national sovereignty or nuclearism is alive and flourishing. And its existence, its pre-eminence, its rituals, gods, priests, and high priests make serious encroachments on all of us. In fact— and this is the second part of our argument—violating our freedom of religion. This state religion not only <u>compels acts that are prohibited by the laws of God</u> but the <u>state religion itself prohibits the free exercise of religion</u>. The state religion compels a quality of loyalty focused on our acceptance of the existence of nuclear weapons as a necessity. Weapons we are expected to pay for, adulate, thank God for, become sacred objects of worship. And such worship is prohibited by the laws of God.

Likewise the state religion prohibits the acts of justice that God's law requires. The acts of justice include not only not killing or preparing to kill, but also the rescuing of victims of murder, or intercession on their behalf. In this time when nuclear weapons threaten all created life, in this time when THE CLOCK[11] stands at three minutes of midnight, in this time when 40,000 children die daily from hunger while the world spends $1.3 million a minute on annihilatory weapons, acts of rescuing victims or intercession on their behalf take the form of direct acts of disarmament. And fulfilling God's law means obedience to the Biblical imperative to beat nuclear swords into plowshares.

Then to use the laws of our land for the purpose of punishing people who carry out acts of nonviolent direct disarmament is unconstitutional. Such <u>application</u> of the law prohibits our free exercise of religion and violates Article I of the Constitution. I refer to the application to our conduct of descriptions of sabotage, destruction of government property, and criminal conspiracy.

We are not asking you to decide this motion now. But, in the interests of justice, that you be open to hearing the issues that cross-cut and define it most clearly. Let us bring into this court, in pretrial hearing, experts who would point up the truth that this religion has been established; that it is unconstitutional; that it amounts to idolatry; that it contributes to the violation of the whole set of checks and balances on which our system has been established. On the basis of such testimony, make your ruling.

It is clear to us that the religion of nuclearism that has deified nuclear weapons not only contradicts the spirit and letter of the Constitution, but is, as well, part of a long evolving phenomenon that has, for over a century and a half, threatened the basic freedoms espoused in the Declaration of Independence and the Constitution. Let me now take a little time to

---

[11] Refers to the Clock of the Bulletin of Atomic Scientists, a clock that is moved nearer to or farther from midnight depending on the scientists' evaluation of the seriousness of the political situation and its impact on the possible use of nuclear weapons.

outline the establishment of our national religion and its encroachment on religious freedom.

Some have argued that CHRISTIANITY IS THE NATIONAL FAITH; others that church and synagogue celebrate only the generalized religion of the AMERICAN WAY OF LIFE; few realized that there exists, alongside of and rather clearly differentiated from the churches, an elaborate and well-institutionalized civil religion in America. It has its own seriousness and integrity and requires the same care in understanding that any other religion does. I want to make it clear that we have no quarrel with what, from the earliest years of the Republic, served as a genuine vehicle of a national religious self-understanding. We simply want to show an evolution from the earliest days of America's civil religion into our more recent history.

The first great event that involved national self-understanding so deeply as to require expression in civil religion was the Revolutionary War. And until the Civil War, American civil religion focused, above all, on the event of the Revolution—seen by our foreparents as the final act of exodus from the "Old Lands" across the sea.

The phrase "civil religion," which many today use to describe the national religion, comes from Rousseau's *Social Contract* in which he outlined the simple dogmas of that religion: the existence of God; life to come; reward of virtue and punishment of vice; exclusion of religious intolerance. Ben Franklin expressed his own faith in a way exactly parallel to Rousseau. Washington did also—seeing religion and morality as "indispensable support . . . the firmest props of the duties of men and citizens."[12] The Declaration of Independence embodied this same spirit, stating that it was "the laws of nature and nature's God" that entitle people to be independent; that our fundamental legitimacy lies in our being "endowed by our Creator with inalienable rights;" and it indicates a God of History who stands in judgment over the world in its appeal to "the

---

[12] Richey, Russell and Jones, Donald. *American Civil Religion.* Harper and Row, New York. 1974. p. 26.

Supreme Judge of the world for the rectitude of our intentions;" and expresses a "firm reliance on the protection of Divine Providence."

Maybe our concern with America's civil religion begins when Jefferson, in his second inaugural, wove the theme of AMERICAN AS THE NEW ISRAEL IN THE PROMISED LAND, a theme that was used, almost from the beginning, as a justification of the shameful treatment of the Indians. The America as the New Israel theme is overtly or implicitly linked to the idea of MANIFEST DESTINY, which was used to justify a number of adventures in IMPERIALISM since the early nineteenth century. Our manifest destiny to overspread the continent allotted to us by PROVIDENCE. Manifest Destiny became an expression of our civil religion—an expansion deigned and favored by God.

The Civil War was the second great event that involved national self-understanding so deeply as to require expression in civil religion. And we have no quarrel with the attempt of our country to come to grips with what Lincoln called "its punishment by God for the sin of slaveholding" (second inaugural address) or with the themes Lincoln, in his Gettysburg Address, introduced into the religious spirit of the country—themes of sacrifice, of death, and resurrection.

The essay by Robert Bellah in *Daedalus*[13] in 1967 gave the phrase "civil religion" a life of its own in this country. The term has been picked up by major media and inspired books, essays and symposia. The debate it inspired centers on two questions: "Does civil religion exist in the United States?" and "Should it exist?" The weight of evidence and opinion is that it is alive and well and, as presently formulated, it is illegal. <u>As presently formulated. WHAT CONCERNS US IN THIS COURT IS WHAT WE</u> MUST CALL A THIRD PHASE IN THE DEVELOPMENT OF OUR RELIGIOUS EXPERIENCE AS A COUNTRY USHERED IN BY THE NUCLEAR AGE which radically altered our lives and values and sense of self.

---

[13] Bellah, Robert. "Civil Religion." *Daedalus.* Winter 1967.

At the explosion of the first atomic weapon (code-named "TRINITY") witnesses were transfixed by the power of it. A passage from the Hindu Scriptures came to Oppenheimer's mind: "I am become death, the shatterer of worlds."[14] That line of scripture was uttered by the Exalted One, Lord of the fate of mortals; Oppenheimer applied it to himself, sensing that into his hands a far too mighty instrument of power had been given. He referred to his work on the bomb as a Faustian bargain with the forces of evil.

All the scientists, even those (the majority) without religious faith, recounted their experience in religious terms: Kistiakowsky—"This was the nearest to doomsday one can possibly imagine. I am sure that at the end of the world . . . the last man will see something very similar to what we have seen." To this William Lawrence, science writer for *The New York Times,* responded—"But it is also possible that if the first man could have been present when God said 'Let there be Light,' he might have seen something very similar to what we have seen . . ." Still another said: "It was like being witness to the Second Coming of Christ."

When Truman was informed of the successful explosion of the atomic bomb on Hiroshima, his response was—"This is the greatest day on earth. Thank God that he has given us the bomb and may we use it in his ways."[15] This then was echoed by Senator Brian McMahon when he told the Senate that the bombing of Hiroshima had been "the greatest event in world history since the birth of Christ."[16]

More than any other person we know, the psychologist Robert J. Lifton has analyzed the way nuclear weapons radically altered our existence so that nothing we feel or do is free of their influence. "Nuclear weapons," he said, "make their possessors either mass murderers or else deceivers and self-de-

---

[14] *Bagavad-Gita.* Chapter II, verse 32.
[15] Lens, Sidney. "The Doomsday Strategy." *The Progressive.* February 1976. p. 19.
[16] Congressional Record for August 1945.

ceivers who fluctuate between feelings of omnipotence and impotence as they gradually loose their hold on ethical tradition and existence itself."[17] Lifton points up the absurdity of being poised to destroy humankind, and living as if we weren't so poised; being unable to imagine nuclear holocaust, yet waiting and preparing for it to happen, the special fear that these weapons inspire and the set of illusions they foster: the illusion that we control them, that we can limit their damage, that we can prepare for and thus protect ourselves in face of nuclear war, that we can recover from nuclear war. We are left, he says, with the radical reality of vulnerability and the loss of FUNDAMENTAL STRUCTURES we have counted on in the past. A significant response to this condition has been an exaggerated restatement of those threatened FUNDAMENTALS that becomes NARROW FUNDAMENTALISM.

So in the 1970s and 1980s we have witnessed what he calls a world-wide outbreak of fundamentalisms: People's Temple in Guyana; the radical right politics of the moral majority; Khomeini in Iran; Jewish "Biblical Politics" in Israel; Hal Lindsley's movement around the celebration of the apocalyptic event. These would be some of the more dramatic examples. Usually such movements would be short-lived, such is the nature of fundamentalism. But, in an era of potential nuclear omnicide, we can expect them to become permanent fixtures in our collective experience. But the gravest fundamentalism (AND THE RELIGION OF OUR COUNTRY TODAY) is "NUCLEARISM," as Lifton and a host of others term it. It is a religion in which the bomb is the new fundamental, the new source of salvation. If this sounds outrageous, we need to listen to the way in which the bomb is described and talked about. Recall William Lawrence's response to the detonation of the hydrogen bomb—an amazing statement in which he moved from a sense of awe at its power to a sense of total security with the bomb

---

[17] Falk, Richard and Lifton, Robert. *Indispensable Weapons: The Political and Psychological Case Against Nuclearism.* Basic Books Publishers. New York. 1982. p. 33.

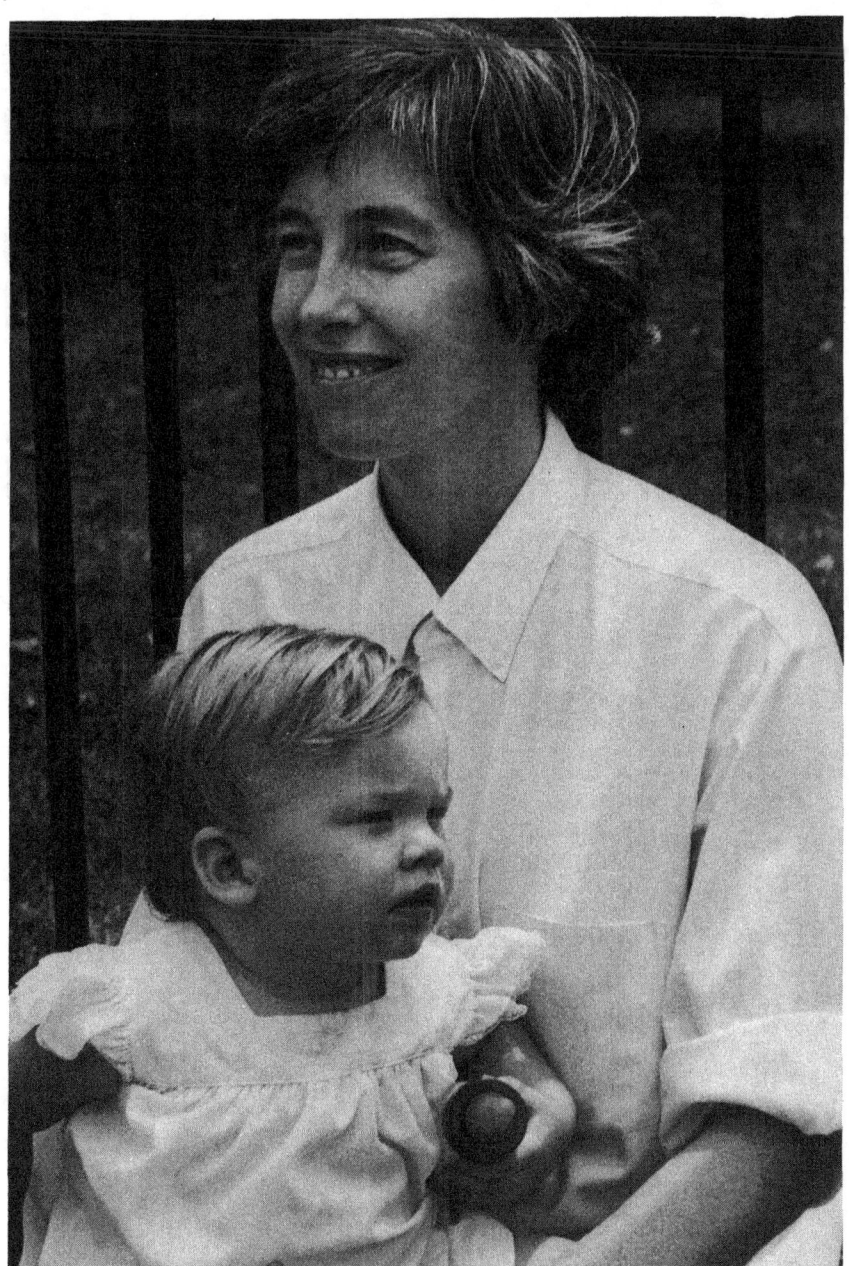

1. 1975—Summer. Liz and Frida at a White House demonstration.

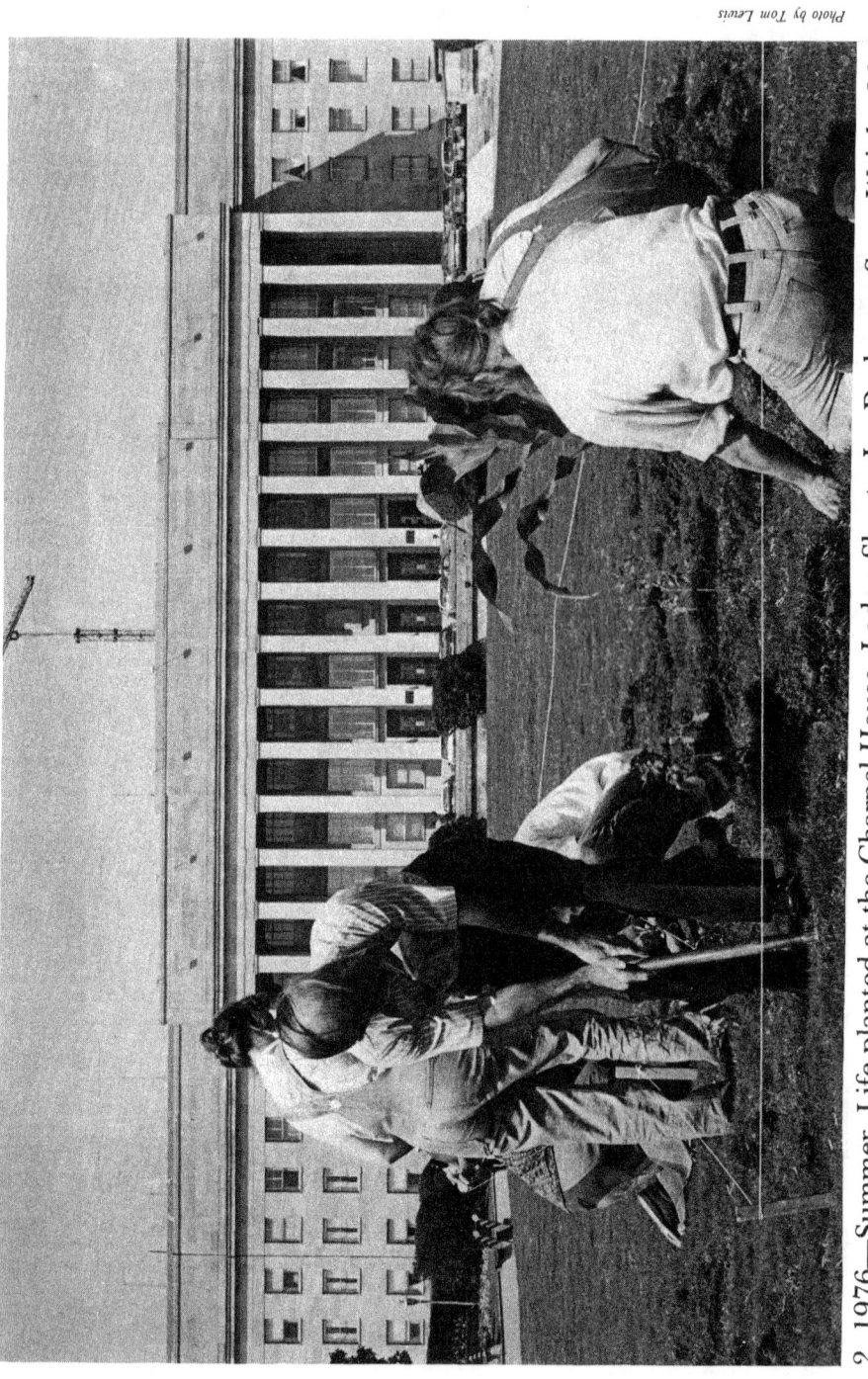

2. 1976—Summer. Life planted at the Charnel House. Ladon Sheats, Jay Dudgeon, Scott Wright, Mary Lyons, and others install a garden on the Pentagon Parade Ground.

*Photo by Tom Lewis*

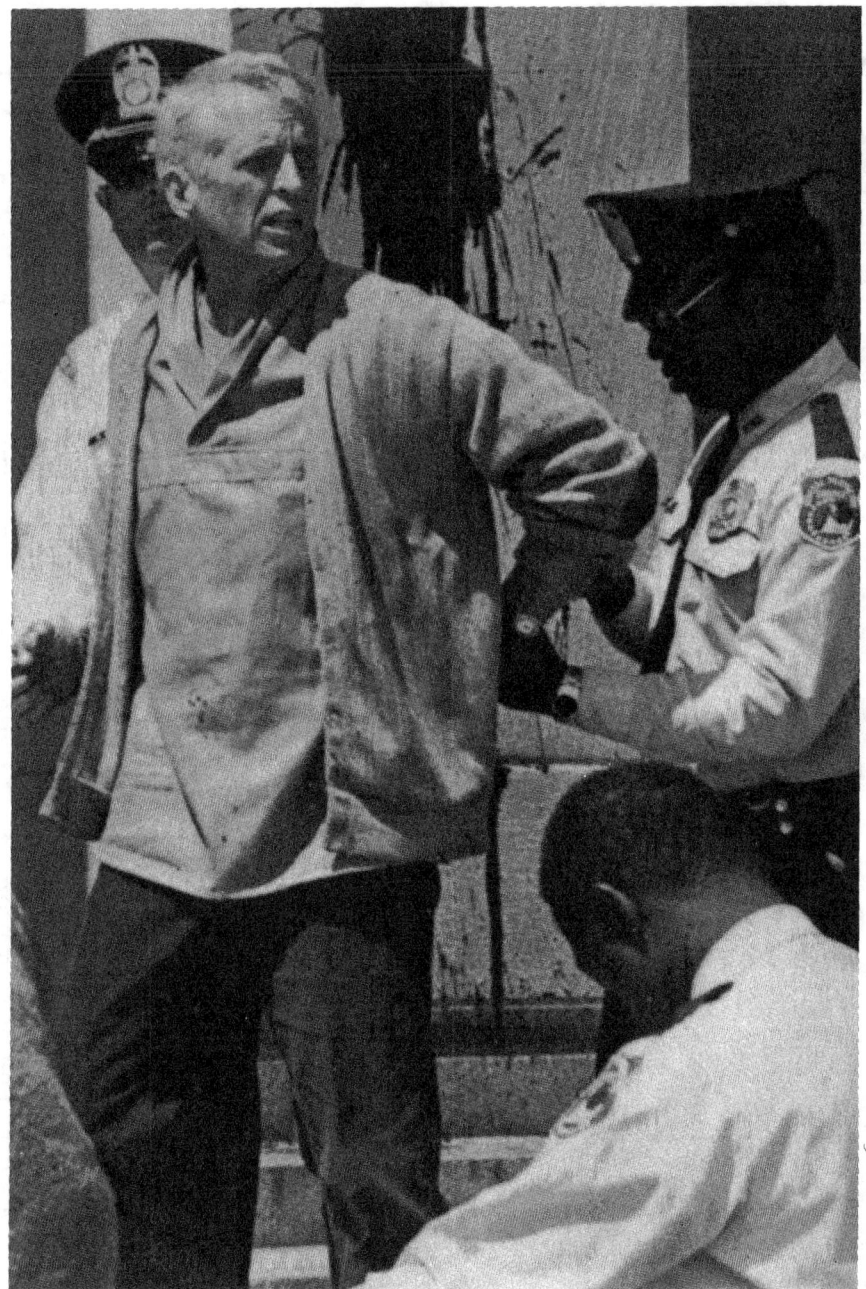

3. 1977—Summer. Blood as unmasking. Phil arrested at the Pentagon.

4. 1977—October. The broken promises of Carter. Mary Lyons, Paul Hood, and Rosemary Maguire are led away from First Baptist Church after speaking out during the service attended by the president. All three were arrested.

5. 1979—November. Anne Montgomery, Kathleen Wilkers, Liz, Dan, and Phil at an early resistance at the Riverside Research Institute, New York City.

Photo by Tom Lewis

6. 1979—Tax Day. Frida at the Federal Building in Baltimore. The other side of her sandwich board read: "We won't have the option."

7. 1979—Tax Day. Jerry at the Federal Building in Baltimore. The other side of his sandwich board read: "We won't have the option."

8. 1980—Feast of the Innocents. Children with a voice hold the banner they made at the Pentagon.

*Photo by Tom Lewis*

9. 1982—Feast of the Innocents. Many bombs, little butter, much homelessness. The militarism/destitution connection is made placing a car painted with "Wandering Jobless" on the Parade Ground. It was swiftly removed.

10. 1982—Feast of the Innocents. Updating St. Matthew's Herod at the Pentagon.

*Photo by Tom Lewis*

11. 1983—Thanksgiving. A bloody handprint on a B-52 being fitted with air launched Cruise Missiles. Part of the work of the Griffiss Plowshares. Written on the plane was "320 Hiroshimas," the payload of one B-52. The numbers can be seen in the photo.

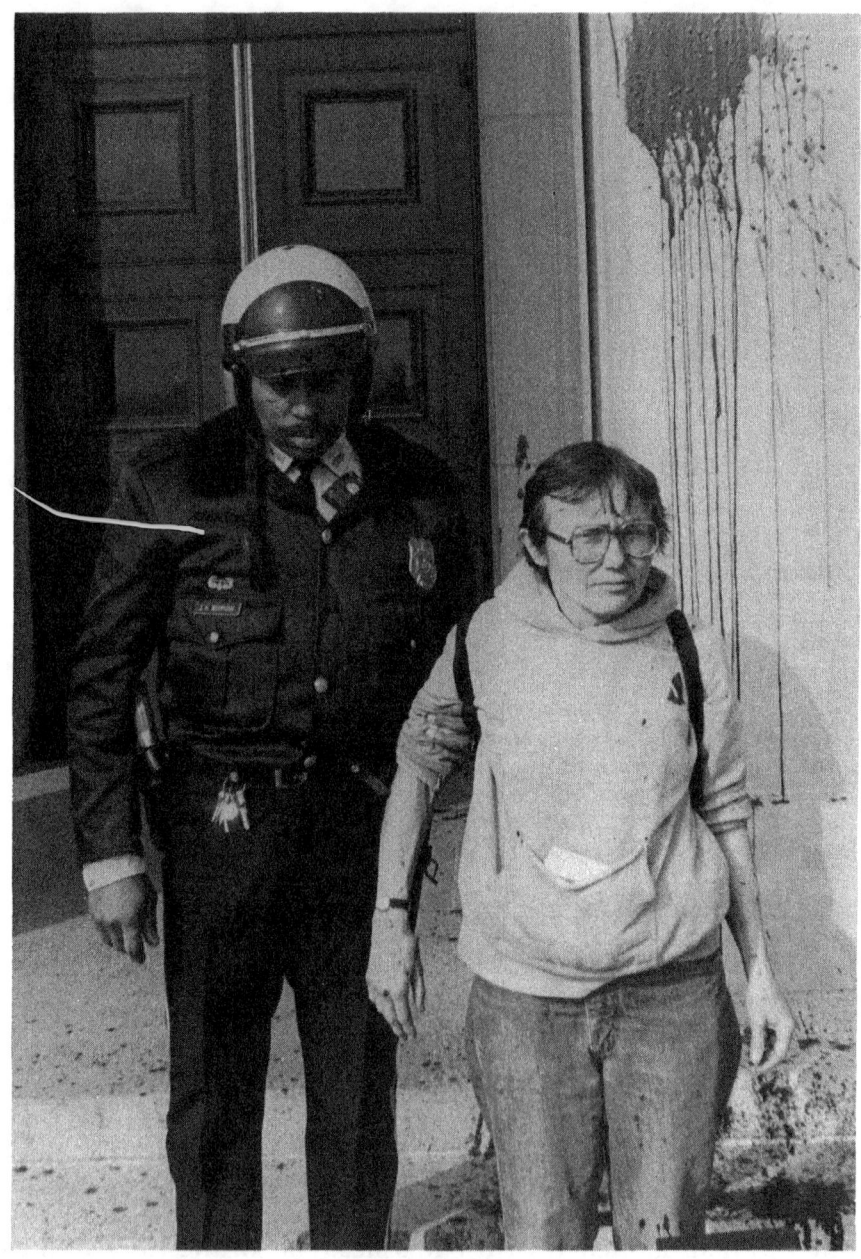

12. 1984—Holy Week. Jean Holladay, grandmother, nurse, resister, Christian, is arrested after labeling the Pentagon with blood.

13. 1984—Holy Week. A symbol less gruesome than the reality. A death specter at the Pentagon.

Photo by Peg Gallagher

14. 1984—Feast of the Innocents. Shamelessness, a national sickness that resistance seeks to heal.

15. 1988—Easter. Before the Nuclear Navy Plowshares action are the activists Margaret McKenna, Greg Boertje, Phil, and Andrew Lawrence with one of their banners.

16. 1988—September. Katy and Phil at the Atlantic Life Community Retreat at Kirkridge just after Phil's release from prison.

as our shield, to seeing (and articulating) the bomb as our salvation.

Nuclearism is the ultimate fundamentalism of our time. Above all, this is the idolatry against which we stand and because of which we stand in this court. And the modern state is the child of the nuclearist religion. In the years since 1945, the modern state has moved steadily in more and more authoritarian directions. The process was subtle. Leaders who insisted that the major stake in international conflict was the fate of democracy were the very ones who steadily eroded democratic content in the name of "National Security." Legally, we have witnessed a constitutional antipathy to standing armies give way to an expanding, permanent military establishment with the Pentagon as the cathedral of the nuclearist religion. We have seen the Executive Branch claim privileges to keep national-security information secret without any correction from the judiciary. Judge Munson, this nuclear, national-security state is a new, as yet largely unanalyzed phenomenon in the long history of political forms and of civil religions.

Being constantly ready to commit the nation and the planet to a war of annihilation in a matter of minutes created a variety of structural necessities that contradict the spirit and substance of democratic government: secrecy, lack of accountability, permanent emergency, concentration of authority, peacetime militarism, plus an extensive apparatus of state intelligence and police. "NO KING EVER CONCENTRATED IN HIS BEING SUCH ABSOLUTE AUTHORITY OVER HUMAN DESTINY."[18]

"The claim by fallible human beings to inflict total devastation for the sake of THE NATIONAL INTERESTS OF ANY PARTICULAR STATE IS AN ACUTE VARIETY OF IDOLATRY."[19]

---

[18] Falk, Richard and Lifton, Robert. *Indispensable Weapons: The Political and Psychological Case Against Nuclearism.* Basic Books Publishers. New York. 1982. p. 262. Emphasis added.

[19] *Ibid.*

We would cite, as further evidence of the direction our democracy is taking, a Council on Foreign Relations study called "Security in the Nuclear Age..." (Brookings Institution, 1975). The report describes and justifies blatant usurpation of the faith and power of the people and subordinates them to non-accountable decisions made, not only by elected officials but as well by bureaucrats, generals, and corporate executives. The process leading to this point has occurred somewhat invisibly, generally obscured by claims of "emergency" and "necessity."

One very clear example of this process was the decision to build the hydrogen bomb. A general advisory commission, headed by Oppenheimer, in October 1949 came to a unanimous conclusion opposing its development. With that recommendation in hand, and on the basis of seven minutes of Cabinet-level discussion, President Truman announced the decision to go ahead with the H-bomb in January 1950. ("... We have no other choice.") Citizens and even Congress were denied any voice or role despite the absence of any pressing emergency or circumstance of war. And it amounted to a quantum leap in the arms race and a threat to all life.

When Congress did get involved in the Atomic Age, it was determined by the McMahon Act that decisions about nuclear weapons, development, and doctrine should be made within the Executive Branch on the basis of secret and technical information. This decision and practice destroyed the healthy relationship envisioned by the Constitution between government and citizens, and it did so in the area most crucial to the future well-being of our society. The military came to enjoy a permanent place in the bureaucracy, a place that is unchallengeable even by elected political leaders. Truman's decision regarding the H-bomb exemplified two major things: one, his "We have no other choice" expressed the Faustian bargain—once the commitment was made to nuclear weapons, *we would be first*. Two, it revealed that only the most aggressive, the most militant were the voices that would survive in the evolving web of violence. The H-bomb also created its own system of loyalty, so that anyone who bucks the "most aggressive" route gets spewed out of the system. Thus, what we have managed to witness by way of dissent from nuclear orthodoxy has come almost exclusively from those who, at or near retirement, renounce nuclearist structure so central to their entire professional lives. This list is a very long one.[20]

And, Judge Munson, this has all been done "legally," and it amounts to a congressionally established religion. "Congress will make *no law with respect to* the establishment of religion . . ." Yet Congress has passed laws approving and funding the Manhattan Project, the continued arms race including the first strike arsenal of cruise, MX, Trident; the new scenario for winning a nuclear war. It requires that our taxes finance these projects. The bomb and nuclearism have been protected too by laws concerning national security, restrictions on free speech by government employees, loyalty and secrecy oaths required for security clearances. And now the laws of sabotage, laws that protect government property from destruction, and the conspiracy laws are used to punish and prosecute those who, from a perspective of conscience and Christian witness, would speak the truth, would resist the evil of nuclearism and the idolatry of nuclear violence. To so use these laws is to prohibit the free exercise of religion and violates the constitutional guarantee of this freedom.

Judge, it is within your power to contradict this trend. It is within your power—it is, as we understand it, part of your responsibility in this government—to be a check against the imperial power of the presidency; to be a check against the unconstitutional use of laws to prohibit and punish those who speak the truth, who resist the idolization of the bomb and carry out direct nonviolent acts of disarmament on the ultimate manifestation of the demonic idols—the weapons themselves. We are (or should be) a nation of laws. These laws are violated daily, and I don't mean by the likes of us. We submit that you

---

[20] The list includes such architects of our nuclear policy as Admiral Hyman Rickover, President Dwight David Eisenhower, J. Robert Oppenheimer, William Lawrence, Henry Stimson.

need to apply to the state the criteria of this court, even as we, as Christians, need to apply to the state the criteria of Christianity. And there is a clear basis in Christian political thought from which our criteria can and must proceed.

The first of these bases is the principle that the state is not the origin of human political society. It is called to serve, not to rule. This idea of service is a fundamental tenet of liberal democracy but it is also applied by the Bible to political power (Romans, 13: 4). The makers of political society are the people; this principle obliges us to act to undo what has been done in our name, yet without our understanding and consent. We must therefore recall our leadership to service as a crucial step in resisting the idolatry of nuclearism.

The second basis is that the state is not the author of law and justice but their servant. Thus, law and justice need to be embodied in institutions above the power of the state. The only good statist power is one that is limited; law and principles need to be stronger than the state. This is a Christian or Biblical view. It is also the view of our own Constitution and the reason we bring these concerns to this court. For too long the authority of the courts has been compromised by the failure of the courts to address the legality of nuclear-weapons deployment and use. And we ask ourselves, "Of what use is the law, if it cannot prevent the killing of all people and the destruction of our beautiful world by nuclear fiat?"

Third, Christian political thought distinguishes between the people and the state. The thrust of power—especially today—is to blur and destroy that distinction; for the state to identify itself with or as the people. The national-security ideologies with which we are saddled today are based on a simple if radical idea of the state. Namely, that the state is the people. The state has become its own power and that power lies in the hands of its most representative (and most violent) bearer, the military. Such developments require our stance of resistance; we believe that they require yours as well.

Judge Munson, from where we stand today, it is our conviction that much as our leaders push the concept as a justification for yet more weaponry, *national security no longer exists.* There is no security with nuclear weapons, and there is no such thing as defense.

We all need to remind ourselves that the B-52s on which we hammered and painted and poured our blood do not drop leaflets or ping-pong balls or food for hungry people. We focused on the B-52 because of the role envisioned for the B-52 at Griffiss Air Force Base. They have been prepared as carrier-launchers for the cruise missiles, which are destabilizing weapons, weapons that violate the United States commitment to nonproliferation treaties, weapons that in Pentagonese have "the highest kill probability against 'hard' targets of any of our forces." The cruise missile system is an integral and indispensable part of the evolving United States' first-strike, offensive, disarming, and war-initiating system.

We were plainly and simply smashing at an idol of our national religion, a religion that is unconstitutional. The laws that exist to protect such weapons exist to protect our national religion. Ours was an act of our religion, including a prayer that all weapons be disarmed. If the courts continue to say that such weapons—and their planning, production, and testing—are legal, when will they be able to say that their use is illegal? It is too late once the weapons are launched. All those dead and dying will not find relief or solace when the courts finally say it was wrong after all. In refusing to rule on the legality of these weapons, the courts are protecting the religion of nuclearism.

Our intent was not to injure national-defense materiel (there being no national defense with nuclear weapons to begin with) but to strengthen our real defense; out intent was not to contaminate, but to purify or cleanse; our intent was not to infect, but to heal and liberate. In view of the realities we all face, the conduct of the seven of us was both more rational and more religious than that of our government. Our intent rose from our religious convictions backed by voices and spirits of religious women and men like Bishop Raymond Hunthausen, who said: "Our security as a people of faith lies not in *demonic weapons* that threaten all life on earth. Our security is in a loving, caring God. We must dismantle our weapons of terror and place our reliance on God."[21]

Conspiracy, in the sense of breathing together, is our proper work in God's spirit. We own it. We seek it. We long for the spirit of community and the unity that was the object of Christ's prayer for us before his death. Contrary to the government's allegation in response to our motion, we reflected and conspired carefully to ensure that *no one would be hurt.* We could have gone into a deadly-force area of Griffiss Air Force Base—we know of at least two such places. There was never a question of our harming anyone; we prepared ourselves to endure rather than inflict harm. But our concern was the possibility of some guard having to live with the knowledge that he had harmed or even killed one or more of us.

We conspired carefully in the hope that our statement would be clear, that each of our voices might be heard. But our conspiracy did not have as its object the commission of offenses against the U.S. government. Rather it amounted to this: planting the seed of our highest hope, the hope that men and women and children might be able to live together on this planet in justice and peace without the domination of weapons of mass destruction over our lives minute by minute. We believed that this was the highest religious and political act possible to us.

Judge Munson, you are being called upon to rule in this case. If there is in you the slightest resonance with what I've been saying, you owe it to yourself, to your profession, to your oath—you owe it to our children and their hope of raising children—to hear more, to hear until you've heard enough to be able to render a just judgment.

---

[21] Hunthausen, Bishop Raymond. "Faith and Disarmament." A speech delivered to the Pacific Northwest Synod for the Lutheran Church in America. June 12, 1981. This talk is available on video tape from Jonah House.

The judge listened intently and allowed that ours was a solid legal argument. He took it under advisement for a month before ruling against a hearing. The substance of his response was that the government didn't create nuclear-arms systems out of religious motivations, but to effect a military purpose of preserving the national defense.

We keep coming on new threads of this reality: that nuclearism is indeed North America's national religion. Dan, for example, addressed his Jesuit brothers for the feast of the Holy Name of Jesus in 1985. America, he said, usurps the name and work of Jesus in its claim to "save," to be "savior." John Whitehead, law instructor at Oral Roberts University, wrote that in modern America the state does not openly claim divine worship, but in effect it is seeking to make itself the center of all human loyalties, the goal of all human aspirations, the source of all human values and the final arbiter of all human destiny. In doing so, without using the language of revelation, it is claiming to be divine.[22]

In 1984 the Department of Energy recommended that the government establish "An Atomic Priesthood" to create and spread "rituals and legends" that will warn the next 300 generations against the dangers of nuclear waste.[23] Early in 1986, Reagan justified his "hijacking" of the Egyptian airliner with: "I will disobey international law if it means catching terrorists." Then the secretary of war asserted that "regardless of Congressional rulings, he would find a way to test nuclear weapons." In explaining the bombing of Libya, April 1986, Reagan used the same bankrupt phrase as Truman when the earlier president decided to develop the H-bomb: "We had no other choice!" We wondered and continue to wonder how often that phrase has been used to justify our oppression of one another on large

---

[22] Whitehead, John W. *The Second American Revolution.* Elgin, Illinois. David C. Cook. 1982. Also recommended is the film version of the book, by the same title. It is produced by Franky Schaeffer V. Productions, P.O. Box 909, Los Gatos, California 95030.

[23] Reid, T.R.. "U.S. Seeks 10,000-Year Warning for Planned Nuclear Waste Dump." *The Washington Post.* November 17, 1984.

scale and small. "We had no other choice" implies that only the most aggressive, the most violent will survive in the evolving web of violence.

How does one say it briefly—Libya bombings, Chernobyl disaster, Irangate, the Pentagon's response to the nuclear scientists' boycott of Star Wars research; our behavior toward Nicaragua and in the Persian Gulf—each event offers awesome evidence that our nation is hell-bent on usurping the power of God.

In response, we of Jonah House have had to learn again and again the meaning of hope, to ground our hope in the promise of God, to struggle for a spirituality that joins us in spirit and life to threatened creation and to one another. Only thus, we know, can we stand outside the idolatry of death.

In Alderson prison, the night after the bombing of Libya (1986), Liz and a small group of women came together with the chaplain for Eucharist. We read from Matthew, Chapter 24, of Christ's prediction of the fall of Jerusalem and the end of the world—a tough chapter, from an exegetical point of view. Sitting inside that chapter is like sitting inside a whirlwind—like sitting inside life today. We look every which way for a measure of assurance or reassurance. None is given. "Flee it!" is the command. Not in the sense of going to a safe place—there being no safe place to go. Flee the consensus. Flee false unanimity. Flee the mad search for clarity from this or that expert. Flee the floundering and rumors.

The need—it came again so clearly—is to find our center: a matter of singleness of mind and heart; a matter of purity of means; a matter of leaving the ends to God's designs. From that center we can take the next step, can be loving and compassionate, can change and be changed—in God's power and that of the Spirit. Only glimmers come to us, hints of this power at work. Still, the more obsessive our leaders become about loyalty and patriotism, the more vulnerable they are before even us, who pledge allegiance only to the God of All, who try to remain pure of heart.

# THE PASSIONATE LIFE: ITS COST, ITS BLESSING

We North Americans pay dearly for our idols. We have an "apartheid" society. Instead of an open and vulnerable society, ours is closed, unassailable, apathetic. The living, open, vulnerable life is poured into steel and concrete. This is the modern death called apathy: life without feeling.

*"I came,"* Jesus said, *"that they may have life, and have it abundantly."* John, 10:10. The single-minded service of God is joined irresistibly to abundant life, to a passion for life. Thus it is disturbing to think about and more disturbing to witness how accustomed our culture has become to death, to death before birth, to death on the street, to death through violence, to death of the soul, to death above life. And the tragedy of tragedies follows; one gradually (or quickly) becomes used to death, accepts it, becomes indifferent to it.

What, we ask, causes such apathy? What reduces life to such a low state that one must hesitate to name it such? Perhaps this: we strive for a life without suffering, for joy without pain, for community without conflict; and we misname our plight "good fortune."

Where do we find the courage truly to live, the power to suffer? For us the central event of the New Testament is the passion of Christ. One understands the history of Christ's suffering only when one grasps the passionate devotion of Christ to God, to us. In this history we can perceive the pain of God and, in the process, discover the pain of our own lives, a pain often suppressed or projected on others.

What in the life of Jesus speaks to us again and again? His life is inspired by the will to live before death, even to live against death. Where the sick are healed, lepers are accepted, sins are forgiven, there life is present. Freed life, redeemed life, divine life is there, in the midst of us. He became one with us, one with our flesh, healed the ill, accepted the oppressed, thawed the frozen relationships between human beings.

Today, too, we find in our midst all the woes of humanity. We see them. Out of the dark corners into which society has condemned them, they emerge into the light, the light that Jesus radiates through his love.

Such passionate devotion to life works contagiously only when it is prepared for suffering. The passion for freedom from death is alive only when the spirit of sacrifice animates it. Wounds are healed only by the wounded. The more we love life, the more we experience the joy of life; and in the very joy we experience the pain of life and the deadliness of death. So the paradox: if we find life, we will lose it; and if we lose life for Christ's sake, we will find it. (A paraphrase of Matthew, 10: 39.)

From apathy into caring! The way is summed up in this instruction of Paul: *"Welcome one another, therefore, as Christ has welcomed you."* Romans, 15: 7. Where acceptance is lacking, the air becomes thin and we languish. We know too well, from Auschwitz to El Salvador, that whoever is not accepted as humanly equal is ostracized and finally exterminated.

Why the alienation from one another? It may be that we accept others, even our neighbors, only from our own vantage point, and so view them through our own preconceptions. Thus we do not at all seek the other, but only ourselves in the other. The other is left in isolation, and so are we. Or we treat each other only in terms of closed-minded or narrow-minded reciprocity.

Granted that we are slow to accept those who are different, another ironic difficulty arises. We at Jonah House, and especially Liz and Phil, tend to refuse to accept those who are "the same," those who fit the profile of the "good American." Our friends accuse us of this at times. At times we accuse ourselves.

Some of us routinely abhor discussions with Pentagon employees, for example, or with workers in war industry, or with hawkish politicians. Our language about them is filled with contemptuous descriptions: hirelings, dupes, ideologues, fascists, and worse. Similarly, we are critical of aspects of "the Left" in our country. Our language about those of the Left highlights what we call their shallowness, bombast, ideological fixations, and low profile. As though we were to say "our purity justifies exclusiveness." And at times we justify our failing. Alas, self-justification is deeply ingrained in us. Even while we know that in order to enlarge our humanity we must continually undergo this displacement, this dislocation—*"Welcome one another, therefore, as Christ has welcomed you!"* Romans, 15: 7.

The pure of heart will see God, will see goodness and justice. Indeed, the pure of heart bring justice. Though the "chances" that justice prevail in our world seem slim to nil, the measure is no human calculus, but an act of God. The "chances" do not rest on the evidence. They rest on the Spirit of God in us. And we know that the nations will become just if the people are single-minded servants of justice, pure of heart, infused with the Spirit of God.

> *Blessed are the peacemakers,*
> *for they shall be called children of God.*
> (A paraphrase of Matthew, 5: 9.)

## CHAPTER SEVEN
# THE PEACEMAKERS

A tale out of ancient India spoke to us deeply when first we read it. The tale has proven useful since, in talks, seminars and retreats. It goes:

> Four royal children were discussing what specialty they should master. And they said: "Let us each learn a science." And after they had agreed on a place where they would meet again, the four started off in different directions. At the allotted time and in the appointed place the sisters and brothers met and asked one another what they had learned. The eldest said: "I have mastered a science that would make it possible for me, if I had nothing but a piece of bone of some creature, to create the flesh that goes with it." The second eldest said, "I know how to grow that creature's skin and hair if there is flesh on the bones." The third said, "I am able to create its limbs if I have the flesh, skin and hair." "And I," concluded the youngest, "know how to give that creature life if its form is complete with limbs." Then the four went into the jungle to find a piece

of bone with which to demonstrate their specialties. Alas, as fate would have it, the bone they found was a lion's and none of them had learned to identify the different bones. One added flesh to the bone, the second grew hide and hair, the third completed it with limbs, and the fourth gave the lion life. The ferocious beast arose, shook its mane, and jumped on its creators. It killed them all and vanished contentedly into the jungle.

Like all good tales, this one remains timely. We too have created the potential for self-destruction. It has become possible for us to destroy not only life, but also the possibility of rebirth, not only for human beings, but for the whole of created life; not only a period of history, but history itself. The future has become an option. Many firmly believe that nuclear annihilation will not be delayed beyond the turn of the century. Unless the present course of events is turned around, we are forced to share that belief.

The future *has* become an option. If there is to be peace, if there is to be continuance of life on this planet, if there is to be any redirection of the present course of mass suicide, a heavy task burdens us. All, in sum, depends on peacemakers.

"We will be happy if we are peacemakers"—indeed, a full-time, life-long business! Peacemakers are those who by patience and judicious intervention spread peace about them.

The summons of the seventh beatitude is to *MAKE* peace and to renounce all violence. In the cause of Christ, it must be understood, nothing is gained by such means. Indeed, it is God who makes peace. So the peacemaker identifies with God in the work of saving the world: To make *The kingdom of the world . . . become the kingdom of our Lord and of his Christ, and he shall reign forever and ever.* Revelation, 11: 15. This touches on a basic life option: we can be at peace, not because we are free of conflict, but because our conflicts are consequent on acts of conscience, acts that seek to have an impact on public morality.

In our efforts at peacemaking, a demonstration or peace witness sometimes is mounted as a response or reaction to some outrage the government has perpetrated in our name. So in recent years, for example, we have held demonstrations or protests when the U.S. invaded Grenada, bombed Libya, underwrote further aid to the Contras in Nicaragua. But mostly our witnessing for peace is the result of conspiring, breathing together, against injustice and on behalf of life. There are many such witnessings on which we could report. We refer here to one, introducing a "calendar of peace witness" that has become, in the course of the years, a succession of "seasons of celebration."

## PEACEMAKING AND SEASONS OF CELEBRATION
### Concerning Thanksgiving—American or Real

For what did Americans thank God on November 25, 1976? For turkey and fixings, for number-one status in the world, for fundamental "rights," for white skin, for "freedom" backed by nuclear weapons? Whatever the substance of gratitude, it hardly bears scrutiny. Enormous waste and jealous harboring of food attend our full stomachs; jobs become more mechanical, trivial, and morally sterile; "rights" evaporate for want of responsible and courageous practice; blacks and foreigners awaken fright and anger at home and abroad; counterforce and first-strike nuclear strategies symbolize our guilt and self-hatred.

A Thanksgiving springing from repentance, from conversion of spirit and heart, as movement toward atonement (at-one-ment), simply eludes us. Repentance for Hiroshima, for Korea and Indochina, for consumption of one-third of the world's food, for violative and militarist diplomacy, for barren consciences and bankrupt lives, this eludes us. Intoxicated by violence and its profitability, we know neither true gratitude nor the means to offer it.

For three days prior to Thanksgiving 1976, the community of Jonah House went with friends to the Pentagon to expose its Thanksgiving which, we thought, coincided wonderfully with the Thanksgiving of most North Americans. In contrast, exposure and resistance became our theme. We were convinced that, as there could be no repentance without resistance, so there could be no at-one-ment without gratitude. We remain convinced also that Pentagons around the world were at the root of beckoning starvation, deranged relationships, and a lock-step march toward mass suicide.

Excerpts from the leaflets circulated during our actions reveal what Thanksgiving requires of vigilant and peaceful people:

*First Day* (November 22)

"Hear the Word of God, you rulers of America.

Attend you her people:
The offering of your gifts at Thanksgiving is useless.
I cannot tolerate your assemblies and festivals,
your sacred seasons and ceremonies I cannot endure.
They have become a burden to me and

I can put up with them no longer.
When you lift your hands outspread in prayer,
though you offer countless prayers, I will not listen.
There is blood on your hands; put away the evil of your deeds, away out of my sight.

Cease to do evil and learn to do right;
pursue justice and champion the oppressed." (A paraphrase of Isaiah, 1: 14-17.)

*Second Day* (November 23)
"I hate, I spurn your Thanksgiving feasts,
I take no pleasure in your church services.
Away with your noisy hymns.
But if you would offer me thanksgiving, then let justice surge like water
and goodness like an unfailing stream." (A paraphrase of Amos, 5: 21-24.)

*Third Day* (November 24)

"When the White Man first came over the wide waters, he was but a little man, very little, very little. His legs were cramped by sitting long in his big boat and he begged for a little land to light his fire on . . . but when the white man had warmed himself before the Indian's fire and filled himself with their hominy, he became very large. With a step he bestrode the mountains, and his feet covered the plains and the valleys . . . (And he said to us) 'Get a little further lest I tread on thee . . . Get a little further lest you are too near. . . .' Then we tried to reason with him saying, 'Why will you take by force what you may obtain by love? Why will you destroy us who supply you with food? What can you get by war? We are unarmed and willing to give you what you ask, if you come in a friendly manner . . . Take away your guns and swords, the cause of your jealousies, or you may die in the same manner. . . .' " (Selections from Speckled Snake, Bigmouth, Powhatach, and Tecumseh.)

Five times we broke the law and the police arrested us.

*First Day*—Dressed as beggars, Ched Myers and Vince Scotti chained themselves to pillars at the River Entrance of the Pentagon. Over them, two specters of death, Liz and Rosemary McGuire, hovered like vultures, personifying the death-dealing weaponry of that institution. Others bore graphics and circulated leaflets as police arrested them.

*Second Day*—The beggars, Ched Myers and Ladon Sheats, representing the world's poor, reappeared. The specters, John Bach and Phil Berrigan, harassed and abused them, all the while exhorting generals, soldiers, and civilian employees to pursue their grisly paperwork. The specters commended the Pentagon's task, called for higher appropriations, for new weapons of "defense," for "stiffening" toward the Soviets, for first-strike war. It seemed to us that military officers and civilians walked through the harangue shamefaced and silent.

That afternoon, caving in to our presence, officials closed off the Pentagon's tours, those macabre displays of American military might. While other citizens were shut out, we were alone in the complex. Consequently, Ed Clark, Ed Gersh, and John Schuchardt penetrated the Pentagon's shopping center. To dramatize the connection between war-making and marketing, they poured blood on the Concourse entrance, and on a portrait of President Ford benignly presiding over all.

*Third Day*—Beggars Bob Smith and Dan Berrigan and specters Phil Berrigan and John Schuchardt again appeared. The specters encouraged workers toward their desks with "haste and enthusiasm." Blank checks for the poor should cease, they said. "They should work or starve. Guns and butter we can have, but only if we have sufficient guns." The police asked the actors repeatedly to leave. They refused and were arrested.

The Pentagon offers frequent Christian services to employees, the Catholic Mass, meditation groups, and prayer breakfasts. Accordingly, a Thanksgiving service was scheduled in the Concourse for noon. Ed Clark, Vince Scotti, and Ladon Sheats disrupted the hypocrisy by simply quoting Jesus on discipleship. One after another they spoke; police would remove the first, another would take up, and so on. Ladon was the last; he condemned forcefully the possibility of Christian worship (or Thanksgiving) in a setting given over to war-making and death. As the police dragged him off, bystanders could hear him declaiming the "blasphemy" of coming to God's altar with nuclear weapons in hand.

The state, through its federal court in Alexandria, was lenient toward us. It muffled resistance, curtained publicity, and imposed token jail sentences. Vince Scotti, John Schuchardt, and Ladon Sheats did six, six, and ten days in jail, respectively: Ed Clark did twenty days, most of the sentence on a water fast.

For what finally did we give thanks? For the Christ who, despite the posturing of generals, is our example. For sisters and brothers of clarity, courage, honor. For strength to face our own duplicity and lassitude; to face as well the public terror of the bomb. For truth, community, life. *For these we thanked God!*

Was this an act of peacemaking? We think so. Throughout we were recalling our history, North American and Biblical. Throughout we were reminding Pentagon employees and visitors of aspects of our history that they, perhaps, were choosing to forget. Throughout we were making visible and audible the sufferings of people in face of skewed North American priorities. Throughout we were offering an alternative form of thanksgiving and of life.

To those who cling to the normal, our witness may have appeared to be little more than negative criticism. But to those who yearn for a life rooted in and reflective of justice, our witness may have been a source of hope and energy, a sign that they too might con-spire to build such a world, such a life.

The question is inevitable: "What about the anger the witness generated?" The anger we felt in ourselves and perceived in those around us was not generated by our action. It was there. It is there, smoldering just below the surface. It cannot not be there. When people are so deeply entrenched in injustice, as people in our country are, they silence conscience only with difficulty. And when conscience is aroused, its first expression is often anger against those whose actions stir the voice within. Irritability, abuse, and excuses inevitably follow.

As would-be peacemakers we must learn again and again to absorb the anger, to respond, not in kind, not in cutting words or hostile gestures, but with love, with willingness to restate the truth as we see it, not accommodating the truth to the hearer. The tensions endemic to such witness are reduced only slowly, only with persistent presence. Fair weather or foul, the peacemaker is committed to constancy and persistence, to restating the truth lovingly and often. Only thus is a climate of acceptance and communication created.

Persistent presence, constant reminding, constant restating; these suggest presence that is beyond the resources of a small community. To do what we can, over the years a kind of calendar has evolved, as a way of celebrating the seasons of our history. Admittedly, our calendar includes ritual. But we do not apologize for this. Ritual in touch with history can be profoundly moving and energizing. It is a way of re-enacting our Biblical and our North American story, to evoke our shared memories and to awaken hope in a common destiny.

Our calendar looks, roughly, like this:

*New Year's Day* is a time for new beginnings. If the community is not involved in a vigil on New Year's Eve, members and friends join in a penance service and Eucharist. Our thinking is that there can be no new beginning without repentance or "turning around." This, then, is the time to look at our past, to seek the pardon of sisters and brothers and of God for the needless pain we've caused each other, and to seek support to change our lives. What is unique about the human person, we believe, is this ability to begin again. God begins; we humans begin again.

*Martin Luther King Jr.'s Birthday* is a time to remember and commit ourselves once more to the far-from-complete struggle for civil rights. Something deep within us decries such celebrations of this man that cap, cork, and bottle his work as if it were ready for storage in files. There can be no civil rights where the right to life is compromised. On this day, traditionally, we join with friends to give public witness to the history and hope of civil rights.

We recall a number of *Valentine's Day* actions in which the images of the day were fruitful for resistance. "Love American Style," a piece of theater done at the Pentagon one Valentine's Day, was a brilliant combination of wit and wisdom. Many employees caught themselves watching and laughing and then meeting the truth in a shocking "recognition scene." So in 1986, when the Atlantic Life Community[1] proposed that we choose a day on which all might act, we chose Valentine's Day. The first ALC Valentine's witness was held in 1987 at GTE Corporation in Worcester, Massachusetts. Each year a different ALC Community will plan resistance on St. Valentine's Day.

*Ash Wednesday, Lent, Holy Week, and Easter* are a unity for most Christians. Often through this time we vigil weekly, if not daily, at one or another site of oppression. Often, too, this time

---

[1] The Atlantic Life Community (ALC) is a network of communities and individuals on the East Coast of the United States that shares a commitment to both nonviolent resistance to the arms race and to growing more deeply in nonviolent living.

includes the sister feast of Passover, with which we share the same theme: a summons to a new exodus, the exodus through which each generation must pass to the hope of new life. This hope was given its most vivid realization in the Resurrection of Jesus, the promise of a future closed against every human alternative.

In our vigils and actions, we try to express the Biblical themes of the season as they apply to the hope of Christians, even in the face of a will to death as ominous and ubiquitous as our nuclear reality. It is a nuclear cross we carry today, a betrayal of humanity for the thirty pieces of silver that pay the mortgage, rent, vacation, and trappings of normality, and for the courtesies of today's imperial power. We try, through the actions, to build to a culmination during Holy Week, which we usually spend at the Pentagon.

*Tax Day* brings us face to face with a North American political reality. We are, we remember, responsible for the deeds of our government as we continue to pay for them. How and where to give that symbolic expression may occupy us for some weeks. But, since most people lack adequate preparation time (tax day is often very close to Holy Week), we go to the Post Office, to which North Americans rush to have their taxes mailed in time, and we are able to talk with and give leaflets to thousands of taxpayers in one evening.

*Pentecost,* named "Peace Pentecost," as a day of peacemaking and peace witness has been the work of Sojourners Community in D.C. This we support and share in wholeheartedly.

Through the *summer* we call ourselves and others to an alternative vacation, to take time with sisters and brothers to consider the task of peacemaking and nonviolence and to create acts of peace out of these considerations. Three or four ten-day sessions or workshops give all participants a mini-experience of nonviolent, resistance community. We have planned these sessions so that one would include *July 4* and another *August 6 and 9.*

On July 4, participants are invited to recall the radical concepts on which our country was founded, and to seek to fulfill them. On August 6 and 9, participants painfully remember the shame of Hiroshima and Nagasaki, memories we all would rather forget. Peace witnessings on those days ask that we look, remember, repent; they provide imaginative access to the horrors that haunt even our quietest moments.

At *Thanksgiving* we try, as in the example shared earlier, to bring to public attention the real meaning of such a day, in contrast to the commercial sham it has become in practice.

In an earlier chapter we have spoken at some length about the season of *Advent* and what it has come to mean in our lives. Throughout Advent we voice one or more themes of the season in public witness and lead up to the celebration of the Feast of the Holy Innocents.

For more than twelve years, the Pentagon has been the site where we most frequently witness the urgent work of peacemaking. Even without direct communication, the officials and police know when we will be coming. We have often arrived there to find their welcome mat: handles removed from doors to prevent our chaining the doors closed; pillars covered in plastic to prevent our blood's "defacing" (revealing the true face of) that institution; police lined across the entrance where they anticipate our assembly.

Our task has been to offer symbols and actions to refute the hopelessness in which people live. In such despair the newness of Christ seems unthinkable, impossible, preposterous. We try to give public expression to the hopes and yearnings of the heart, denied for so long that they lie dormant, nearly dead. We try to celebrate that hope; and in so doing invite wonder, and even invite adversaries to the possibility of friendship and solidarity. The acts of witness themselves are full of song and hope, of theater and art, as well as judgment upon systematic injustice.

There are other places for our witness for peace—in D.C. and elsewhere. But always we find we must return to the Pentagon, one of the few government buildings in the D.C. area that lack a name written in stone across its face. By our presence, we name it for the temple of death that indeed it is; without such a presence, the place would remain nameless, secure in the darkness where its evil deeds can be perpetrated.

## THE PUNISHMENT FOR PEACEMAKING

At the end of the docu-drama "In the King of Prussia" on the action of the Plowshares 8, Ramsey Clark stands on the steps of the courthouse in Norristown, Pennsylvania, announcing to the press the sentences just handed down by Judge Salus against the eight. "It just shows," Ramsey concludes, "how hard it is to make peace in America!" Four of the eight were sentenced to three to ten years in prison; three of them were sentenced to one and a half to five years; and Molly Rush, to two to five years. Fines and long probations in addition to the sentences were meant to ensure that these women and men would be immobilized for many years to come, in prison or out.

It did not happen; it has not happened. No one is immobilized; no one, given God's grace, ever will be, whether "The Plowshares Eight" are imprisoned or not.

On the Feast of the Innocents 1976, as we've already indicated, both Liz and Phil were arrested at the Pentagon. Prior to sentencing, January 31, for his part in the action, Phil made this statement to the court:

> We have been told repeatedly to dissent within the limits of the law. "Peaceful protest is available to you," we are told. Implying, of course, that if one breaks the law, however unjust or repressive the law, one ceases to be peaceful, one ceases to be nonviolent. Thus we are advised: "Carry your signs, hold your rallies, seek march permits, talk with your Congresspeople, write your newspaper editors." Which is like advising the passengers aboard a sinking liner to circulate a petition protesting the flooding decks. The advice meets neither the dire necessity of the situation, nor the unlawful action of government, nor the deadly lethargy afflicting the public.

Once again, I hope to share with this court what motivated me to come to the Pentagon on December 28, what motivated me to "break the law," as the indictment charges.

The following are quoted from Air Force launch officers stationed at Whiteman Air Force Base, near Sedalia, Missouri. One of their missiles, the Minuteman II, tipped with a 1.2 megaton warhead, has the explosive yield to vaporize an urban population of a million people. One of these officers, a Captain Beal, said this in an interview: "The fact is, it is possible for four officers in a Minuteman squadron to launch and start World War III.[2] If four officers in two capsules decide to turn their keys and launch, they can do so without orders from anyone. There is no absolute guarantee that orders [from the top] have to be followed. Naturally, this would be illegal, but who would be around to punish them?"

Another officer, a Captain Ted Wye, said this: "A single crew also could transmit over radio and teletype communication a proper launch message which could result in all the nation's missiles being launched. There is simply no way to withhold the essential codes from the crews if they are going to be able to respond to a launch message. No guarantees exist that a hawk crew could not use the materials at their disposal for starting a nuclear war."

Captain Wye commented further on mistakes and miscalculations within a missile capsule. "World-War-III-type messages have come as a result of honest error. A controller at Strategic Air Command headquarters once mumbled a missile alert over a live mike while practicing. Realizing his error, he closed with 'Oh shit!' Less than one-

---

[2] The quotations of air launch officers came from personal interviews conducted by Bill Wickersham, a professor of peace studies at the University of Missouri. Bill sent the unpublished text of these interviews to Jonah House. He refered to the conversations with the missileers in "One Man's Nucleomitaphobia." *Saturday Review.* Volume 3. April 17, 1976. pp. 22-23.

half the missile wings responded properly, even though we are taught to react to any correctly decoded message no matter how received."

Later, he told the interviewer: "One crew, just for fun, recorded a launch message with near perfect authenticity. They played it after a crew, composed of good friends, came to the capsule to relieve them. The new crew was so overwhelmed at hearing what happened to be a valid launch message that they were paralyzed."

Obviously, there is no moral capacity to control such weapons—from a president who would threaten first strike, to launch crews playing tricks upon their friends with launch messages. There is no moral capacity to control these weapons because there is no moral right to have them, let alone use them. And so, we have the madness related by Captains Beal and Wye; we have a trillion and a half dollars invested in war-making since 1946; we have the official willingness to strike first with our nuclear arsenal; we have the tragedies of Hiroshima and Nagasaki; we have near nuclear escapes from Berlin, the Suez, and Cuba; we have the cruise missile, Trident, and MX; we have 220 million Americans virtually unanimous in paying for mass suicide.

In contrast, there is the sanity and reverence of Jesus: *But if any one strikes you on the right cheek, turn . . . the other also.* Matthew, 5: 39. *Love your enemies and pray for those who persecute you . . .* Matthew, 5: 44. And you are blessed, if you work for peace among people. (A restatement of the seventh beatitude.)

As for us, we will try to go with Jesus; we will try to remain faithful to Him. And this will mean, inevitably, a reminder to pharaohs and public alike—as often as our feeble resources can make it, at the White House, at the War Department, and elsewhere, in the courts and on the streets—"You are mad; you will kill us all if you continue; you will curse God and creation; you will kill Christ once again—this time in his people." Yes, we will try to go with Jesus, as long as he gives us the strength to do so.

The judge imposed a sentence of sixty days in jail. Once confined, Phil had a more or less typical discussion with himself, in his journal, which he ended with this:

Do it, Phil, do it!

Do time for Christ Jesus and his Kingdom!

Do it for Frida and Jerry and the world's kids!
Do it again—after 44 months' imprisonment!
Do it for the sisters and brothers of conscience
struggling against the bomb!
Do it for the old federal judge!
Do it to remember the dead, but to fight like hell for the living!
*My grace is sufficient for you.* 2 Corinthians, 12: 9.
Do it, Phil, do it!

Reason and self-interest would argue against being here: seventy prisoners in a dormitory cattle-car. Food pitiful in quality, short in quantity. Noise pollution of the boob tube eighteen hours a day. Family and community need me. Frida and Jerry need me; Liz needs me; the resistance needs me. Is prison counter-productive?

Faith and corporate interest argue for being here: there is the invitation: if you will save your life, you will lose it; if you lose your life for Jesus' sake, you will save it. (A paraphrase of Luke, 9: 24.) There is the promise: *I also saw . . . those who had conquered the Beast and its image, and the number of its name.* Revelation, 15: 2-3. There is the testimony of Acts. Nearly every chapter relates witness against the state by the disciples. The consequences: disgrace, rejection, stoning, stripes, imprisonment, death. Then there is the realization that steps toward nuclear suicide are a counter-creation and a counter-redemption. They are insane, blasphemous, demonic. Witnessing to their true nature is to witness to God's creation and redemption. And that is the true primary moral and political duty of our time! Then there is the chemistry of complicity. Those who are not with Jesus are against him; and those who do not gather with him, scatter. (A paraphrase of Luke, 11: 23.) One makes peace or one makes war! I could give "promises" to the Beast, effecting immediate release, but I'll stay where I am and later conspire to return.

## PEACEMAKING IN A NUCLEAR WORLD

In July and August 1980, thousands sought to remember the birth of the bomb thirty-five years earlier, and to penetrate the national numbness. Simultaneously, the scientists who had worked on the first atomic bombs had their own reunion at Los Alamos to celebrate the thirty-fifth anniversary of the "Trinity" test at Alamogordo.

THEN : Nobody knew why Dr. Robert Oppenheimer named the first atomic test site "Trinity"—part of the enigma or the moral schizophrenia of the man. But Los Alamos, New Mexico, appears obsessed with the name. For example, there is the Trinity Bible Church, Trinity Shopping Plaza, Trinity Street, Trinity Housing Project. (We recall the insight of the Book of Revelation that Satan is the ape of God; the demonic mimic. Why then Trinity for Los Alamos, except that it was a place where Dragon, Sea Beast and Land Beast came to accord on that hellish instrument, the bomb?)

Los Alamos boasts more churches and liquor stores than towns twice its size, but almost no book stores. One woman, Judy Blume, an author herself and the wife of a physicist, claimed the town was possessed by fear and called it "Stepford" after the novel in which housewives were transformed into mechanical dolls.[3] The reference is to what work on the bomb did to the wives of physicists. She says: "People at Los Alamos are afraid of people in Santa Fe. It's not safe in Santa Fe. There

---

[3] Levin, Ira. *The Stepford Wives*. Random House, New York. 1972.

are those who carry guns with them when they go to Santa Fe. What are they afraid of? I wish I knew. The kids who grow up at Los Alamos can't wait to get out but they always come running back."[4] "There is as well," she said, "the fear of personal safety. People on bikes wear crash helmets. They're building enough bombs to blow up the world and they wear crash helmets when they ride bicycles."

At Los Alamos, the difficult things make sense, the simple things seem too complicated. Stan Ulam, a Polish scientist who worked with Teller on the H-bomb, has a wooden puzzle on his coffee table, like a Turkish puzzle ring. "It's very hard," he said. "I can't do it, Enrico Fermi and John von Neumann could never put it together. They would spend hours on it, then a child would walk in and put it together in an instant." Fermi would lose at tennis six to four and would excuse his loss by saying, "It doesn't count because the difference is less than the square root of the sum of the number of games."

What strikes us about the scientists is an astonishing political naivete and a blind enthusiasm for scientism, as though science indeed were the art of the gods. Stealing fire from Heaven—successful Prometheans. The bomb is of course value free. The scientist must have latitude to experiment, especially if political sanction supports him. So there was no mention at the scientists' reunion of "Counterforce," no regret for the 400,000 Japanese dead, not the slightest openness to vexing moral questions. The most thoughtless and ruthless were the North Americans. The simple official lies were enough for them. One, a Dr. Agnew, justified his role: "I believe in helping to preserve the integrity and well-being of the United States." Another past director of Los Alamos, Norris Bradbury, said this: "What frightens me is that some damn fool might start a war. But I'm never safe from a madman walking down the street. If your leader is a madman, you're in trouble." Another, Stan Ulam, said this of Fermi: "He

---

[4] Quinn, Sally. "The Sweet Sin of the Atomic City: Reunion at Los Alamos." *The Washington Post.* June 29, 1980. pp. G1-G4. The quotations that follow are all taken from this article.

was very pessimistic about humanity." Fermi, considered by his colleagues to be a modern Galileo, was never pessimistic about his own humanity. He took bets before the first test in 1945 as to whether it would ignite the hydrogen in the air and sea water, start a chain reaction, and blow up the world.

As for Oppenheimer, he was philosophically brighter than most of his colleagues, but that merely worsened his condition of mind. Years after Hiroshima and Nagasaki, he would say: "When you see something that is technically sweet, you go ahead and do it and you argue about what to do about it only after you had your technical success. That is the way it was with the atomic bomb." Note the political naivete here. After Alamogordo, only generals and politicians argued about what to do with the bomb. Not Oppenheimer or Szilard or von Neumann or Fermi. Their job was to make it. Once the bomb was made, the scientists had nothing to say about its use; as in the earlier case of Einstein, they were totally ignored, once their "job" was finished.

Yet Oppenheimer fruitlessly attempted to be moderate with the bomb. He quoted the *Bhagavad Gita* after the first test. He agonized over personal guilt to the point of annoying everyone at Los Alamos. The moral ambivalence of the scientist is powerfully displayed by Francoise Ulam, the wife of one of the Los Alamos team. She reflected on 1944 and early 1945. "During the days of the 'super debates' [i.e., as to whether the bomb could be built], Stan [her husband] refused to become politically or administratively involved. Yet I knew that he felt intense relief when he spearheaded the research that convincingly proved that such a weapon could not be built. The irony is that all hopes were dashed the day he said 'I think I have found a way to make it work!' " The rest is history!

NOW: We need to focus on that history and on some of the suicidal realities humanity faces in consequence. American policy is now first strike, counterforce (FTO—Flexible and Strategic Targeting Options). The nuclear-war stance is now "hair trigger," as the abortive rescue mission of hostages in Iran in 1980 displayed, as the bombing of Libya displayed, as the invasion of Grenada displayed, as the stance toward Central America displayed, as Irangate displayed. In 1983, the Western European strategic system was deployed. It is a computerized LAUNCH ON WARNING system made up of Pershing II and cruise missiles capable of striking targets deep inside Russia. Killer lasers and SIPAPU (ironically, sacred fire) subatomic neutral particles, aimed from a space station against hostile satellites and missiles—all these are in the works and projected for operation before 1995.

What is the spirit of such suicidal derangement?

It is the spirit of imperial "hubris"—of a people schooled in getting its way by crushing Native Americans, by putting Blacks in the furrow.

It is the spirit of politicians whose moral and cultural mediocrity is sadly and universally evident.

It is the spirit of generals and bomb makers and technicians who work in symbiotic concert, for ideology or profit, and who manipulate the politicians as mouthpieces and legal marionettes.

It is the spirit of you and us—whenever fear or egocentrism or personal agendas withdraw us from establishment of the Kingdom, from struggle against the Beast, from securing, however little, justice, disarmament, peace.

Bluntly and specifically, it is the spirit of Henry Kissinger—the architect of American Counterforce, adulator of the wealthy and powerful, protege of the Rockefellers, and beyond doubt or debate, genocidal war criminal.

Kissinger has been and is the surpassing imperial theorist of the marriage between military force and diplomacy. Whether in or out of power, he exerts a central influence. The American war machine was designed around his ideas and infused with his derring-do and ruthlessness. All and any politicians pay fealty to him—Schlesinger, Brzezinski, Carter, Reagan. Student of Metternich, and to some lesser extent Clausewitz and Machiavelli, Kissinger devises a doctrine that quickly and decisively applies U.S. power against the Soviets; at the same time, he stuns the uncommitted with a nightmarish ferocity.

In his fundamental book—*Nuclear Weapons and Foreign Policy*[5]—he saw the bomb as a political tool, and limited nuclear war as a strategic option. "The basic strategic problem of the nuclear age," he wrote, "is to discover whether it is possible to find intermediate application of our military strength, whether our strategic thinking can develop concepts of war which *bring power into balance with the willingness to use it.*"[6]

Kissinger's essay, "Limited War: Conventional or Nuclear? A Reappraisal" stated:

"Conventional forces should not be considered a substitute for a limited nuclear war capability but a complement to it . . . *Conventional war can be kept conventional only if we maintain, together with our retaliatory force, an adequate capability for limited nuclear war.*"[7]

Notice that statement. One might think exactly the opposite; that conventional war can be kept conventional only if neither side possesses limited nuclear war capacity. But the logic of power-mongering is the reverse. As alternative to nuclear war, Kissinger proposed the doctrine of limited war and suggested scenarios less cataclysmic than a thermonuclear holocaust.[8] These scenarios would apply to gray areas—Africa, Asia and the Middle East—answering a need he perceived for a weapons system translating our technological advantage into local superiority.

In other words, the Kissinger universe raises such questions as these: how can the empire derive political (translate eco-

---

[5] Kissinger, Henry A. *Nuclear Weapons and Foreign Policy.* Harper and Brothers (for the Council on Foreign Relations), New York. 1957.

[6] Kissinger, Henry A. "Military Policy and Defense of the 'Gray Areas.' " *Foreign Affairs, XXXIII.* April 1955. pp. 416-428.

[7] Kissinger, Henry A. *The Necessity for Choice: Prospects of American Foreign Policy.* Harper and Brothers, New York. 1961. pp. 89-90. Emphasis added.

[8] Kissinger, Henry A. "Limited War: Conventional or Nuclear? A Reappraisal." *Daedalus.* Fall 1960. pp. 800-817.

nomic) advantage from nuclear overkill? How can it restore balance between the very real power the United States possesses in its nuclear arsenal and the willingness to use it? Such a doctrine gives potency to diplomatic threats and ultimatums, for example, Korea ('50-'51), Dien Bien Phu ('54), Paris Peace Negotiations ('72), Middle East War ('73)—to cite several of some fifteen examples.

No empire survives without militarism. Militarism protects the incestuous marriage of power and money. Between 1947 and 1970, the United States intervened militarily (all for our "freedoms" of course) on an average of once every fourteen months: Korea, Indochina, Chile, Guatemala, Nicaragua, Dominican Republic, Lebanon, the Congo, Indonesia, and Iran. These are just a few of the more flagrant examples. Needless to say, these limited wars, often called "invisible" wars, were invisible only to the American people. They were not invisible to the Cambodians, Laotians, or Chileans.

Indochina and our defeat in Saigon (April 1975) killed this approach to limited war. The fall of Saigon was a serious wound to the American Empire, perhaps a fatal wound, at the least a critical factor in our dissolution as an empire. The task in the next six years (1975-1980) was to heal the wound and declare the empire as stronger still. By its own logic, our empire is stronger if Indochina is weaker. The military conflict clearly lost, the U.S. continued the war by other means: an economic embargo, CIA subversion, the mobilization of international propaganda against the Vietnamese. Beyond our refusal to pay reparations to Vietnam, as we had agreed under the Paris Peace Accords, we refused to normalize diplomatic relations; we refused to supply Vietnam with maps and technical advice for the hundreds of thousands of duds (unexploded ordnance) left behind in Vietnam soil; we allied ourselves with China and tacitly approved its invasion of Vietnam. In a word, we did our utmost, short of war itself, to overthrow the revolution and to return the peninsula to our control. The performance has been characteristically vengeful and ruthless.

The nature of our war, its TOTAL character, would seem to guarantee a weakened Vietnam. The revolution was undoubtedly triumphant: the Provisional Revolutionary Government in Vietnam, the Pathet Lao in Laos, the Khmer Rouge in Cambodia. America left devastation, poison, millions of dead and crippled people, a shambles of what had existed before we came. The plague receded, leaving in its wake a century's desecration, poison, terror. Nonetheless, the plague receded—intrigue and assassination, insane doses of firepower, airborne poison, forced resettlement, calculated civil war, nuclear threats—the whole spectacle of a United States gone mad with delusion of power and waste—all gone.

A plague receding from one area must find a new home.[9] The empire rebounded from shame and defeat in Indochina with astonishing resiliency and mad vigor. It can be said that the defeat in Indochina, a war waged with conventional troops and unconventional means, made us more daring with unconscionable means, nuclear weaponry. The timing was too precise. Sidney Lens[10] and others have revealed that a nuclear "win formula" has always been the covert military objective. It became overt in the final year of that war. How could America maintain the illusion of victory, victory denied? A way must be found to say: "We won't be a paper tiger!" "We won't be defeated!" "If we can't win with conventional means, we yet have the power to destroy all and the willingness to use it!"

Accordingly, the Ford administration returned to the Cold War, and the process of heating it up. Schlesinger first, then Kissinger and Ford began talking openly of Flexible and Strategic Targeting Options, the notorious counterforce policy. Military appropriations swelled, strategic weapons once more targeted Soviet ICBM sites, command posts, sub pens, and bomber bases; a new round of phobic propaganda was an-

---

[9] Cf. Johnson, Paul. *Modern Times: The World from the Twenties to the Eighties.* Harper and Row, Publishers. New York. 1983.

[10] Lens, Sidney. *The Day Before Doomsday: An Anatomy of the Nuclear Arms Race.* Doubleday and Company. New York. 1977.

nounced—"for real, THE RUSSIANS WERE COMING AGAIN"—in Africa, in Cuba, in Salt II, in Afghanistan. . . .

The propaganda has worked; the image of vitality remains intact. But the reality is something else. Almost all levels of our society gave the Vietnam war decisive and enthusiastic support. With its failure, they regarded themselves as absolved from personal responsibility. Our nation has never worked through, as the psychologists say, the Vietnamese experience. We have refused to remember horrifying crimes, have failed to confess our violence. Our people, a people contemptuous of humanity, refused all guilt, all personal recognition of direct or implicit involvement. Yet only such a confession can prevent the automatic projection of guilt and hostility onto others, a process some have pondered with horror through the Iran and Afghanistan crises.

The failure to remember and repent of Vietnam has made our people full participants in the illusions of the beast of empire. A frenetic busyness obsesses us; a preoccupation with technical problems, apathy about civil and political rights, a sense of political unreality, disinterest, the shambles of accurate "disinformation," absorption in routine. Thus in the years since we were ousted from Saigon, authorities have moved with astonishing speed to a nuclear intention, nuclear war planning, first-strike weaponry. Some experts say twenty years, some say five, some say two. Then nuclear war.

With the defeat in Saigon, the American leadership continued to victimize our people, already morally exhausted by the war. Victimization included a systematic program of "disinformation," a massive increase in the development of nuclear weapons systems, wrapped tightly in the flag, and sanctions against all who dared to expose the truth. As for the movement for peace, it shared the overall malaise; it was fragmented and inert. It failed to give voice, in any compelling way, to the crimes of that war.

In another shift of tactic after 1975, the U.S. began to employ surrogates or mercenaries. Kissinger's geopolitics, embraced by Carter with variations, had three features: First, it established detente as a policy, including both antagonistic collaboration with the U.S.S.R., and American-Chinese detente as a trump card in the Washington-Moscow poker game. Second, it included the Nixon Doctrine: a low-profile, low-cost strategy designed to smother domestic resistance against Third-World intervention, while exploiting the Third-World wealth of rich clients such as Iran and Indonesia. The Nixon Doctrine implied promotion of regional concentrations of pro-American powers in critical areas of the world. Third, it provided for the shake-up of U.S. armed forces into a "high-technology, capital-intensive service" to support the armies of threatened allies, and a greater readiness to use nuclear weapons in any circumstance threatening American "interests." The Carter administration considered Brazil, Iran, Israel, Greece, Turkey, Portugal, Indonesia, and South Africa as our regional bastions of power.[11]

By mid-1974, and continuing through the late Seventies, the Nixon-Kissinger formula for imperial peace was in shreds. Portugal, Greece, Ethiopia, Iran, and Israel—all fell or were in increasing trouble. Saudi Arabia proved weak. Angola, Mozambique, and Guinea-Bissau rose to power; Turkey became alienated from Cyprus. Carter poured new wine in old skins and went with Kissinger. So, said Carter, we need more Pentagon dollars, more even than requested. We must sell more conventional arms and nuclear technology. We must develop the neutron bomb against superior tank forces. We need Trident, MX, and cruise, a new penetrating bomber. We must equal Soviet space-warfare achievements. We need the "Central Command"[12] and more bases for logistics. We need registration and the draft. We need, in sum, to be number one again, lest the Soviets try a move toward the Persian Gulf. The sentiments, it goes without saying, have been fervently huckstered by Ronald Reagan and his cohorts.

---

[11] Ahmad, Eqbal. "Iran and the West: A Century of Subjugation." *Christianity and Crisis.* March 3, 1980. pp. 41-42.

[12] Central Command is the new name given to the Rapid Deployment Force.

US: Between such suicidal derangement and its logical consequences stand peacemakers. Between intentions, preparations, scenarios, and weapons of thermonuclear war, between these and war itself, stand peacemakers. On the one hand it is said, God alone can save us; and of course the statement is right. For there has been no identifiable human counterpoise to nuclear madness in spite of the beatitude, which speaks of peacemakers as being children of God, those who inherit and share in the work of God, the work of peace.

Others say, "We alone can save ourselves! We must get off our asses, take on the war-makers nonviolently, struggle as though our souls and lives were at stake, or the world will go up in mushroom clouds!" They too are right.

What then is the course of truth and realism? To believe as though God will not abandon us, as though God is truly Lord of all things; and at the same time, to live as though we alone are responsible, to resist as though we alone can resist, to resist as though we were God's children, as though we alone can secure a future for the children.

We suggest that the truth of faith, the truth of the seventh beatitude, and the realism of justice *must* entail resistance to a body of law which is criminal and lunatic: a body of law, international, inter-Superpower, federal, even regulatory, designed only for the prospering of the War Department. Resistance, we know, will entail Holy Obedience, (a better term than "civil disobedience") as often as conscience and a mature community dictate. This holy obedience will testify at the war managerial centers, such as the Department of Energy and the Department of "Defense;" at the residences of war-makers, such as the White House; at the bomb factories; at the ICBM lairs in Missouri, Kansas, Montana, the Dakotas, Wyoming, Arizona, Arkansas, wherever.

Resistance, furthermore, will invest the whole person: spirit, convictions, body, and freedom. For the believer, civil disobedience—as it is generally known—identifies one's life with the outlaw Christ, the sinless and lawful one whom the law made outlaw, criminal, and cursed for our sake. For those more pragmatically inclined, civil disobedience must entail resistance to a body of law which makes international psychopathology and nuclear terrorism acceptable, normal, sane, utterly rational, legal.

It is clear that if the arms race can be halted, it will be because peacemakers take serious steps to stop it. Thus the beating of Mark 12A warheads, Trident submarines, MX components, cruise and Pershing components, missile silos, and any other weapon into plowshares. It is incumbent upon each, we believe, to find a way or ways to say "No More," ways that are consistent with our faith; ways that involve us in greater risk than we've embraced before.

Experience has taught that the weapons factories, military bases, and storage facilities are not as securely "protected" as their guardians believe. Nor are they as secure as we've been led to believe. Time and again, the illusion was shattered as the hammers fell. Shattering illusions, revealing the truth in love, releasing into our world the spirit of disarmament by seeking to live a disarmed life—all this has to be part of the work of peacemakers, part of the work of the children of God.

*Blessed are those who are persecuted for righteousness' sake, for theirs is the kingdom of heaven.*
Matthew, 5: 10.

# CHAPTER EIGHT
# THOSE WHO ARE PERSECUTED

The consequences of being poor (the first beatitude) and suffering persecution (the last beatitude) are stated in the present tense. The consequences of every other beatitude stand as promises: . . . they *will* be comforted, . . . they *will* inherit, . . . they *will* be satisfied, . . . they *will* be shown mercy, . . . they *will* see God, . . . they *will* be called children of God! But in the first and the last we are told "the kingdom of heaven *is* theirs!" The Beatitudes imply that the moment we know our need of God, the moment we suffer persecution for justice's sake, two startling events occur. We enter the Kingdom of God, and the Kingdom becomes available through our deeds. That is true whether those deeds are chosen or accepted.

The key reality in the last beatitude is not persecution as such, but persecution for the sake of justice, for doing what God requires. Life apportions to each of us a dole of troubles, pains, persecutions even. Some arise from arrogance and indifference, mistakes, guilty consciences. When we name such "persecutions" and lay claim to this beatitude, we nullify spirit, letter, and process. But suffering persecution for doing what God requires, that is, for the sake of justice, flows from serious, public work, the work of peacemaking.

In our meditations on the Beatitudes, we have noted a sublime yet subtle flow. Thus the last beatitude suggests not an ending but a new beginning. When we suffer persecution for justice, we undergo a peak experience: the need of God, a need deeper than we have ever known. Thus the last beatitude brings us back to the first, to suggest our starting over at a deeper level. The suggestion becomes a mandate; we recall that the Christ who counsels our attitude toward persecution is the Christ who speaks repeatedly of the Cross, the Christ whose death on the Cross was his decisive critique of the death inherent in the status quo. He announced the end of death and took death to himself. He stood, not over against death but within it. His ultimate criticism of his own culture was not his triumph but his compassion that undermined the world of competence and competition.

## PERSECUTION AND TRUE FREEDOM

In First Corinthians, Paul describes this spirit of Christ:

> *For since, in the wisdom of God, the world did not know God through wisdom, it pleased God through the folly of what we preach to save those who believe. For Jews demand signs and Greeks seek wisdom, but we preach Christ crucified, a stumbling block to Jews and folly to Gentiles, but to those who are called, both Jews and Greeks, Christ the power of God and the wisdom of God.* 1 Corinthians, 1: 21-24.

And again:

> *For I decided to know nothing among you except Jesus Christ and him crucified.* 1 Corinthians, 2: 2.

Paul's thought echoes an emphasis of Christ himself: Those who would follow me must deny themselves; they must take up the Cross. (A paraphrase of Mark, 8: 34.) This apparently is how the redemption of Jesus saves us—first, the command "Follow me!" as spoken to virtually all the disciples, and then, a threefold response, deny the false self, pick up the cross (daily), and follow after Christ.

It is curious and humbling how often Christ spoke of himself and of us in the same terms. He said, *I am the light of the world*, John, 8: 12, but also said, *You are the light of the world*. Matthew, 5: 14. He spoke of himself as *the truth*, John, 14: 6, and told us, *the truth will set you free*, John, 8: 32, suggesting that with freedom we become the truth. He told us that we were the *salt of the earth*, Matthew, 5: 13, because he was salt and leaven for all of humanity. And there is this instruction, one which he rigorously applied to himself in every detail: If you love your life you will lose it; and if you hate your life now, you will keep it forever. (A paraphrase of John, 12: 25.) And then, there is this mysterious teaching: If you serve me, you must follow me. Where I am, there will you be also. (A paraphrase of John, 12: 26.)

While Liz was in The Federal Correctional Institution in Alderson, West Virginia (1984-1986) with six other Plowshares women, a friend sent Kathleen Rumpf[1] a set of notes smuggled out of prison by Soviet dissident Mihailo Mihailov. They were entitled "The Mystical Experience of the Loss of Freedom," printed in single space on nine ditto pages. Through the notes, this exemplary prisoner sought to record and communicate an experience shared by men and women in different Soviet prisons, prisoners who had little in common outside their circumstances. Enduring the worst forms of psychic and physical suffering, Mihailo wrote, some of these prisoners experienced, simultaneously, moments of utter happiness. They felt love and hate, despair and hope intensely. They lived with the basic questions of human existence; they knew their oneness with the universe.

---

[1] Kathleen was one of the Griffiss Plowshares witnesses.

Such prisoners establish empirically what Jesus predicted would happen: those who insist on preserving their spirits are often able as well to preserve their bodies and physical existence. Their experience teaches us that in the depths of the human soul there is an unexplained force that is stronger than the forces of oppression and destruction. If people obey that voice, deep in the soul, subject to no rational control, many roads open which lead not only to preserving the life that they have given up for lost, but also to the fulfillment of their *deepest desires*.

By "deepest desires" Mihailo had to be referring to desires in harmony with the cosmic consciousness, rather than desires attached to personal gratification. Indeed, a false dichotomy has arisen, dividing cosmic consciousness—a consciousness of the oneness of all creation—on the one hand, and prophetic consciousness on the other. The two come together in our understanding that *the whole creation has been groaning in travail until now.* Romans, 8: 22.

The terrible experiences of the prisoners about whom Mihailo wrote made them free. The key was their individual and often-repeated decision to choose freedom rather than submit to their fate. Their choice informs our hearts' insight: that people need, not power, but freedom. We find that freedom not by knowledge, but by faith. Prisoners, and even ourselves, may yet learn, beyond concentrated power of evil, that the power of goodness is stronger.

It's true! If the outer world were stronger than the inner life, oppression could not be removed. But if the outer world obeys the inner spirit, our fate is in our own hands, as is the moral responsibility for the direction history takes, as is the possibility of the Kingdom of God breaking into our time.

Freedom, the insight goes, begins when there is nothing more to lose. The body responds with incredible toughness to strong spiritual concentration. Conversely, loss of spirit, loss of faith leads to spiritual disintegration. And the mystery goes further. The whole universe and the coming of the Kingdom are linked—in ways of which we know little or nothing—to the depths of spirit we summon in favor of life.

The phenomena recorded by Mihailo Mihailov are complementary to the spiritual experiences of many, if not part of the same web of spirit and life. Those who let go, who live thereafter by faith (the name we must give to the inner voice) discover, astonishingly, this mysterious yet real force at work, not only within themselves but also in the world as well. They discover as well that they are not the masters but the servants of that force. Thus we speak about persecution for doing what God and faith require. What we might read as an astonishing discovery is familiar (but no less astonishing) to those who hearken to God's Word. Something like this mystical experience of the loss of freedom is part of what is promised in this eighth beatitude. What inexpressible magnanimity! That God and his Christ summon us to the design of reclaiming creation and our human family from the ravages of death. To awaken to this reality is to be called and to respond.

While he walked among us, Christ witnessed to the Father— *The son can do . . . only what he sees his Parent doing.* (A paraphrase of John, 5:19.) And the Holy Spirit witnessed to Christ. Christ said that the Spirit would remain with us forever. The Holy Spirit whom the Parent would send, would teach us everything, and make us remember all that Jesus told us. (Cf. John, 15 and16.) In other words, the charge given just prior to Christ's death was no less than a share in his redemption. In Acts, just prior to the Ascension, Christ returns to this essential vocation of the disciples. *You shall receive power when the Holy Spirit has come upon you; and you shall be my witnesses in Jerusalem, and in all Judea and Samaria, and to the end of the earth.* Acts, 1: 8.

If we shift to the scene of John's vision in the fifteenth chapter of Revelation, we find yet another version of Jesus' hope for his witnesses:

*And I saw what appeared to be a sea of glass mingled with fire, and those who had conquered the beast and its image and the number of its name, standing beside the sea of glass with harps of God in their hands. And they sing the song of Moses, the servant of God, and the song of the Lamb, saying, "Great and wonderful are thy deeds, O . . . God the Almighty! Just and true are thy ways, O King of the ages!* Revelation, 15: 2-4.

The rich imagery deserves some attention. The text speaks only of those faithful to the Lamb. They stand by the sea, a metaphor for the source of life. That sea is now transfixed, frozen, timeless. Its life is purified and confirmed by the victory of the faithful. They, in obedience to the Lamb, had triumphed over the Beast, its image, and over the one whose name is given by a number. Their triumph is revealed in the *"mixed with fire"* image and in *"the harps"* that they now hold. The *"number of its name"* recalls chapter thirteen of the same book: the Beast of Empire (anti-Kingdom of God), the Beast's image (anti-Spirit of God), and the one whose name is given by a number (the contemporary version of empire—North American, Soviet, Chinese).[2]

The Lamb (Christ), the text implies, has done but two things in his witness. First, he has identified himself as the source and protector of life. Christ is consonant with the image of the sea of glass, the sea as the source of life. Second, he has named the Beast, its image, and the one whose name is given by a number. The apocalyptic or unmasking chapters of Matthew, Mark, and Luke reveal this; so do Jesus' words in Gethsemane and his words from the Cross. Above all, his Resurrection names them, because it reveals their deadliness, their irrelevance, and their final futility.

So also with us. The disciple will resist any beast, which is to say, any principality or power dominating, exploiting, abusing life. The disciple will resist any image maker of the Beast, any institution, any church, any media, any campus that "wires

---

[2] In circles of power, it is staunchly denied that the United States is an empire. Its imperial claims and policies require that it be so named. The naming is part of the unmasking. The same applies to Soviet and Chinese imperial claims.

the image of the emperor for sound." Further, the disciple will resist, not just the idea of empire but specific empires, the North American one, the Soviet one, this or that one with the bomb and the nuke.

"Naming" suggests the truth for us: first, the vision granted to John in Revelation is an unmasking, a laying bare and exposing of the evil lurking at the heart of Satan, and of us. Second, God limits the destruction flowing from that evil. The earth suffers regionally. Herein lies a clue for us: we must expose at every turn, in season and out, the lies, deceits, and pretensions, both of our own and of the empire. We must limit the destruction (which we can certainly do in ourselves.) We must ensure, as Albert Camus put it, that it be harder for one more child to be murdered.

We must expose the beast in ourselves: our treachery toward God and his Christ (we run from him as the disciples ran); our neutrality toward evil; our concessions to fear and appetite. The bomb and the nuke speak about us, and most Americans: the hair-trigger temper, the poisoned moral sense, the militarized spirit. Further, we must expose the beast at the Pentagon. We must unmask that vainglorious and murderous enterprise, as its scenario writers, technicians, and generals dare to decide who is to live and who is to die.

A Cleveland newspaper reported some years ago that in a West Cleveland neighborhood there lived a recluse by the name of Mr. Wesley. Neighbors were accustomed to not seeing Mr. Wesley for periods of time. But when they noticed his newspapers and mail stacking up on his porch and received no answer to ringings of phone or doorbell, they grew alarmed and called the police. The police broke in and discovered Mr. Wesley dead in bed, surrounded by rifles, pistols, and guns of every description, boxes of shells and cartridges. Mr. Wesley held a knife in his dead hand, and against the open refrigerator door—the refrigerator was empty—leaned a harpoon.

The autopsy revealed starvation. One could claim, we think, that "defense" killed Mr. Wesley. He reveals the antithesis of the Soviet prisoners mentioned by Mihailo Mihailov. In his paranoia about burglars, Mr. Wesley spent every nickel from his Social Security check and pension on guns and ammunition to defend his unhappy person and his empty refrigerator. Mr. Wesley should have shared with our all-knowing government a simple fact: "You can't have guns and butter!" Indeed, famine rides with the horsemen of war and death. Indeed also, the arms race threatens everyone in the world, and meantime robs the poor.

"Defense," as our leaders euphemistically call it, is sure to starve multitudes, if not us, and is certain to kill everyone if it continues to grow in strength. Only when we reject the pitiful example of Mr. Wesley can we dare to entreat God to number us among those standing by the sea of glass, singing the Song of Moses and of the Lamb, the song of liberation, the song of redemption. This song, we submit, is central both to resistance and peacemaking, to witness and persecution. Apart from the song of praise, our acts can be reduced, all too quickly, to mere ideology. The song enthrones God who is the inner voice, the outer summons. We would obey. Because it is the Kingdom of God to which we point, in which we long to live, even now.

## SOME CLARIFICATIONS ON SUFFERING PERSECUTION FOR JUSTICE'S SAKE

We need to slow down for a moment, to pause and reflect. Otherwise we risk drawing conclusions without adequate foundations or making questionable parallels. This is especially important for us; for we are often accused of trying to be martyrs. Some think we seek prison as a form of persecution, that we like going to jail. This oft-repeated criticism has forced us to look more closely at our motivation.

One does not seek persecution in order to claim God's Kingdom. One does not seek prison to find freedom. To do so we know would be foolish, sick, or destructive. Rather, in the spirit of Christ, we seek to bring to public expression the deceit, lawlessness, immorality, danger, and death at work in our imperial (and personal) life. Then we seek to give voice to the pain and grief awakened by the human predicament. Simultaneously we voice the hope of humanity and of creation. Thus we seek to create alternatives, other ways to live.

Unlike our leaders, Christians do have options; we need not accept imperial premises or conclusions, for Christ brought us a vision of life that redefines all social perceptions. This vision is as close to us as our next breath, if we but reach for it. Animated by that faith, we plead with each other to live that freedom in every possible (and seemingly impossible) way. Animated by that faith, we seek to hold up the Christ of history beyond history who *will reign for ever and ever.* Exodus, 15: 18.

Contrary to the assumptions of some, we do not seek prison or persecution. But we do try to accept unpleasant consequences when they occur—and to learn from them. Liz expressed something of this spirit to Magistrate Grimsley[3] at one sentencing:

> On January 7, 1977, I was sentenced to six months in jail for defacing government property. I have appealed that sentence on the grounds of prejudicial treatment and denial of the right of allocution.[4] I am before you today because Judge Bryant determined that the right of allocution was indeed denied.
>
> My friends and I have been before this court many times. You, Judge Grimsely, and Mr. Ackerman[5] tell us over and over that you respect (indeed share) our motivations and

---

[3] Harris Grimsley was a federal magistrate (judicial inferior to a federal judge) in the Northern District of Virginia. He heard many of the cases stemming from our witnesses for peace at the Pentagon.

[4] Allocution is the formal address allowed to defendants prior to sentencing. It is the time in a trial when defendants may speak freely about their motivations, about their lives, about anything that might mitigate their sentences. Liz and others were given one minute to make a statement but it could be neither moral, nor religious, nor political.

[5] Oliver Ackerman was a retired federal magistrate who heard cases periodically.

our consciences, but you listen neither to what we say at the Pentagon nor to what we say in this court. Your expressed attitude is: "I have heard it all; I am judging on the fine points of law." Therefore each time we come before you, we receive higher sentences—"a deterrent to your actions!" says the prosecutor as he demands them ... "a way of trying to silence your voices!" Seven sisters and brothers are in jail here now serving sentences of thirty to 120 days; others in other parts of the country, even more. Three of us expect to join them soon.

You have not heard us; you have totally missed the point. Bombs are being built ever day in the country with full protection of the law. These bombs will be used with the full protection of the law—the law that you and this court so staunchly guard. You and your children, I and mine will be destroyed as well as all who look to this court to protect their way of life. And it will all be perfectly legal. It will be so because you refuse to listen to what we and a few others are trying to say. Because you hide your humanity and conscience behind that bench and say you respect our conscience, but you never act on your own. You contribute by your decisions to mass suicide, every much a victim of the national run toward suicide as was Gary Gilmore.[6]

As a man, as a member of this human family standing under the threat of mass suicide (and I call it suicide since we invite nuclear annihilation by refusing to speak and act against it), what do you think your chances are personally—our chances are collectively—of surviving nuclear war; what kind of law will you practice when it comes; whom will you prosecute? Or, rather than look to the future, what should people do now to stop its happening? What does your conscience tell you to do?

---

[6] Gary Gilmore was the first death-row defendant executed when the ban on executions was lifted. Gary Gilmore was executed on January 17, 1977.

We act, we speak, we invite others to act and speak. The actions are a witness and a call. You say you admire the witness; but you have never heard the call. You tell us we have broken a law; that we must respect the law. I ask you—how can we, how can you, respect a law that makes preparation for mass suicide legal? We invite you to say: "Until the law begins to come down on those who draw up the plans, who manufacture the parts, who make the bombs, who strategize about war plans and the hoax of bomb shelters, I will not bring the law to bear against those who witness to protect life." We invite you, in short, to a species of civil disobedience as a witness to your fellow lawyers and judges, because as a federal magistrate you have the legal power to work against this criminal act of nuclear annihilation. Until you do, this court is nothing but an extension of and cover for the war-making establishment of this country. I am not that much concerned about what happens today; in my heart I have already accepted the consequences.

Think about these things, because you will see us again and again.

## SOME ASPECTS OF THE PRISON EXPERIENCE

We believe it is inaccurate to equate prison with persecution, especially in this country. North American prisons are not like the Gulag the Soviet dissidents experience. Prison is in fact a multilayered reality. The brothers at Marion Prison, in lockdown and sensory deprivation,[7] know what many Soviet dissidents know. Their experiences may be parallel. Parallel too are

---

[7] Marion, a maximum security prison for men in Marion, Illinois, has been in lock-down since a riot there in 1983. All inmates of this behavior-modification facility are locked in their cells for twenty-three hours of every day, with little to no human interaction and severely limited access to materials for reading and writing.

the sufferings of political prisoners whom our government has labeled "terrorists," a label it would broaden to include peace activists.[8] And there are prisoners—Liz and the women in the Alderson "community" knew a number of them—who are persecuted repeatedly by the system: by the FBI, prosecutors, and judges, and, later, by parole officers and parole board members. These are women who, because they kept faith with husbands or friends, found their own offenses "aggravated."[9] Thus insinuation and innuendo replace evidence, and crucial years are placed in jeopardy. So misused, these women are forced to a hard choice between fidelity and freedom. Those who choose fidelity shine in inner freedom. They inspire and strengthen all whom they touch; their friendship is a priceless gift of the Alderson experience.

Prison has become part of our lives, our experience, our growth. To many it appears as a kind of death or doom. Yet, accompanying the moments of persecution are far different moments in prison when, as Mihailov's Soviets learned, we can experience the Kingdom of God in and about us—growing, alive, real. Phil wrote about a moment of deep freedom in prison in 1977:

> Our second day here, Vince Scotti and I. Despite overcrowding—twenty-two prisoners in a sixteen-person dormitory—this human warren strikes me as somewhat more human than others I've experienced.

---

[8] In 1984, when a large group of resisters were imprisoned for their Plowshares witness, all were placed on CIM (Central Inmate Monitoring) status, a status that involves special supervision of each person. Any special permission, transfer, travel had to be cleared through the Bureau of Prisons in Washington. The "justification" for this act was that the resisters were members of a "terrorist" group that was plotting the overthrow of the government.

[9] Aggravated is a technical term which the parole board can apply to a prisoner's record and which allows the parole board members—who control the time of release for prisoners—to raise the seriousness of a person's offense to a higher level, thus adding, in many cases, years to a prisoner's sentence.

Vince and I spent an hour or two on Philippians. Once again, I noticed how the Bible cleaves through the ambiguities of other "truth" to fundamentals and sustenance for the spirit. It is the letter of a prisoner to us prisoners. *Do nothing from selfishness or conceit; but in humility count others better than yourselves . . . Have this mind among yourselves, which is yours in Christ Jesus, who, though he was in the form of God. . . . emptied himself, taking the form of a servant . . . obedient unto death, even death on a cross.* Philippians, 2: 3ff.

The kenosis (the word means self-emptying) of Christ is precisely what we find most threatening. Perhaps for two reasons: because kenosis enjoins destruction of false gods like ego, property, attachments to others (frequently, domination of them), subservience to a cannibal state and ejection of the demons symbiotically clinging to the idols; and kenosis is threatening because it requires obedience to the real God in the person of Christ, with his limitless compassion, justice, fearlessness, and freedom. We find both sides of the process abhorrent; toppling the false gods leaves the self with no familiar anchor. And because the incomprehensible freedom of Christ leaves us trembling and revolted. As Dostoevsky says in the remarkable Grand Inquisitor scene: "people find nothing so intolerable as freedom."[10]

In the same vein, who can think of others as superior to self? The psychological meanderings—too indulgent and imperial to deserve the term psychology—hold as axiomatic that self is first, self alone is the court of last appeal. Such distortion—also at the heart of capitalistic, national "interest"—is profoundly bewildering and destructive. It destroys the sovereignty of God; it destroys the superiority and equality of others. The God who abased divinity by becoming human, and who welcomed abasement further by assuming the condition of a slave and a criminal doomed

---

[10] Dostoevsky, Fyodor. *The Brothers Karamazov.* Great Books of the Western World. Volume 52. 1952. pp. 127-136.

to crucifixion, becomes a nursery-school teacher, or an outpatient clinician. As for others, we regard them as property, fit only for consumption.

The Church, for its part, will neither preach kenosis nor practice it. By default, then, the state becomes Church, and digests the Church into itself, making it a courtesan.

Consequently, a handful of believers encounter the spectacle of an exterminating state, armed with the weapons of mass suicide, and a flabby, devious, and cowardly Church. Both are blind leading blind; both are purveyors of confusion and violence. Together, they may bring down the world—the state by its addiction to war; the Church by idolatry and omission.

Closer to us as we write this is Liz's recent incarceration in Alderson, West Virginia. Her sentence was three years; she was given mandatory release at the end of twenty-five months. Considering the process leading to the Griffiss Plowshares action, trial, and sentencing, it consumed three years of her life. We talked at great length about that experience, and share here a few insights and reflections.

## PRISON AS DISPLACEMENT

One needs to begin with the displacement, with the separation from all whom we love so much. And that is full of loneliness and fear. We can feel their embraces, hear their voices, see their expressions, intuit their ups and downs and live, in part, in the remembering. But then we need to free them to live and free ourselves to be where we are—in the here and now.

In the first month of this imprisonment, Liz's mother suffered a severe stroke. For days her life was in the balance. It was a time to be with her and we could not. It was a time to be with brothers and sisters, brothers-in-law, sisters-in-law, nieces, nephews, Mom's grandchildren and to prepare together for her death and, in some way, for our own; but we could not.

Our youngest, Katy, turned three. She was frail, haunted by ill health. And we could not guess how much of her problem was physical and how much was emotional, a child's grief. That plagued us for a long time. The communication between us was clear, though our fear that we'd lose her, a fear that ate at us both, was harder to admit or wrestle with.

The older children were physically robust, but what was the effect on them? In some respects it may have been even harder for them. They did not readily accept a substitute Mom or Dad. Consciously or unconsciously, friends have tried to be that toward them. The children's antennae were well tuned to this gaming and they switched channels immediately. Friends they welcomed but not alter-parents. In this critical stage of their development (they were eight and nine at the beginning of the separation) there was much they needed to talk about, much they had no way of articulating, much they wanted help in clarifying. Only a few people could do this for or with them. Were the children being injured by this time? Could we have done anything to strengthen them? Their Dad learned to be Mom and Dad. It was both a burden and a gift of relationship with his children that too few fathers enjoy. We shared concerns when they became argumentative, quarrelsome, selfish, when they performed poorly in school.

Having experienced in Harrisburg the publicizing of our correspondence, with all our quirks and complaints, we were careful, even cryptic in our letters through this time. Instead, we used time in each prison visit to talk about the pain and the problems, to acknowledge them, to try to share them, to encourage each other, to avoid pretense. The spirit we brought to our visits was one of: "This is hard for us all but we can come through it, grow through it by being honest and by helping each other." But, because so much expectation was brought to these visits, often the hopes could not be met, and one or more of us would go from them with a nagging disappointment.

There is a paranoia that goes with prison and we humorously remind each other, "Just because we're paranoid, it doesn't mean they're not out to get us." The unease comes from being constantly under observation, from having details of behavior recorded and editorialized upon, much of it untrue. There is no way of altering the suspicion with which a prisoner is regarded. Associations and friendships are noted and evaluated as threat, as conspiracy, as illicit intimacy—one never knows.

There is a real lack of "freedoms." Each day is circumscribed. What you can eat or drink or buy, the people with whom you can associate, the resources for spiritual, intellectual and emotional growth and health care, all are severely limited. Kathleen Rumpf[11] felt the official neglect most severely during their time in prison. Helen, serving an eighteen-year sentence, continues to endure.

Out of many years' experience, the question we ask first of one another about a jail or prison concerns the noise level. "Can you read and write?" "Can you think and pray?" If there is space for this, then you can make it. Despite the "displacement," you can grow where you are planted. One of the greatest agonies of prison is the noise, the lack of silence for real growth. This is more marked in jails than in prisons, but it plagues all the government's warehouses.

## PRISON AS ENTERING INTO THE GRIEF OF OTHERS

The crush of humanity gets to you; all the inmates carry so much tragedy in their lives. To dwell in prison is to know shared pain, a life in solidarity with others whose lives have been disrupted by the wheels of justice (and injustice). To be there is to be where it hurts, enter a place where pain is part of life, to share in the brokenness, anguish, and fear, to become vulnerable. Within minutes you talk with a person just back from court bearing a thirty-year sentence. She, her three young children, her parents and friends are all in shock. Then you rejoice with another whose sentence has been cut to eighteen months;

---

[11] Kathleen Rumpf was one of the "Griffiss Plowshares" with Liz. She suffered from back trouble and arthritis.

she can begin to see daylight and a normal life for her family. One reels in rage at the administration that is responsible for this scene. While Liz was in Alderson, Reagan was in the White House. Liz often thought: "Before he's finished, Reagan will have appointed about three-quarters of the federal judges in this country. Each is carefully screened to comply ideologically with Reagan's party line: get tough on crime; fudge the Bill of Rights; give harsh sentences. Prisons become more crowded; they work less and less to anyone's benefit."

Aside from the pain of others, none of us is free of personal pain. Pain is pain. It doesn't compare.

## PRISON AS CONFRONTING ONESELF AND ONE'S GROWTH

Bishop Walter Sullivan of the Richmond Diocese in Virginia adopted the Plowshares women at the Federal Correctional Institution, Alderson. With Eileen Dooley, who heads the Diocesan Commission on Justice and Peace, he came every three months for a visit. These were precious times for us all.

At one visit, Bishop Sullivan shared with us the information that the American bishops were contemplating a pastoral letter on women in the Church. The Richmond people developed a reflection process called "Women Listening to Women" that was used in retreats by women throughout the diocese. Insights and experiences from the retreats were culled so the bishop could bring them to the national council preparing the pastoral letter. A group of us at the prison spent a weekend considering the "Women Listening to Women" format. From its simple questions, we probed our own experiences as women in the Church. Our thoughts were sent to Richmond and were part of "The Word" that helped convince the American bishops that they were in no position to write a pastoral letter on women in the Church.

The "Women Listening to Women" retreat was astonishing, Liz wrote, "A gift of eyes into both my past and my present. Unquestionably my past has been unique for a woman in the

Church. As a Religious of the Sacred Heart of Mary,[12] I was alive to the spirit of "aggiornamento" (renewal) that arose through the Second Vatican Council. Participants in the council visited and talked with our community, answered questions, and encouraged the searchings of our sisters. I recall a sponge-like existence in those years, listening, looking, reaching to understand what it all meant. I was challenged in every fiber of my being to become a daughter of this Church, a sister to these women."

During the "Women Listening to Women" weekend, we almost forgot we were in prison. The place was transformed, for a time, into a vital women's space where we were helping each other to accept our past, to be in our present, to grow into the future. But given the nature of prison, that spirit was short-lived.

In so many ways, religious life prepared both Liz and Phil well for prison. Indeed, in many ways, prison life seemed easier than the religious formation we recall. The parallels deserve some mention:

—There is in both a radical displacement from home and loved ones and periodic, formalized visiting time with them.
—There is in both the enclosure, the cell, and authorization required to move about.
—One's possessions are as limited and circumscribed in prison as they are in religious life.
—We were prepared for the enforced celibacy of prison life and had learned better ways to live with that special kind of pain.
—One obeys in prison or meets heavy consequences of lock-down and privation. There are sanctions in religious life, too, for disobedience.

---

[12] The religious community to which Liz belonged for fourteen years; the North American branch is centered in Tarrytown, New York.

—We have learned better reasons than fear for this obedience—reasons grounded in respect and the almost limitless demands of love.
—We have learned as well that there are times when obedience to God and conscience require disobedience to specific orders.
—One prays in prison and in religious life or rapidly meets a death of spirit. And there are few diversions with which to excuse the failure to pray.

It is the ways in which prison differs from religious life that make it a hard place, nearly impossible even to describe as a human space. Prison spirit and morale are terrible—of necessity. A necessity born of the fact that no one wants to be there, that few accept being there, that fewer still try to make something creative out of the time. Hatred for the place spills over into utter disregard for others. And there is often a self-hatred that eats at people's insides like cancer. So many prisoners have absorbed so much hate in their lives that they know little more than how to perpetuate it; the language reflects it, the names used, talk punctuated with obscenities. People go to pieces in prison in many ways; wasted by society, they waste themselves.

One needs to go to existentialist literature, to the theater of the absurd, for appropriate imagery. There is an appropriate image C. S. Lewis traces in *The Great Divorce*. It was his image of hell; a place from which people could travel to heaven—to the outskirts, at least—on a bus that left at regular intervals. But the place from which they left was a vast wilderness of abandoned houses. From that wasteland the residents moved farther and farther into a wilder wasteland simply because they couldn't bear to exist with one another.

In a deeper sense, prison is a mirror in which our culture is starkly and depressingly revealed. What one did or will do on the street, in the "free world" is more real than the present moment. The illusion is to regard the world outside—freedom—as if it were a place one could walk into, rather than a spiritual reality one creates with others. Most prisoners never learn that freedom is something other than an object or a possession or a presence. Few learn that it's a relationship, something we have with others.

The reality is that the now, the kairos, is all we have. It is now that we make peace, build just relationships, become more human. "We would rather be ruined than changed. We would rather die in our dread than climb the cross of the present moment and let our illusions die."[13] In this sense people in prison are no different from millions on the streets who also cherish illusions of freedom. Prisoners or outsiders, all need the service of peacemakers to begin to see reality, to choose the present moment, to build a free society.

## PRISON AS PURIFICATION

When our witness for peace is tainted by desire for attention, it can become self-serving. And when is motivation pure or untrammeled by ego? Prison can help purify one's sense of fidelity. James Douglass has described prison as a kind of contemporary monastery:

> One way of seeing jail today is to regard it as the new monastery. In a society preparing for nuclear war and ignoring its poor, jail is an appropriate setting in which to give one's life to prayer. In a nation which has legalized preparations for the destruction of all life on earth, going to jail for peace—through nonviolent civil disobedience—can be seen as a prayer. In reflecting today on the Lord's Prayer, I think that going to jail as a way of saying "thy kingdom come, thy will be done" may be the most basic prayer we can offer in the nuclear security state. Because we have accepted the greatest evil conceivable as a substitute for divine security, we have become a nation of atheists and blasphemers. The nuclear security state, U.S.

---

[13] Auden, W.H. *The Age of Anxiety.* Random House. New York. 1946. p. 134.

or U.S.S.R., is blasphemous by definition. As members of such a nation, we need to pray for the freedom to do God's will by non-cooperating with the ultimate evil it is preparing. Civil disobedience done in a loving spirit is itself that kind of prayer.[14]

It can be and it is. There is a prison discipline that can free people to probe more deeply into their lives. Consequently there are fewer distractions and diversions. Prisoners can immerse themselves in work that is really important. The uselessness of prison, if kept in perspective, is similar to the uselessness of the monk's life. The utility of the useless. It is useless as art is useless, or prayer, or death. And once in a while we are gifted with a flicker of perspective into its utility. Between one flicker and the next, we live on faith, on hope, and above all on the love of creation that drives us to act and accept the consequences.

## PRISON AS AN EXPERIENCE OF DISARMAMENT

We claim dedication to disarmament; or we so aspire. "Aspire" is a necessary addition, since there are endless aspects of disarmament. The reality becomes all-inclusive. We long to see the annihilatory weapons disarmed, and we assume responsibility in our actions. We plead and preach and pray for that end.

But there is also a disarming of our own spirits to consider. This means, among other things, disarming the "stand-offs," the separations that divide people into "we-they" for whatever reason. Disarmament is not possible, is not even a hope, as

---

[14] James Douglass is a long-time peace activist, founder of the Ground Zero Community of resistance, Bangor, Washington. This passage first appeared in the March 1986 *Fellowship Magazine*. It was reprinted in *Swords into Plowshares*. Harper & Row, Publishers, San Francisco. 1987.

long as we accept this "we-they" frame of reference. Until we understand our oneness with all of humanity, with all of life, we will construct some kind of missile or bomb to protect us from each other.

Prisons are constructed on the stand-off between jailer and jailed. They function by nurturing stand-offs within the prison population; racial differences, informing, other enmities are fostered as control mechanisms. The names people call one another in prison are ugly often precisely because they deny the humanity and human potential of each individual. You hear nigger, slut, bitch, queen, girlfriend. Girlfriend, in this context, differs radically from "sister." The former is sexual; the latter calls us into family, into community, into building together in this place. The names given the cops reinforce the walls between us. They fail to summon us and them to our mutual task, which implies dismantling the whole apparatus of prison—a threatening prospect, and not to the officials alone.

The insight we have gained into this disarming is that, from the perspective of the staff, the barriers between jailer and jailed must be maintained at all costs. The least suspicion that the walls are crumbling causes them to be reinforced. Perhaps the walls must be transcended. But that can happen only when one's freedom is interior and when the respect one gives is rooted in a common humanity and, again, in the almost limitless demands of love.

An example of that love can be seen in an amazing sequence in Mark's Gospel describing Christ's Passion in a series of "handing-overs." *Judas . . . kept looking for an opportunity to hand him over,* Mark,14:11, to the chief priests. The chief priests . . . *handed him over to Pilate.* Mark, 15:1; and Pilate . . . *handed him over to be crucified . . .* Mark, 15: 15. Things are done to Jesus; he is victim. It struck us so forcefully one day that there is a direct parallel in what happens to every prisoner—"handed over" from arresting officer to court, from court to U.S. marshals, from U.S. marshals to jailers. Then Luke's Gospel tells of the moment that Jesus took control of this process and transformed it. *Crying out in a loud voice, ". . . Into thy hands I commit my spirit!"* (Jesus handed himself into death.) Luke, 23: 46. Like him, we are asked to give our lives, as opposed to having them taken away. The difference makes all the difference. We are victims no longer; jailers, no longer victimizers; the barriers can be transcended.

The barriers among the prisoners are harder to transcend precisely because there are so many. It seems that when we concentrate on controlling one of the "we/theys," the others grow stronger. Turn to another aspect and the former has restructured itself. The effort is constant; it is exhausting. And it speaks profoundly to the way prison can wear one down, can erode what is most deeply human in us. It is often with a sense of failure that we have had to admit to feelings of racism, sexism, classism toward other prisoners—feelings we thought had no home in us.

There are ruts in prison, too, places in which we hide from one another and ourselves. But love can bring us out of the ruts if we let it. In love's light we can learn of ourselves and how far we have to travel to be disarmed people. Maybe we have to experience this failure in ourselves to grow strong or to reach the deeper inner person. And maybe there's a wisdom that comes from failure that nothing else can provide. We reflect that the crucifixion of Jesus, the paradigm of enduring persecution for justice's sake, shows us that our work is not dismantling but living out the new life Christ inaugurated. This life, undeserved as it is, finds us in failure, more receptive, less grudging and plaintive.

The crucifixion articulates God's odd freedom, his strange justice, his peculiar power. It lets us know that without the Cross, without suffering and persecution, our peacemaking is apt to become as strident and destructive as the warmaking it criticizes. The Cross, suffering, and persecution become the insurance policy, our only real credential, a guarantee even, of discipleship. Through the Cross, through suffering, and through persecution, the peacemakers enter a kind of death; the pain of their own failure—and thus know their need of God, know their need of forgiveness, know their need of continuing to search the mandates and lessons of the Beatitudes. They are able to turn back to the first beatitude to begin the journey through yet another time.

*APPENDIX A*
*Advent*
*Reflections*

## DAY 1—THE HOPE OF ADVENT

The Spirit of God has come to me.
This Spirit has commissioned me to preach
to the poor the good news of God.
She has sent me to proclaim freedom to prisoners,
sight to the blind,
liberty to the oppressed.
(A paraphrase of Isaiah, 61: 1-2.)

The hope the Bible talks about, the hope of this season, is a passion for the impossible. Not impossible, however, because our hope is rooted in the promise of God, with whom nothing is impossible. So it is not an idle hope. Because we have this promise of God (like the words Jesus quoted above) there is for us both the possibility and the command to do it—to make that history.

Our advent hope calls on us to write, with our lives, a new history, the history of lives lived in justice and peace.

## DAY 2—THE PROMISE

Then I saw a new heaven and a new earth; for the first heaven and the first earth had passed away and the sea was no more . . . I heard a loud voice from the throne saying, "He will dwell with them and they shall be his people. And he will wipe away every tear from their eyes, and death shall be no more, neither shall there be mourning nor crying nor pain anymore" . . . Behold I am coming soon.
(A paraphrase of Revelation, 21:1, 4; 22: 7.)

Such a promise! And the God who makes it is the same God who, out of nothing, made this splendid universe; the same God who raised Jesus to new life after his shameful death on the Cross.

In advent, we reach out to God the Creator and Parent of Jesus and to the promise God made of new life. We reach out in the midst of our own pain and the pain in our world and remember this promise and, in prayer and faith, expect, demand fulfillment.

## DAY 3—AWAKE

*Besides this you know what hour it is, how it is full time now for you to wake from sleep. . . . The night is far gone, the day is at hand. . . . Let us conduct ourselves becomingly as in the day.*
Romans, 13: 11-13.
*Awake, my soul! Awake, lyre and harp,*
*I mean to wake the dawn!*
*I mean to thank you among the peoples,*
*to sing your praise among the nations.*
Psalm 57: 8-9.

Being awake is so important. So many of us sleep-walk through life and we miss the sounds and smells and sights and feel and taste of life. The call of Advent is a call to live wide awake so that we can be alert to God working in us and in our world to bring about the Kingdom. Awareness is another way of talking about being awake. Work today to be aware of the needs of people around you, because God calls us through those very needs. Each time we answer to them, the Kingdom of God comes nearer.

## DAY 7—PREPARE

*The voice of one crying in the wilderness: Prepare the way of the Lord
... Every valley shall be filled, and every mountain and hill shall be
brought low, and the crooked shall be made straight, and the rough ways
shall be made smooth; and all flesh shall see the salvation of God.
... Go through the gates, prepare the way for the people; ... build
up the highway, clear it of stones, lift up an ensign over the peoples. ...
Your salvation comes.*
Luke, 3: 4-6; Isaiah, 62: 10-11.

It is easy to imagine what boulders and bumps on a highway can do to a car and the people in it. We want a clear way on a journey. Clear the way for God. The Scripture reveals what boulders we need to remove: *It is your injustice that is the barrier between you and God.* Isaiah, 59: 2. So preparing for God means removing selfishness and bickering and laziness as much as we can. *For the sake of the kingdom . . . I will speak out until the people's righteousnes shines forth.* Isaiah, 62: 1.

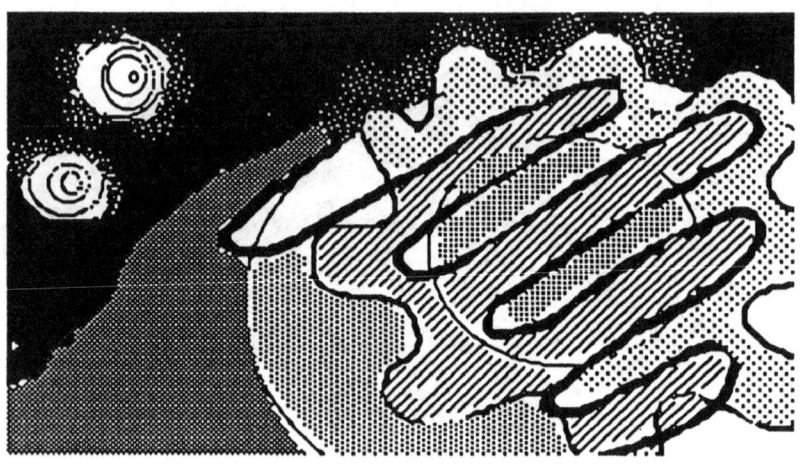

## DAY 6—CRY OUT

*You have seen, Yahweh. Do not be silent. Do not be far from me! Awake! Defend me! Side with me, my God.*

*Will your promise be unfulfilled? Have you forgotten how to be gracious? Have you withheld your compassion in anger? Has your right hand changed? Is the arm of the Most High powerless?*

*O God, do not be silent; do not hold your peace.*
Psalms 35: 22-23; 77: 8-10; 83: 1.

Advent makes us see ourselves as acutal beggars for the Spirit of God. Especially because, it seems, God's Spirit has been taken away from our world. Our work of Advent hope is to incite God to come, no longer in weakness and humility, but also in glory. We cry out to God to beg him not to turn away from us. And we do it for ourselves, for our world, for all of creation—groaning for its freedom through us, God's children.

## DAY 4—WAITING

*For still the vision awaits its time;
it hastens to the end—it will not lie.
If it seem slow, wait for it;
it will surely come, it will not delay.*
Habakkuk, 2: 3.

We know what it is to be waiting today. "I can't wait...." You say it all the time. You wait for the joys and fun of Christmas, for the next outing, for Mom or Dad to come home. In Advent, we wait for God's Kingdom to be established here and now, for justice and peace, for the deepest longings of our hearts to be fulfilled. How we wait is so important. Nothing will happen unless people like us believe in God's promise and base our lives on its fulfillment. Let's try to understand the connections between the things we long for and the kind of world God has promised.

## DAY 5—WATCH

*Watch therefore, for you do not know on what day your Lord is coming ... For the Son of man is coming at an hour you do not expect.* Matthew, 24: 42-44.

> "Be of love a little more careful than of anything."
> e.e.cummings.

What is this watchfulness that Advent calls us to but awareness—a fruit of being awake especially to what is important?

You use the expression: "You'd better watch it!" What does it mean? Here God calls us to careful attention (with a hint of warning too). God can come silently into our lives and we can miss him—to our great loss and the loss of all the community. Let's transform, in this Advent, the expression, "You'd better watch it!" so it reminds us to watch for God's coming.

## DAY 8—DAWN

*The people who walked in darkness have seen a great light; those who dwelt in a land of deep darkness, on them has light shined. Thou hast multiplied the nation, thou hast increased its joy . . .*
Isaiah, 9: 2.
*O that today you would hear God's voice: "Do not harden your hearts. . . ."*
Psalm 95: 7-8.

Dawn is the beginning of a new day. Christ and his coming not only promised a new day for our world (a total change of our world) but he began to realize it. From the time of Christ, the old order of death and sorrow and greed is moving to its end. A sun has risen that knows no setting. An energy was released in Christ that will not rest until all darkness is made light. Advent asks us to be filled, moved by that energy—to make the work of Christ our work.

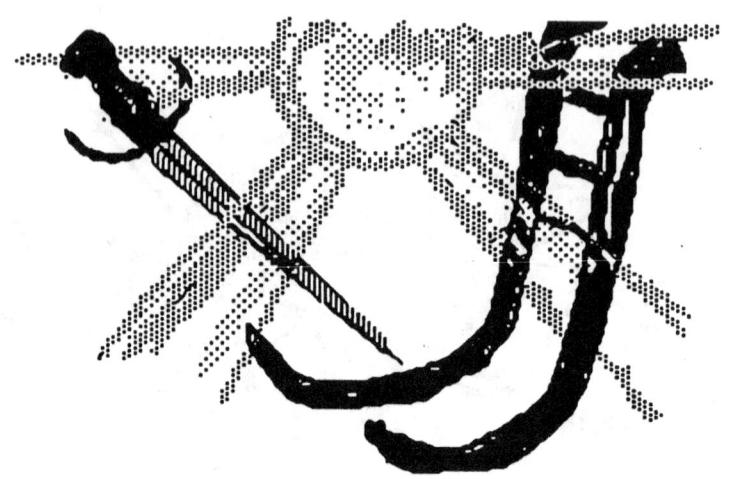

## DAY 9—SWORDS INTO PLOWSHARES

*It shall come to pass in the latter days that the mountain of the house of the Lord shall be established as the highest of the mountains, and shall be raised above the hills; and all the nations shall flow to it . . . God shall judge between the nations, and shall decide for many peoples; and they shall beat their swords into plowshares, and their spears into pruning hooks; nation shall not lift up sword against nation, neither shall they learn war any more.*
Isaiah, 2: 2-4.

The "days to come" are. Christ is the dawn of those days. Today as we try to learn the way and obey the Christ, the light shines more brightly and the impossible (that nations not prepare for war anymore) becomes possible. If the ways of humanity are to be dramatically changed, people must do what God requires. We have cause to rejoice this Advent as more obey the call and still more live acceptingly with the consequences.

## DAY 10—THE KINGDOM OF GOD

*The wilderness and the dry land shall be glad, the desert shall rejoice and blossom . . . it shall blossom abundantly. . . . They will see the glory of the Lord. Strengthen the weak hands, and make firm the feeble knees. Say to those who are of a fearful heart: "Be strong, fear not! Behold your God." . . . Then the eyes of the blind shall be opened, and the ears of the deaf unstopped . . . For waters shall break forth in the wilderness, and streams in the desert.*
Isaiah, 35: 1-10.

"Kingdom of God" appears 122 times in the New Testament, ninety times on the lips of Jesus. What is it? Isaiah tries to describe what the Kingdom will mean. Clearly it is not some other world but a transformation of this world, a total about-face. Christ's coming brings it—an event that sings and shouts of God intervening in our history—making sure, making sense, making love. God took our deepest longing, used our language, and gave it the new meaning of total liberation and absolute hope. The Kingdom of God is no longer unattainable because nothing is impossible with God.

## DAY 11—KEY OF DAVID

... *The words of the holy one, the true one, who has the key of David, who opens and no one shall shut, who shuts and no one opens, I know your works. Behold I have set before you an open door, which no one is able to shut ... Because you have kept my word of patient endurance, I will keep you from the hour of trial ...*
Revelation, 3: 7-11.

Jesus is the key that has opened the way to the Kingdom and no one can close it. He invites us to live the Kingdom now, that is, to live justly and lovingly now. There is no more friend or enemy, neighbor or stranger; there are only sisters and brothers. If evil people exist, it is because we have closed our hearts and not helped others to grow. The Key of David also promises an opening of the prisons and release to the captives and so it becomes very personal to those of us who have friends in prison.

## DAY 12—JOY

*Rejoice in the Lord always; again I will say, Rejoice. . . . The Lord is at hand. Have no anxiety about anything, but in everything by prayer and supplication with thanksgiving let your requests be made known to God. And the peace of God, which passes all understanding, will keep your hearts and your minds in Christ Jesus.*
Philippians, 4: 4-7.

Today, when the world is so full of sadness and oppression, someone must lift the veil of sadness, believe in joy, and proclaim it in our world. The apostle Paul announces, in this second week of Advent, a call to joy, even in the midst of darkness, oppression, and sadness. More than a call, it is a command—to recognize joy, trust it, believe it, and begin to live it because God is near (is here). This joy is a fruit of hope. We can be joyful *because* we know that, in Christ, suffering and pain are ended. Our fears, doubts, discouragement are rooted out by the power of God's love for us.

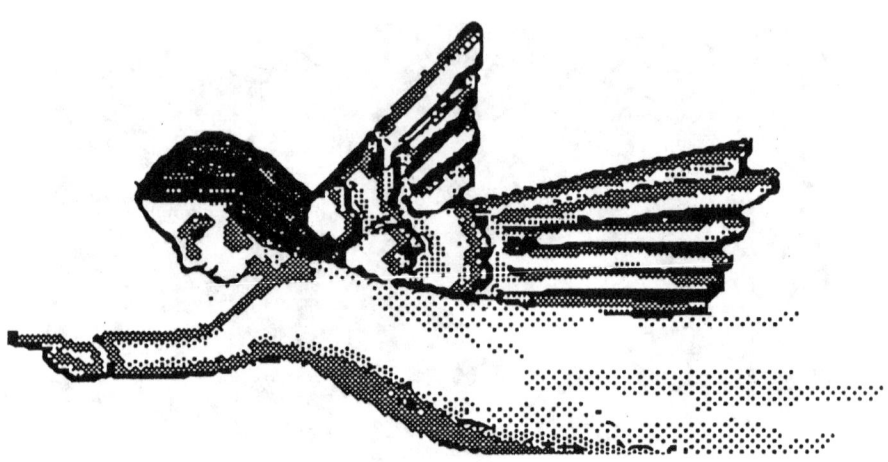

## DAY 13—THE ANGEL

*And there appeared to (Zechariah) an angel*
*In the sixth month the angel Gabriel was sent from God to a city of Galilee named Nazareth.*
*... An angel ... appeared ... saying, "Joseph ... do not fear to take Mary your wife."*
*And suddenly there was with the angel a multitude of the heavenly host, praising God....*
*... An angel ... appeared to Joseph in a dream.... "Rise, take the child and his mother, and flee to Egypt."*
Luke, 1:11,26. Matthew, 1: 20. Luke, 2: 13. Matthew, 2: 13.

There are many messengers who bring the good news of Christ's Advent and prepare for the Kingdom of God. First among them are the angels. Usually they come and speak to people when people are silent and ready to hear. Part of our Advent work of waiting is the silent listening to God's message. The other part is becoming messengers of the word that we hear, so that others also may know. Try to be silent for some time each day to hear God's message and messengers.

## DAY 14—THE SPIRIT OF GOD

God will pour out the Spirit on all the earth. All the children of God will be prophets. Old people and young people alike will dream dreams and see visions. (A paraphrase of Joel, 2:28.)
*The Spirit . . . will convince the world concerning sin and righteousness and judgment . . .*
*. . . The Holy Spirit will come upon you and the power of the Most High will overshadow you; . . . the child to be born will be called holy, the Son of God.*
John, 16: 8; Luke, 1: 35.

The Spirit is more than a messenger—the Spirit is God. And, because of Jesus, this Spirit lives within us. And when we don't know how to pray as we ought, the Spirit herself pleads for us.

We need to join our prayer with that of the Spirit within us to plead with God for an end of injustice and suffering, for the fulfillment of all God's promises. Of course, it is more than praying for it; it is a matter of living in the "light" of that promise as if the promises were fulfilled. That is, living justly, lovingly now.

## DAY 15—THE STAR

*I will give portents in the heavens and on the earth, blood and fire and columns of smoke.*
Joel, 2: 30.
*Where is he who has been born king of the Jews? For we have seen his star in the East. . . . The star which they had seen . . . went before them (and) came to rest over the place where the child was.*
Matthew, 2: 2, 9.

The Scripture tells us how important it is to read the signs of the times—be attentive. We cannot mess with the earth and the heavens without messing over our own spirits and bodies. So we learn to read the heavens (in praise of God and for better understanding).

To send the message of Christ's birth, a star appeared, actually a coming together of Jupiter and Saturn in the constellation of Pisces; but how few saw and understood it. Advent brings home its message: to be awake, aware, listening, looking, waiting.

## DAY 16—JOHN THE BAPTIST

*Now when John heard in prison about the deeds of the Christ, he sent word by his disciples and said to him, "Are you he who is to come or shall we look for another?" Jesus answered them: "Go and tell John what you hear and see: the blind receive their sight and the lame walk, lepers are cleansed and the deaf hear, and the dead are raised up, and the poor have good news preached to them."... Jesus began to speak to the crowds concerning John.... "This is he of whom it is written, 'Behold, I send my messenger ... who shall prepare thy way before thee.'"*
Matthew, 11: 2-10.

The Baptist was a messenger with his whole being. So we meet him often in Advent and try not only to hear him but to imitate his commitment and his question to Jesus: *Are you the one who is to come?* During Advent, let us put this question to Jesus, urging him to use us as messengers and come, pleading with him to fill the gap between his promises and the reality today of so much suffering and injustice.

## DAY 17—PEACE

*I will hear what you, God, proclaim: a voice that speaks of peace—peace for your faithful and those who turn to you in hope. . . . Love and faithfulness have met; justice and peace have embraced.*
Psalm 85: 8-10.
*A multitude of the heavenly host praising God and saying, "Glory to God in the highest, and on earth peace . . ."*
Luke, 2: 14.

Of the messages the messengers bring, the first is peace. Christ is our peace. And Christ makes a proposal to us. Whenever we feel responsible or whenever we feel a challenge to go outside ourselves, to accept others, to assume a task, God is making a proposal and trying to make peace. The proposal may come within our lives, in the signs of the times, in prayer. Whenever we are called to love, to grow, to open ourselves to others and to God, a faithful response is demanded. If we are open and respond, we become women and men of peace.

## DAY 18—JUSTICE

*When the promised of God comes ...*
*The wolf shall dwell with the lamb, and the leopard shall lie down with the kid, and the calf and the lion and the fatling together, and a little child shall lead them The cow and the bear shall feed; their young shall lie down together; and the lion shall eat straw like the ox ... They shall not hurt or destroy in all my holy mountain; for the earth shall be full of the knowledge of the Lord as the waters cover the sea.*
Isaiah, 11: 6-7, 9.

The justice Christ comes to bring is a whole new order of life and relationships. It is easy to live within laws that foresee and determine everything. It is difficult to follow a norm of behavior inspired by love, because love knows no limit. It calls for creative imagination, for putting ourselves at the service of others. The birth and life of Christ is for us a permanent and disturbing memory of what we ought to be and are not.

## DAY 19—LIGHT

The life of Christ was the light of all humankind. The light shines in the darkness, and the darkness has never conquered it . . . The light that enlightens all the world, was coming into the world.
(A paraphrase of John,1: 4-5, 9.)
*The people who walked in darkness have seen a great light; those who dwelt in the land of deep darkness, on them has light shined.*
Isaiah, 9: 2-3.

Today we face a darkness so vast as to snuff out even the sun. We long for the light to overcome the darkness. The light coming into the darkness gives us a new hope and a new start. We can walk in the light and spread the light. We can, indeed we must, like Christ, become light. We can, indeed we must, like Christ, enlighten the dark places of our world.

## DAY 20—A PAUSE FOR PRAYER

*Oh that thou wouldst rend the heavens and come down, that the mountains might quake at thy presence. . . . When thou didst terrible things which we looked not for . . . No eye has seen a God besides thee, who works for those who wait for him.*
Isaiah, 64: 1-4.

    We pause now, after staying with the themes and messengers and messages of Advent, and before entering the spirit of the journey that marks each life fully lived. We want to reflect a bit longer on the promise and hope of Advent and to make this plea of Isaiah with all our hearts and minds and bodies.
    And we remember that it is all of creation and not only people that are transformed by Christ's coming. Creation groans awaiting its transformation through us. *Oh, that you would rend the heavens and come!*

## DAY 21—ONE JOURNEY

*In those days a decree went out from Caesar Augustus that all the world should be enrolled. . . . . And Joseph also went up from Galilee, from the city of Nazareth, to Judea, to the city of David, which is called Bethlehem . . . to be enrolled with Mary his bethrothed, who was with child.*
Luke, 2: 1-5.

We tend to think of a journey merely as going someplace, and we look to the end of the trip rather than to the journeying. As we think of journey Biblically, we are asked to remember the journey of God's people (under the leadership of Moses) for forty years through the desert. A journey to the Promised Land. Why so long? God saw the need that the Israelites had, coming out of Egypt, to learn what freedom meant; to learn to be a people. Their journey is a symbol for our journey during which God teaches us what freedom means, during which God teaches us to be a people.

## DAY 22—A SECOND JOURNEY

*I see him, but not now; I behold him, but not nigh; a star shall come forth out of Jacob. . . .*
Numbers, 24: 17.
Shine now; for our light has come. God's glory has risen among us. Though darkness cover the earth, our God will arise, and God's glory will be upon us.
(A paraphrase of Isaiah, 60: 1-3.)

The Magi are the first kings of many to acknowledge the king and the Kingdom of God. They point to the day when all the nations will be one people under God, when the Kingdom of God will be understood as kin-dom. They let us see that, in the words of *Numbers*, "I see it (in them), but not yet (in its fullness); I behold (that day), but not near." The journey of the kings to Christ forces us to reflect on the journey still ahead for the nations and for us. Like them, we have to leave so much behind, to let go of so much, to make the journey at all.

## DAY 23—A THIRD JOURNEY

*When the angels went away from them into heaven, the shepherds said to one another: "Let us go over to Bethlehem and see this thing that has happened, which the Lord has made known to us." And they went with haste and found Mary and Joseph, and the babe lying in the manger.*
Luke, 2: 8-16.

They went in haste on their journey, probably leaving their flocks on the hillside—leaving all they possessed to go and worship the Christ. Shepherds were looked down on in their world. They were not that clean; they were seldom able to go to church; they were not well versed in the Jewish law. But to them was given the message of Christ's birth. From the very beginning of his life, Christ shows special love for this kind of person and asks us to be very careful of things like privilege, possessions, power, and prestige.

## DAY 24—CHRISTMAS EVE

*The people who walked in darkness
have seen a great light;
those who dwelt in a land of deep darkness,
on them has light shined.
For a child is born to us,
a son is given;
and the government will be upon his shoulder.*
Isaiah, 9: 2, 6.

We walk, so often, like blind people in the midst of miracles and don't see them happening and don't wonder about them or praise God for them. God came to the world quietly. So God comes today. To us.

As we wait for this coming, we ask for a little foretaste of the joy we will know when the fullness of God's glory fills the earth.

We pray God to give us better vision to see the rising of the dawn of the kin-dom in our midst.

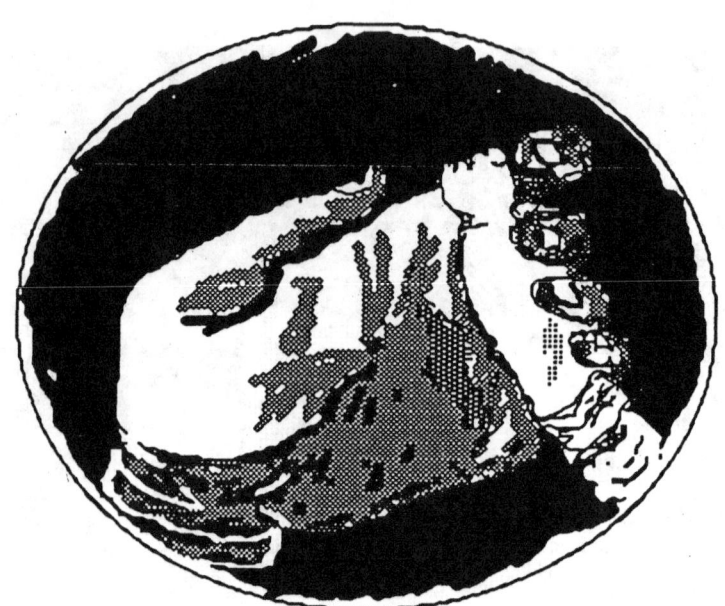

## DAY 25—CHRISTMAS

*And in the morning you shall see the glory . . .*
*Yahweh, you are faithful in all your words and holy in all your works.*
Exodus, 16: 7; Psalm 145: 13.

And God's promise is this—there is present in the heart of history a new future, here within time. Jesus is the new human being, the first to arrive at that goal. We will follow.

The Franciscans used to say that Christ would have become human even if sin did not exist. Without Christ something would have been missing in creation and we could never become, as human beings, what we are meant to be. We live expecting Christ, because we want to be all we can be (that is, children of and one with God). And this is the dynamism at the heart of creation. Christ is the one who raises the hope that we have full humanity as our end. Alleluia.

*APPENDIX B*
*The Chronicle*
*of Hope*

# THE CHRONICLE OF HOPE

A capsule history of the actions
that have come out of the experience of Jonah House.

*White House Pray-Ins—Summer 1973*

With a number of Notre Dame Sisters, including Judith LaFemina of Jonah House, the White House Pray-Ins began July 5 (a month after Jonah House began). They continued each day the White House was opened to tourists (Tuesday through Saturday) until August 15. The pray-ins called for a halt to the intense bombing then under way in Cambodia.

Each day the police arrested two to six people for kneeling and praying during the White House tour. Everyone at Jonah House except Phil, who was then on parole, participated in this action, making every effort to speak with tourists, and to invite their resistance. Initially, protesters served up to ten days in jail; later, prosecutors frequently dropped charges.

*Thanksgiving Day 1973*

Joining with the Community for Creative Nonviolence, Jonah House gathered at the home of Secretary of State Henry Kissinger. A liturgy of Thanksgiving. We presented Dr. Kissinger with a world globe into which was plunged a carving knife and fork. In other words, the world was Dr. Kissinger's turkey.

*Baltimore Shopping Mall—December 1973*

With friends, several members of Jonah House confronted an Army recruiting team which boasted a huge dummy missile and a lavishly equipped public relations van. While the management strenuously objected to our presence for peace, it was clear that it desired the Army there as a spur to Christmas sales. The police were called, but we insisted on the right to stay. In the interest of presenting "both sides," the management desisted, sputtering. Death specters silently followed the recruiters, hovering over every move and conversation. One specter sat atop the missile. By midafternoon, the Army judged the effort a loss and withdrew.

*Christmas 1973*

Again with the Community for Creative Nonviolence, Jonah House celebrated Christmas at the White House, communicating the radical lesson of the Feast of the Holy Innocents—that power's reaction to the Christ child was and is murder; therefore, Christmas promised the Massacre of the Innocents. Indeed, the terrible Christmas bombings of North Vietnam were under way.

Near the Treasury Building, directly across from the White House, we performed the sixteenth century morality play, *Herod and the Kings,* contemporizing it by changing the names. A Eucharist followed. At the "Go, you are sent forth!" people moved across the street toward the White House, and the waiting police. Five figures robed as specters of death and carrying photographs of the ravaged children of Indochina, handcuffed themselves to the White House fence. While they had police occupied, two others walked down Pennsylvania Avenue, climbed the fence and proceeded across the lawn with the intent of presenting their photographs to President Nixon, who was comfortably eating his Christmas dinner. All seven were arrested. Later, another demonstrator threw the mutilated and bloodied dolls from the theater presentation onto the lawn.

*Anniversary of the Signing of the Paris Peace Accords—January 27, 1974*

Jonah House, with Baltimore and Washington friends, staged another theater, this time in front of the White House. The scenario: General Thieu spoke of his indebtedness to Nixon and Kissinger and answered critics of his Saigon regime. Later, four persons (Ned Murphy, Lee Randol, Lee Kohns, and Sal Scafidi) offered themselves at the guardhouse as "hostages" (substitutes) for Vietnamese political prisoners and were arrested.

*Lenten Series, 1974.*

Each Friday of Lent, Jonah House, joined by sisters and brothers from Baltimore and Washington, demonstrated at a seat of oppression:

1. The Baltimore City Jail and Maryland State Penitentiary—prisoners depicting the overwhelming presence of the poor in jails and prisons, were marched in chains from the courthouse through the city streets to the jails, where a vigil was held.

2. The Maryland National Bank, which had lent huge sums of money to the Union of South Africa despite that country's apartheid policies—Mr. Pig E. Bank effusively greeted patrons as they entered or left, telling them to protect their common (dollar) sense, and to ignore demonstrators, who, chained to him, depicted the South African victims of apartheid.

3. The National Security Agency, the elite American intelligence community, whose budget remains a classified item and which monitors every international call—commercial, military and private—which knows the constant whereabouts of every Russian diplomat or agent, whose mechanical and human spies penetrate virtually everywhere—we held a liturgy under the nervous scrutiny of five different species of police, finally attempting to bring the fruit of the service (a cross hung with images of repression made possible by NSA "intelligence") across the military lines to the director. The military, from Fort Meade, Maryland, intervened at that point and arrested Joan Cavanagh, Rosemary Bramble, and Joe Cronin, turning them over later to the local police.

4. The Catholic Center and Cathedral—a silent vigil in the rain addressed the complicit silence of the Church in the face

of official warmongering, malign neglect of the poor, and racism. Clergy and laity officed in the Center watched as demonstrators and graphics pleaded for a return to Gospel spirit and fidelity.

5. The Westinghouse Plant in Baltimore. Westinghouse built this corporate fortress in close proximity to the Baltimore-Washington International Airport, through which it maintains a constant influx and efflux of equipment, technical expertise, and production. The plant is one of the most heavily guarded in the Northeast, a fact betraying its warmaking alliance with the government. Demonstrators dug graves on the lawn of the Administration Building, erected crosses engraved with weapons systems produced by Westinghouse. A flag reading *Death* replaced the big *W* on the flagpole. Leaflets were distributed to workers as they changed shifts.

6. On Good Friday, demonstrators from the previous actions carried the cross through downtown Baltimore, stopping to pray at fourteen stations of oppression. That same cross, the central symbol throughout Lent, was finally burned at the end of the procession in Hopkins Plaza, suggesting resurrection and the ultimate triumph of Christ.

*Vietnamese Overseas Procurement Office—First Action—Lent 1974.*

This agency, financed by Washington's Food for Peace Program, was secretly engaged in weapons procurement for the Saigon regime. Thus, on that same Good Friday, two members of the community (Ned Murphy and Debbie Daniell) entered it with Mike Bucci and Mitchell Snyder and poured their blood on the office files, staying until arrest.

This action made it abundantly clear that Food for Peace money, intended by Congress for the South Vietnamese poor, went to the corrupt plutocrats of Thieu, who used it to purchase American favors and arms in Washington. The agency in question served both purpses—it channeled funds, and it purchased weapons.

*Vietnamese overseas Procurement Office—Second Action.*

On July 10, as the first action groups went to trial, a second group—Rosemary Bramble, Joan Cavanagh, Bill Murphy, and Hank Skrypeck (three of whom were Jonah House members)—repeated the blood pouring because of continued U.S. violation of the 1973 Paris Peace Accords, and to support their friends on trial.

In trials emerging from both actions, a pattern of defense evolved, drawn largely from the trials of Socrates, and especially from the trial of Jesus. Pro-se defense became the rule; all accurate evidence of "crime" was stipulated (admitted); the legal figments, which invariably masked the complicity of the courts in official crimes, were dispensed with. Defendants kept their counsel, except for a statement at sentencing before the trial judge, clarifying their motivation in civil disobedience, indicting the government's criminality and appealing to the responsible conscience of the bench. All were convicted.

*Tiger Cage on The Capitol Steps—July 10 through August 9.*

Almost simultaneously with the first trial, and the second blood pouring action, a group of supporters carried a tiger cage from the Federal Court Building to the Capitol. When stopped by police at the Capitol steps, they, resigned to arrest, insisted on a site at the top of the steps outside the Rotunda. The police proved to be surprisingly flexible. Negotiations followed and the tiger cage went outside the Rotunda.

For several weeks, protesters from such cities as Baltimore, Washington, Philadelphia, New York, and Boston chained themselves inside the tiger cage, fasted on water, and prayed, leafleted, witnessed, talked with tourists. The last week, leading to August 9, three peacemakers (Carol Bragg, Mitch Snyder, and another young woman) occupied the cage around-the-clock (the police would not allow them to sleep at night), and fasted on water. The series and the fast ended with a superb Vietnamese meal.

*Occupation of the Baltimore Gas and Electric Tower—September 30, 1974.*

Before dawn, three members of the community—Hank Skrypeck, Stan Clark, and Joan Cavanagh—with Rosemary Bramble and Marjorie Colchin, climbed a huge gas tank adjacent to Route 83 running to downtown Baltimore, and displayed a mammoth banner calling for cessation of B-52 raids and U.S. withdrawal from Indochina. After ten hours, the police were clever enough to divide them on several levels of the tank, trick them, and remove them to jail. A Baltimore judge sentenced them to several weeks' imprisonment. Demonstrations at the judge's home freed them after several days in jail.

*Occupation—National Catholic Shrine, Washington, D.C. November 1974.*

This demonstration addressed the American Catholic bishops during their annual conference at the Statler-Hilton Hotel in DC. Three members of Jonah House—Deborah Budd, Jim Budd, and Chris Moore—accompanied by Mitch Snyder and Mary Ellen Hombs—gained access to the Shrine's bell tower, and then dropped two huge banners reading, "If they come for the innocent without stepping over our bodies, cursed be our religion and our life!" and "Famine and War—Scripture connects them, do you?"

Firefighters brought heavy equipment to break through two levels in the tower, and police arrested them. The next day, two demonstrators were arrested in the lobby of the Statler-Hilton for leafletting. Finally, Rosemary Bramble read a statement at the Bishop's Mass, in the National Shrine of the Immaculate Conception. She was promptly arrested.

*Paris Peace Accords Readings at the White House—January 1975.*

Demonstrators, sometimes two, sometimes more, were arrested daily at the White House for reading the Paris Peace

Accords from the tourist line. All members of Jonah House, save Phil (still on parole) were arrested, several, two or more times. The culmination of the month-long campaign came with Scripture readings in the vestibule of the White House. Then, Chris Moore and Ron Riech took down the flag, threw the Accords on it and poured blood on both. The judge gave them a month in jail, but after a few days, their prosecutor filed an unprecedented brief asking for release after time served.

*The White House Arrests—Amnesty Issue, March 1, 1975*

Sixty-two people, including Dan Berrigan, Liz, Joan Burds, Ladon Sheats, Joan Cavanagh, and Ed Clark from Jonah House, were arrested at the White House for sitting in as a protest to President Ford's vindictive amnesty program. The previous Friday, six ex-prisoner draft resisters sat in at Director of Amnesty Charles Goodell's office.

*Mobile Tiger Cage Demonstration—White House, March 20, 1975*

Three demonstrators, including Phil, chained within a tiger cage on a flat-bed truck, were arrested on Executive Drive outside the White House for protesting the plight of South Vietnamese political prisoners. The parole board took no action against Berrigan. Charges were dropped.

*Vigils at the Homes of Secretary of State Kissinger and Secretary of War Schlesinger—Holy Week, 1975*

A cross hung with graphics depicting the victims of Indochina was carried from the State Department to Mr. Kissinger's Georgetown home, where a round-the-clock vigil commenced. Concurrently, another vigil was held at Mr. Schlesinger's home. Both lasted until an Easter Eucharist at Haines Point on the Potomac.

*The Hiroshima and Nagasaki Bombs on Capitol Hill—Summer 1975*

This presence was initiated as a response to the Counterforce, or "first-strike" policy announced by Ford, Kissinger, and Schlesinger after the United States defeat in Indochina, on April 30, 1975. Every day, for five weeks, exact replicas of "Little Boy," the Hiroshima bomb, and "Fat Man," the Nagasaki bomb, were carried to the Capitol steps to mourn the bombings of 1945, to remind a forgetful people of these colossal crimes, and to warn tourists of our first-strike policy. On August 6, the anniversary of the bombing of Hiroshima, a press conference was held near the bombs, but was largely blacked out by the media. On August 9, the anniversary of the bombing of Nagasaki, peacemakers destroyed the Nagasaki bomb, using its components as a crude altar for the Eucharist.

*Pratt and Whitney Air Show—East Hartford, Connecticut, October 1975*

Pratt and Whitney celebrated its 50th anniversary as the United States' foremost builder of military and commercial plane engines. The company created a carnival atmosphere for worker families and tourists, and encouraged all New Englanders to attend. The earliest and latest military and commercial aircraft from four wars were proudly displayed. Rumblings of demonstrations aborted plans for the presence of a B-52, but at center stage were an F-111, an F-4, an F-15, and a Boeing 747.

Demonstrators, working in groups of three or four, poured blood in or on cockpits, and painted "death" on fuselages and tails. The five planes hit were all nuclear bomb carriers. After the second plane was "defaced," the crowd became ugly. Police had to protect the resisters. Joan Burds, Joan Cavanagh, Lee Griffith, Ladon Sheets, Jay Dudgeon, and Phil Berrigan from Jonah House were arrested with sixteen others. Some did thirty days in jail.

*The Nuclear Embassies—November 1975*

To foretell the "Disarm or Dig Graves," witness at the White House, and to give evidence of non-discriminatory treatment, Dan Sanders, Jim McNeil, and Phil Berrigan painted "Disarm Now" at the embassies of the nuclear club—Britain, India, and France. Police guarded the Chinese Embassy much too heavily for the attempt, and a wrong address for the Russian Embassy foiled our effort there. At 2:00 a.m., while hunting for the Russian post, the three were arrested by police, who held them overnight and released them when the British, the only ones to react, dropped charges.

*Dig-In at the White House—Day before Thanksgiving 1975*

The "Disarm or Dig Graves" campaign was a response to the lunatic plan of the War Department to employ abandoned mines around the country as evacuation centers and bomb shelters in case of nuclear war. The graves stated that, given a nuclear exchange, the mine shafts would become mass graves. We sought to resist that nightmare by digging symbolic graves at selected governmental sites.

Some twenty-five peacemakers filed through the White House tour and emerged on the Pennsylvania Avenue side and displayed banners and revealed Uncle Sam walking with death specters. The police, noticing the press and other demonstrators beyond the fence, allowed an unprecedented demonstration on the driveway until nearly noon. Then Uncle Sam and the specters of death crossed the chain fence, and, taking shovels passed to them through the fence, dug a grave on the White House lawn. Dan Berrigan was arrested as well as all the members of Jonah House except Liz, who planned to keep the shop open. Thirteen people served from ten to thirty days for this resistance.

*Dig-In at the Pentagon—January 6, 1976*

Continuing the "Disarm or Dig Graves" campaign . . . While some resisters tried to enter the Pentagon to issue an invitation to Secreatry of War Donald Rumsfeld to debate nuclear weapons policy, death specters dug a grave on the Parade Ground overlooking the Potomac. When they had gone deeply enough, the specters buried Uncle Sam, suggesting that atomic death will, in all probability, bury Americans in mass graves. Sixteen were arrested, seven of them Jonah House members.

*The Pentagon and Rumsfeld's Home—Holy Week 1976*

Through the early days of Holy Week about forty resisters held concurrent round-the-clock vigils at the War Department and at the secretary of war's home. At the latter, complaints finally arose from the neighborhood or from the Rumsfelds, and after refusing to leave, four people were arrested. On Holy Thursday, which coincided with April 15 (Tax Day), 1040 tax forms were burned in wire baskets on the steps of the River Entrance, and demonstrators marked the columns of the Pentagon with blood. Seven people from Jonah House were arrested. A dig-in planned for Rumsfeld's home was abandoned for the time.

*Blood Pouring at the Pentagon—April 30, 1976*

To support those on trial from the Holy Thursday action, and to label the Pentagon "Temple of Blood" again, five resisters, with two death specters standing by, anointed the columns of the River Entrance. All were arrested.

*Summer Sessions at the Pentagon—May through September 1976*

1. Liz and Lee Griffith facilitated. Guerrilla Theater in the Pentagon concourse resulted in four arrests. Later in the week, they were arrested again for pouring blood on classified Navy files. They performed the resistance while taking a Pentagon tour.
2. Ladon Sheats and Jay Dudgeon coordinated this series. On July 15, four resisters threw ashes on the main steps of the

River Entrance, explaining. "The Pentagon madness will bury everyone in radioactive ash." The following day, two vegetable gardens were planted on the Parade Ground below the River Entrance. "Choose life then!" was the theme. Police arrested twelve. Six received sentences of one to six weeks.

3. Joan Cavanagh and Jim McNeil coordinated. They managed the first lockout of the River Entrance, shutting out civilians and military for twenty to thirty minutes, handcuffing themselves to the chains. The theme: "The world is chained with us to these doors!" Eight arrests resulted.

4. Joan Burds and Phil Berrigan coordinated. Five demonstrators poured blood again on the River Entrance. Each received ten-day sentences. The five dug a symbolic grave on the Parade Ground. These received suspended sentences. The next day, three dug a grave on the lawn of Secretary of War Rumsfeld's home. They were sentenced to ten days in jail.

*Thanksgiving 1976*

The theme of the three days of demonstration was the nexus between world hunger and United States militarism. On each of the days, two death specters taunted beggars chained to the pillars at the Pentagon entrance. Then at the Pentagon Thanksgiving Service, a statement was read conveying the true spirit of the day, followed by a blood pouring on the entrances to the Pentagon from the Pentagon Shopping Mall. Police arrested nineteen people, several of them twice. Arrestees included all from Jonah House.

*Feast of the Holy Innocents—December 28, 1976*

This demonstration compared Herod's slaughter of the children to the probable atomic slaughter of the world's children contemplated by our present day Herods. Resisters, using locks and chains, locked two main entrances to the Pentagon for almost half an hour and poured blood on each of thirty columns. About eighty people participated; twenty-nine were arrested.

All from Jonah House except Ladon Sheats were arrested. Many served up to four months in jail.

*Pre-Inauguration—Plains, Georgia 1977*

After lengthy negotiations with the Carter "team," Ladon Sheats, Ed Clark, John Schuchardt, and Phil Berrigan drove to Plains and attempted to speak with the president-elect. Carter being otherwise occupied, the witnesses threw up banners outside his home, violating town ordinances. Seven were arrested and spent several days in Georgia jails before being released.

*Holy Week—The War Department 1977*

In a spirited demonstration, labeling the Pentagon as "The Temple of Death" with large letters at each of the columns, nine people were arrested for blocking the doors, and for interrupting the Good Friday Service in the Concourse.

*Anti-Trident March—Connecticut, May 21, 1977*

Following on the heels of the Seabrook Occupation (in which one person from Jonah House participated), many marched twelve miles through New London and Groton carrying a Trident Monster. Afterward, they planted trees and erected other life symbols at the naval base and at the Electric Boat Company, which builds the Trident submarines. Finally, resisters poured blood on the submarine construction display outside. There were sixteen arrests, including Ladon Sheats, John Schuchardt, and John Ragusa.

*Summer Sessions—May 28 through September 2, 1977*

These sessions were similar to those of the previous summer. Participants came from near and far to pray, educate themselves, dialogue, and make democratic decisions before acting. Starting out as groups of individuals, they ended up as communities of resistance, however modest.

1. Joan Burds and Joan Cavanagh from Jonah/Advaita houses facilitated a session of women alone who sought to clarify the connection between sexism and militarism. Leaflets at the Pentagon were passed only to women and guerrilla theater was performed on the Concourse.

2. John Schuchardt and Ladon Sheats coordinated a session that focused on the recently announced neutron bomb. Their community poured blood at the Environmental Research and Development Administration, the agency responsible for funding and developing the neutron bomb project. Then another blood pouring took place at the Pentagon. Seven were arrested.

3. Liz and Jim McNeil facilitated this session that concentrated on the thirty-second anniversary of the bombings of Hiroshima and Nagasaki. Five people fasted on water for ten days. On August 6, five poured blood and dumped ashes on the Pentagon. The driveway to the River Entrance was blockaded on August 9, and three were arrested on the Pentagon tour. Total arrests were eighteen.

4. Ed Clark and Phil Berrigan worked with this community repenting for America's Cold War crimes. Five persons chained themselves to the White House fence to illustrate the spiritual enslavement of neutron bombs and other nuclear weapons. Then four poured blood on entrances to the Pentagon leading from the Concourse. Four more scattered ashes into the blood. Thirteen were arrested.

*Carter's Church—October 1977–April 1978*

This series of witnesses was intended to anticipate the president's decision on the deployment of the neutron bomb in Central Europe. The presence with leaflets, banners and prayer continued each Sunday into the spring of 1978 with periodic "incursions" into the worship service itself.

*White House Presence—August 6–November 19, 1977*

Every Thursday and Saturday during this period, members of Jonah and Advaita houses demonstrate outside the White House on the driveway exit leading to Pennsylvania Avenue. As with the demonstration at Carter's church, we were protesting the decision to deploy the neutron bomb. On one occasion, Ed Clark, Phil Berrigan and three others were arrested, tried, and acquitted.

*Thanksgiving—1977*

Some thirty friends were on hand to focus on the neutron bomb. As a Thanksgiving symbol, a huge cornucopia was stuffed with depictions of the American arsenal—missiles, tanks, planes, and guns. Demonstrators greeted the French war minister with the symbol at a Pentagon parade, also upraising banners and chanting: John Schuchardt lowered the Pentagon flag twice—once during the anthems of France and the United States. Others interrupted the Thanksgiving service and were arrested. Finally, others marched with the symbol to the White House and left it on the lawn there. Nine were arrested in all.

*Feast of the Innocents—1977*

About 100 people participated at a peace witness at the Pentagon. We were based at the United Church of Christ. There were actions at the Pentagon on December 28 and 30. On the 28th there were eight arrests for blocking of entrances and spattering blood on the pillars of the Pentagon. Carl Kabat was given a year for his participation; Bob Randols and Ladon Sheats, thirty days; Pauline Swift, Gil Corby, and Brian Terrell, ten days; Jim McNeil and Mary West never came to trial. On the 30th, twenty-one were arrested for blocking entrances. Paper work for all twenty-one was "lost" and charges were dropped.

*Valentine's Day—1978*

Following Dan Berrigan's week of teaching at Georgetown University, about thirty-five people assembled in the Pentagon Concourse. Eight were arrested for spreading blood and ashes in front of the entrances to the building following a litany of repentance: Phil Berrigan, Esther and Barry Cassidy, Ed Clark, Ellen Kleylein, John Schuchardt, John Shiel, and Brendan Walsh. Dan Berrigan was also a participant but was overlooked by the police. Phil was charged with scattering ashes when, in truth, he poured blood. On his own testimony, he was found not guilty. Charges against the others were joined to subsequent charges and most served time in jail.

*Holy Week—1978*

About 100 people participated in the Holy Week witness. We were centered at St. Stephen and the Incarnation Church in D.C.
March 22—A silent vigil was held at the Pentagon.
March 23—A litany in the concourse was concluded by a die-in, people coming to grips with and revealing the death of nuclear war. Ten people were arrested.
March 24—Thirteen people held letters reading "TEMPLE OF DEATH" in front of the pillars of the River Entrance. A siren went off and eight people re-enacted the death of nuclear war; four others poured blood and ashes. The twelve were arrested. Later in the day, four others were arrested when they labeled a cross composed of weapons with their blood. Phil Berrigan, Ladon Sheats, John Schuchardt, and Ellen Kleylein from Jonah House were among those arrested. Phil, Ladon, John, and Ed began six-month sentences and joined Carl Kabat at Allenwood.

*The First U.N. Special Session on Disarmament*

It was held in New York City. About eight people from Jonah House participated in civil disobedience at the session in New York.

*Summer Sessions—1978*

1. Ellen Kleylein, Jean Fazzino, Paul Hood, and Ray Torres were arrested for labeling a cruise missile on display inside the Pentagon with their blood. Ellen served six months in prison for this act; Paul, sixty days; Ray, thirty days; and Jean, six months suspended. Eight people participated in the ten-day session.
2. Sixteen people participated. On August 6, eight people entered the First Baptist Church to make a statement and were arrested for unlawful entry. On August 9, two were arrested for labeling the Pentagon as a House of Blood—Mary Lyons and Gene Brake.
3. Thirty-five people participated. There was civil disobedience at the Pentagon on September 1 in which twenty-one people were arrested for locking the Pentagon entrances and pouring blood on the pillars. People served sentences of from five to thirty days; some were given suspended sentences.

*The Annual Associations of the U.S. Army Convention at the Sheraton Park Hotel in D.C.—October 17, 1978*

Sixteen people were arrested. The witnesses against this display of arms included people chaining themselves to balconies, even to the arms displays themselves, and speaking to any who would listen. There was also a die-in by some who had poured blood on themselves.

*Feast of the Innocents—1978*

On the eve of the International Year of the Child, this was our first incorporation of children into a session of resistance. 250 adults and forty children and about thirty Hispanic teenagers participated for the three days.
December 28—A massive presence in the Pentagon Concourse included the children in a serious, yet festive atmosphere.

December 29—The adults locked the Pentagon closed at three entrances and labeled it with their blood. Twelve people were arrested. At noon in the Concourse, twenty people staged a die-in aided by survivors who wiped the ashes and blood from their bodies and prayed over them. The blood and ashes were spilled by six sisters and brothers. For half an hour following the die-in all sang "All we are saying, is give peace a chance," in hushed voices to a stunned crowd of onlookers. All who "died" were cuffed and lined up by the police like so many corpses in a morgue. The arrests intensified the impact of the die-in. Meanwhile, the children brought letters they had written and their own presence to the State Department, to Amy Carter at the White House, and to the Air and Space Museum.

*Arms Bazaar in Chicago—February 18-20, 1979*

Joan Burds was working on organizing for the Arms Bazaar. Joan, Carl Kabat, Peter de Mott, and Ed Taylor were among those arrested. They closed the bazaar not only for that year but for subsequent years as well.

*Lent—1979*

A newly formed community in Washington, D.C., fasted throughout the season of Lent for an end to the arms race. Each Friday night there was a presentation to a large group on issues of peacemaking in the nuclear age.

*Launching of the first Trident submarine in Connecticut—April 7, 1979*

There was a mass demonstration against the Trident and mass civil disobedience. Five people from Jonah House participated in the civil disobedience.

*Holy Week—1979*

About 120 people participated in the session from April 10-13. It was centered at St. Stephen and the Incarnation Church in D.C.

April 12—The group split between the D.O.E. (Department of Energy), to protest the handling of the Three-Mile Island nuclear accident, and the White House. At the White House, two people labeled that sepulcher with blood, backed by seven others who bannered and leafleted in the drive of the White House. Nine were arrested. Carl Kabat served two months for this action; Liz McAlister, thirty days; Emma Wiktor, five days. Others were given suspended sentences or, after repeated appearances for trial and constant delays, refused again to appear.

April 13—Four people were arrested at the Pentagon for the use of blood there.

*May 29, 1979*

Mary Lyons was arrested in Connecticut as part of a demonstration against United Technologies and served fifteen days in jail.

*Summer Sessions—1979*

1. Fifteen people participated. Four occupied James Schlesinger's office at the Department of Energy on July 9.

2. Twenty five people participated. Twice on August 6 and 9, twelve to fifteen people lay on the inflexible stone of the War Department and experienced—in so far as possible—the death of the world by the bomb. On August 9 they also marked the porticos of the War Department with blood. Carl Kabat served nine months for this; Louie de Benedette, three months.

3. Thirty participated. There were ten arrests of people who portrayed their fear of our nation's policies of nuclear madness—three for blocking entrances; seven for christening the

building with blood (two for dipping their fingers into the pool of blood and writing "DEATH" with blood on the pillars).

*Arms Bazaar Protest, Washington, D.C.—September 16, 1979*

Two people poured blood on the registration desk and destroyed computer cards that kept the system going; eight enacted a die-in amid the blood; two poured ashes and blood on the cruise missile model at the bazaar iteslf. A large protest outside, organized by Sojourners Community, culminated in civil disobedience with eleven arrests.

*Rocky Flats Nuclear Weapons Plant in Colorado—September 26, 1979*

Seven people, including two from Jonah House and the Baltimore community, entered the plant, having cut the barbed wire fence. Ladon Sheats, J. Dudgeon, and Kathy Jennings served six months for this prayerful entrance into the darkness; Jack Gibson, Peter Weber, Peter Sprunger-Froese, and Al Zook served three months each.

*Department of Energy in D.C.—October 28, 1979*

There was a major action at the Department of Energy with a parallel action at Wall Street in N.Y.C. Jonah House participated fully in the action in which several hundred people risked arrest; no arrests were made but no one entered or left the building except over the bodies of protesters. Carl Kabat was rearrested that day after mistakenly being released from D.C. jail at the end of September.

*Feast of the Innocents—1979*

A brief presence was mounted due to the forthcoming Year of Election. About 120 people participated. December 28, the group went to the Pentagon with the themes of mourning and of hope. Fourteen people acted so as to unmask our country's military violence, though the police chose to arrest only four.

*The Year of Election—1980*

This has been detailed in the manuscript. We will not reiterate it here. Other acts of resistance through 1980, not specifically connected to the "Year of Election," include:

*A mass demonstration at the Pentagon—April 25, 1980*

It was organized by the Coalition for a Non-Nuclear World. No one went to or from work that day without walking over bodies—an appropriate symbol of the reality of the Pentagon. 500 were arrested, including five from Jonah House.

*The Plowshares 8—September 9, 1980*

The first act of disarmament took place at the G.E. facility in King of Prussia, Pennsylvania. This involved three people from Jonah House—Phil Berrigan, Carl Kabat, and John Schuchardt. They joined Dan Berrigan, Dean Hammer, Elmer Maas, Anne Montgomery, and Molly Rush.

*Women's Pentagon Action—November 17, 1980*

2,000 women came to the Pentagon. They gathered in mourning, shouted in rage, and encircled it in unity and empowerment; they blockaded all its entrances in defiance. 140 women were arrested; most were jailed for periods of from ten to thirty days.

*The Pruning Hooks—December 13, 1980*

Peter de Mott of Jonah House engaged in the second act of disarmament using an Electric Boat Company van as a mobile battering ram against a Trident submarine under construction in Groton, Connecticut. Peter was given a year in jail for this service to humanity.

*Pantex Plant—February 10, 1981*

Six people, including Ladon Sheats, intervened in business-as-usual at Amarillo, Texas. They climbed the security fence and prayed on the grounds for an end of nuclear madness. Two were given a year in jail; two, nine months and two, six months.

*Lent—1981*

Jonah House sponsored a weekly presence at local facilities that constitute the war in our own back yard. On each of the six Fridays in Lent we went with banners, leaflets, and ourselves to one of these facilities, including The Johns Hopkins University Applied Physics Lab, Martin Marietta, Litton Industries, Westinghouse, and the AAI.

*Holy Week—1981*

About ninety people gathered at St. Stephen and the Incarnation Church.

April 15 at the White House (tax day), four people poured blood on the pillars of that building, one poured blood on tax forms in the drive, and four others held banners and leafleted in the drive. Mike Miles, Karl Smith, and John Shiel were given six months in jail; Louie de Benedette, four months; George Veasey, three months; Sally Kearsley, thirty days; James Cunningham, five days; and Brigette Cooke and Mary Rose Eagleston, suspended sentences.

April 16 at the State Department, three people entered Secretary Haig's office and held there a liturgy of exorcism. They prayed and spread blood and ash. Theresa Guisti, Macy Morse, and Tom Reed were arrested and given fifty-two days in jail.

April 17 at the Pentagon, Jeanne Clarke and Marcia Timmel were arrested for pouring their blood on the portico of the

Pentagon and given thirty days in jail; two others were arrested in the Concourse also for the use of the symbol of blood. This was in the context of an enactment of nuclear death—the siren, the ashes, the blood, the die-in.

*Call to Prayer and Resistance at the White House—June 2–July 3, 1981*

Each Tuesday through Saturday, Jonah House and the Community for Creative Nonviolence invited friends to enter the White House prepared to address the real and imminent threat to life today through acts of prayer in order to encourage the Congress and the American people to reject the Reagan administration effort to deregulate oil and gas and pump yet more billions into weapons programs. There were groups of six to twelve people each day that month. In all, 242 arrests were made that month at the White House. Most received suspended sentences; a few served three to ten days in jail. But George Veasey of Jonah House, for the same action, was given six months (the maximum) in D.C. Detention Center.

*Sentencing for Plowshares 8—July 28, 1981*

Phil and Dan Berrigan, Carl Kabat, and John Schuchardt were sentenced to three to ten years in prison; Dean Hammer, Elmer Maas, and Anne Montgomery to one and a half to five years in prison, and Molly Rush to two to five years in prison.

*Summer Sessions—1981*

1. Fifteen folks gathered for this ten-day period and determined to witness at the Pentagon on the anniversary of the bombing of Hiroshima. Judy Beaumont, Shayamali Tan, Sunshine Appleby, Gerry Tyrell, and Karl Smith were arrested for a protest made during a Pentagon tour. They chose to stop at a painting depicting a young family kneeling at an altar in the Air Force Academy with the caption: "Here I am, Lord, send

me!" from the prophet Isaiah. Gerry received a sentence of ten days, the others two days. On August 9, the group went to the Air and Space Museum, where they labeled the Minuteman missile and the cruise missile display with their blood.

2. Nine people came together and engaged in life sharing, the viewing of films, and almost daily vigils at the White House and/or War Department.

*Arms Bazaar Protest—September 16*

Jonah House supported the "Bread Not Bombs" theme and presence coordinated by Sojourners Community against the Air Force Association "arms bazaar" at the Sheraton Washington Hotel in D.C. Fifty-one people were arrested, including Rosemary Maguire and Marcia Timmel of Baltimore.

*Feast of the Innocents—1981*

More than 120 people, many with children, gathered with members of Jonah House for four days of resistance and community development. "Reagan/Herod" was sprayed on the pillars of the River Entrance to the Pentagon as an appropriate backdrop for the action there on December 28. Anne and Jim Clune and Theresa Guisti poured blood in the form of a cross on the steps at the River Entrance. They were tried January 15 and given thirty, sixty, and ninety days in jail, respectively. After a day of reflection the groups went again to the Pentagon and again poured blood and ashes at the River Entrance. Jerry Berrigan, Chris Redding, and Tom Joyce were arrested and served three months or thirty days in prison.

*Get Us Out of the Arms Race, Mr. Weinberger—May 27, 1982*

As Caspar Weinberger addressed a crowd at the Hyatt Regency in Baltimore, Peter DeMott and George Veasey rose and said: "That's a lie. Caspar Weinberger, I call on you to get us out of the arms race . . ." They were first detained and then escorted out of the hotel.

*Trident Nein—July 4, 1982*

Judy Beaumont, a Benedictine sister from Chicago; Anne Montgomery, of the Plowshares Eight; James Cunningham, an ex-lawyer from Jonah House; George Veasey, a Vietnam veteran also from Jonah House; Tim Quinn, expectant father and housepainter from Hartford, Connecticut; Anne Bennis, teacher from Philadelphia; Bill Hartman, peace worker from Philadelphia; Vincent Kay, housepainter and poet from New Haven, and Art Laffin, member of the Covenant Peace Community in New Haven, entered Electric Boat to make a "declaration of independence" from the Trident submarine and all nuclear weapons. They were convicted of criminal mischief, conspiracy, and criminal trespass and ordered to pay restitution to the Navy. They were sentenced to jail for up to one year.

*August 5 through 9—1982*

A group of people assembled in D.C. for the five-day period. The days were marked by three distinct actions: a re-enactment of the death of Hiroshima at the Pentagon on the sixth; a bold and revealing action at the Air and Space Museum on the eighth; and a blocking of the River Entrance to the Pentagon amid blood spilling and sprinkling of ashes on the ninth. There were two arrests on the sixth; thirteen on the ninth. No jail sentences were given those who were arrested.

*Election Day—November 2, 1982*

On the evening of November 1, 200 friends gathered in community at St. Stephen's Church to prepare to witness at the Pentagon on November 2. They joined voices to say "No" to first strike, Presidential Directive 59, cruise, and other idols of death. Twenty-nine people were arrested either for blocking the entrances or labeling the building with their blood.

### Plowshares Number Four—November 14, 1982

Five days after the Trident Nein sentencing, John and Ellen Grady, brother and sister from Ithaca, New York; Peter DeMott, of Plowshares Number Two; Jean Holladay, grandmother and nurse from Massachusetts; Roger Ludwig, a poet and musician working with the poor in Washington, D.C.; Marcia Timmel, and Elmer Maas entered Electric Boat. They hammered and poured blood on several missile hatches of "USS Georgia" and on Trident components. They were denied a justification defense at trial and, like the Trident Nein, were convicted and received prison sentences ranging from two months to a year.

### Local Baltimore Actions

We sponsored an evening of poetry and song with Dan Berrigan on December 11, 1982, and a demonstration in downtown Baltimore on December 18 that included a children's theater at the Inner Harbor.

### Feast of the Innocents—1982

On the feast some 150 of us went to the Pentagon and, in repeat of the previous year, spray painted "REAGAN/HEROD" on the pillars of the River Entrance. We planted some twenty crosses in the parade ground commemorating the dead caused by militarism. Tom Joyce and John Pendleton were arrested for pouring blood on the steps and Nancy Ballon for pouring ashes.

The next day we returned to the Pentagon in a spirit of solidarity with the poor, setting up a soup line at the River Entrance and distributing soup and bread. Finally, we marched from CCNV's cardboard boxes in front of City Hall to the Pentagon and staged a blocking of the entrances. Police arrested sixteen for blockading. Meanwhile, a shantytown, called "The last resort," was erected on the parade ground and a car, spray painted with the words, "This is the home the Pentagon Built," was delivered to the same spot.

## State of the Union—January 25, 1983

CCNV called for an occupation of the Capitol Rotunda as a response to Reagan's State of the Union Message which revealed the state of the Union more than the counterpart. 400 people were arrested, including most of the Jonah House community. It was a first arrest for Frida Berrigan, age nine.

## Prayer at Pantex, Amarillo, Texas—February 16, 1983

Ladon Sheats, Kathy Jennings, and Christine Eirene entered the Pantex Bomb Plant in Amarillo, Texas, to pray at the site where the bombs are assembled and turned out. They were convicted of trespass and sentenced to a year (Ladon) and to six months in prison.

## Holy Week—1983

About eighty of us went to the White House, going through the tour with a litany of crimes related to the arms race, crimes for which we begged God's mercy. Outside we enacted a die-in. On April 1 we did the Way of the Cross, beginning at the Capitol and proceeding through the city of D.C., culminating our procession at the Pentagon. There we gathered for a brief reflection before entering the Concourse to block the ramps into the building proper. At each set of ramps we staged a die-in amid blood and ash. There were seven arrests. The presence culminated at the River Entrance, where we saw the preparations they had made for our arrival. All the pillars were wrapped in plastic and one handle was removed from each set of doors to prevent them from being locked shut.

## AVCO Plowshares—July 14, 1983

Agnes Bauerlein, mother and grandmother from Ambler, Pennsylvania; Macy Morse, mother and grandmother from Nashua, New Hampshire; Mary Lyons, mother and grandmother and teacher from Hartford, Connecticut; Frank Panopoulos, member of the Cor Jesu community from New York City; Jean Holladay of the Plowshares Number Four; John Pendleton, member of Jonah House, and John Schuchardt of the Plowshares Eight entered the AVCO Systems Division in Wilmington, Massachusetts, where MX and Pershing II nuclear weapon components are produced. They hammered on computer equipment and poured blood on blueprints labeled MX "Peacekeeper." They also served AVCO and its co-conspirators with an indictment for committing crimes against God and humanity by manufacturing for profit weapons of genocide. During their jury trial they were able to present a justification defense but it was disallowed by the judge prior to jury deliberation. They were convicted of wanton destruction and trespass and sentenced to jail for up to three and a half months.

## Women's Peace Encampment at Seneca Army Depot—Summer 1983

Those of us who are women (and children) gave what support we could to the Peace Encampment with the support of the entire community. In order not to detract from it, we made no other plans for summer resistance than August 6 and 9.

## August 5 through 9—1983

There were three witnesses that occupied the eighty people who participated on these days. On the sixth we witnessed at the White House with banner and leaflets as well as going through the tour and speaking out as we went. There were no arrests.

On the eighth we went to the Air and Space Museum where, amid an enactment of the death of Hiroshima and Nagasaki,

Helen Woodson and Brigette Cooke poured blood on the Minuteman and cruise missiles. A banner was unfurled and leaflets were dropped from the balcony while about twenty people staged a die-in around the missile pit. Brigette and Helen were arrested; Helen was sentenced to six months in D.C. jail.

On the ninth we went to the Pentagon and removed the protective plastic from the pillars and poured blood on the entrance steps in the form of a cross. Four people, including Phil Berrigan and George Veasey, were arrested.

*The Lone but not Lonely Sentry*

In the context of the above witness, Kathleen Rumpf determined to return to the Pentagon with a sign "IT'S A SIN TO BUILD A NUCLEAR WEAPON," and remain alone and vulnerable there through three days and three nights, a sentry for peace. Her vigil inspired us to make a modest proposal for an immodest year—1984.

*International Day of Disarmament—October 22, 1983*

In conjunction with actions planned throughout the western world, we sponsored an action at the Pentagon at which about 250 people marched to the Pentagon and blocked entrances and poured blood and ash on the pillars of the River Entrance.

*Griffiss Plowshares—November 24, 1983*

Thanksgiving morning, Jackie Allen, a nursery school teacher from Hartford, Connecticut; Clare Grady, an artist and potter from Ithaca, New York; Dean Hammer, father and member of the Plowshares Eight; Elizabeth McAlister, mother and co-founder of Jonah House; Vern Rossman, minister, father and grandfather from Boston; Kathleen Rumpf, a Catholic Worker from Marlboro, New York; and Karl Smith, member of Jonah House, entered Griffiss Air Force Base in Rome, New York. They hammered and poured blood on a B-52 bomber converted to carry cruise missiles and did the same on B-52 engines. They left an indictment of the base and United States government, pointing to the war crimes of preparing for nuclear war and depicting how the new state religion of "nuclearism" denies constitutional rights and punishes acts of conscience. They were convicted of conspiracy and destruction of government property (but acquitted of charges under the sabotage act) and sentenced to two and three years in prison.

*Plowshares Number Seven—December 4, 1983*

Carl Kabat of the Plowshares Eight and three West Germans—Herwig Jantschik, Dr. Wolfgang Sternstein and Karin Vix—entered a United States Army base in Schwabisch-Gmund, West Germany, and carried out the first Plowshares action in Europe. They hammered and poured blood on a Pershing II missile launcher. Within fifteen minutes they were apprehended by armed guards. Carl was deported. The three Germans were tried and convicted and moderate fines were imposed.

*Feast of the Innocents—1983*

Over 200 people gathered the evening of December 27. The next morning six people sprayed "HEROD/REAGAN" on the pillars of the River Entrance; ten others poured blood in the doorway and on the pillars and a dozen blocked the doors. Pedestrian traffic was rerouted to the Mall entrance. After arrests were made the group staged a die-in.

On December 29, after a march to the Pentagon, we did a piece of theater (including the "Twelve days of Christmas" written for the occasion) in the Concourse.

On December 30, with "Father Time Bomb" we blocked at the South Entrance. The doors were chained shut; blood was spilled—an unexpected event at that entrance. Father Time-Bomb was unexpectedly arrested as were thirteen other blockers.

*A Modest Proposal for an Immodest Year—1984*

Inspired by the example of Kathleen Rumpf and her three-day and three-night vigil at the Pentagon (The Lone but not Lonely Sentry), people responded to an invitation to maintain a presence at the Pentagon throughout 1984. Dorothy Day Catholic Worker Community in D.C. offered hospitality and individuals and small groups maintained the presence—each working day some one or more were there from 6:00 a.m. until 6:00 p.m. Some stayed through the nights as well. These learned that activists were not the only Pentagon vigilers. In the small hours of the mornings, they found that many homeless people were finding their homes in the nooks and crannies of the Pentagon Concourse and much was shared with them.

*Friday, April 13—Baptist Fundamentalist Convention, 1984*

Five people, including two from Jonah House, were arrested at the Washington, D.C., Convention Center when they interrupted a speech given by President Reagan to the Fundamentalist Baptists. Thirteen participated in the witness for truth.

*Holy Week—1984*

College, university, and seminary students from Minnesota and Iowa joined their spring break to our Holy Week witness. A blockade of the Pentagon on Holy Thursday resulted in the repeated moving of the blockaders. On Good Friday, we enacted the Stations of the Cross across the River Entrance, culminating in the labeling of the building with blood and a half-hour die-in. Five people were arrested.

*Pershing Plowshares—Easter 1984*

Eight peace activists entered a Martin Marietta weapons facility in Orlando, Florida, and used blood and hammers on a Pershing II launcher/carrier and cut hydraulic cables. They also opened a crate prepared for shipment to Germany and removed five or six elements and hammered on them and poured their blood. They were held in lieu of $100,000 bail each. The eight were later released, tried, convicted and imprisoned for three years each.

*August 5 through 9—1984*

The friends who gathered for resistance had their ranks depleated by many still in prison. Nonetheless, they acted at the Pentagon, the White House, and the Air and Space Museum.

*A Harvest of Shame—October 1–November 2, 1984*

The Community for Creative Nonviolence sponsored this civil disobedience campaign to focus attention on Reagan's policies and programs and voice opposition to his re-election. All from Jonah House—those not already in prison—participated in at least one of these days. Frida and Jerry (ages nine and eight) were also arrested as part of this protest.

*Trident II Plowshares—October 1, 1984*

Jean Holladay, Frank Panopoulos, Bill Boston, Leo Schiff, and John Pendleton entered General Dynamics Electric Boat Shipyard in Quonset Point, Rhode Island, and rendered six missile tubes harmless (disarmed). All served a year in prison.

*One Silo Silenced—November 12, 1984*

Helen Woodson, Larry Cloud Morgan, and Fathers Carl and Paul Kabat used an airhammer and sledge hammers against the hatch cover of a Minuteman silo in Missouri. They received sentences of eighteen, ten, and eight years in prison.

*Feast of the Innocents—1984*

Eighty people participated in the three-day session for reflection and resistance. On December 28 they blocked the doors at the Mall entrance and used the symbol of blood on the entrance. Seven were arrested and were given fines or a day or two in jail. On the 29th there was a procession around the White House that culminated in a demonstration in front of the tour line. One person was arrested and served several days in jail.

*Trident II Pruning Hooks—1985*

On April 18, 1985, Suzanne Schmidt, Sheila Parks, Greg Boertje, John Heid, George Veasey, and Roger Ludwig entered the same shipyard as the Trident II Plowshares and with blood and household hammers they committed the thirteenth Plowshares action. They poured blood and hammered upon three Trident II (D-5) nuclear missile tubes. Each of them served a year in prison for their action.

*Holy Week—1985*

Students from the Midwest joined in the witness, centered at the Pentagon. For three days, people vigiled, bannered, leafleted, and sought to confront the war-making capability of our country with their peace-making.

*Thanksgiving—1985*

On the second anniversary of the Griffiss Plowshares, a group of friends entered the base and were arrested. It included Dan, Jerry, and Phil Berrigan, Brian Barrett, Bill Cuddy, George Ostensen, Suzanne Schmidt, and Shirley Lockwood. When they refused to pay the fine, they were jailed for five days in the Public Safety Building in Syracuse, New York.

*August 5 through 9—1986*

Two were arrested at the Pentagon for painting the shadows of nuclear victims on the steps of the River entrance. They were part of a witness of about forty people. There were witnesses on subsequent days at the Capitol and at the Air and Space Museum, with no arrests.

*APL-Johns Hopkins University Campaign—1986-present*

In conjunction with friends in the Baltimore area, Jonah House renewed a periodic campaign directed at Johns Hopkins University's Applied Physics Lab. Johns Hopkins University is the number one university recipient of military contracts in the country. The campaign involves frequent leafleting and demonstrating both at the lab and at the university. Among the actions that grew out of the campaign are:

Rooftop 6 No.1—September 12, 1986. Six people climbed the roof of the Kasiakoff center at Johns Hopkins Applied Physics Lab. They were supported by about thirty friends who distributed leaflets and held banners until they were forced to leave the premises. The six were tried in November and given suspended fines and six months' unsupervised probation.

Rooftop 6 No. 2—November 11, 1986. Celebrating with walkers from the Great Peace March, six people climbed the roof of one of the buildings of the Applied Physics Lab and suspended a banner that read: "APL Death Lab." The six, and one who remained at the foot of the banner, were arrested. About forty people participated in the demonstration, including "Dr. Doom" and his missile launcher.

Rooftop 6 No. 3—January 15, 1987. "We still have a dream, Dr. King, Stars without Star Wars" was the banner held by the children from the roof of the same APL building where the previous two actions occurred. Kate Walsh and Jerry and Frida Berrigan (all children) were joined by the children at heart—Rick Kramer, John Heid, and Betty Schroeder—to complete the number six. The children were released to their parents after being removed from the roof. The adults were arrested, tried, and sentenced to ten days in jail when they refused to pay their fines.

Rooftop 6 No. 4—March 30, 1987. Six people climbed to the roof of the Milton Eisenhower Library at the university. They were arrested, removed from the roof, tried, and convicted. They gave donations to local charities in lieu of paying fines that the court sought to impose.

*Welcome Reagan—October 15, 1986*

The president came to Baltimore to support a local candidate in a hundred-dollar-a-plate luncheon. The streets were cordoned off and demonstrators were pushed out of all sight and hearing by mounted police. Unexpectedly, arrests were made, including three from Jonah House, and a number of demonstrators were run over by horses.

*Riverside Research Institute—Baltimore action, October 27, 1986*

Kairos and the campaign at RRI had asked friends to participate so that there might be actions at RRI each week of the year. Baltimore chose this day, and thirteen people were arrested for blocking the entrance to the lab.

*Department of Energy blockade—November 17, 1986*

Members of Jonah House supported the resistance celebrating the end of the Great Peace March by blockading the Department of Energy. Four from the community and Jim Berrigan were among hundreds who risked arrest.

*Thanksgiving—1986*

On the eve of Thanksgiving, the APL action group delivered a cornucopia filled with weapons to Dr. Bostrom, director of the lab, and a turkey filled with weapons to Dr. Muller, president of Johns Hopkins University.

*Feast of the Innocents—1986*

We brought the message of "SHAME" to the Pentagon and the White House in these days. Shame was painted on the pillars in the early morning of December 28, blood was added in opening hours of work, theater was done, and people blocked the entrance in a powerful witness. At the White House on the thirtieth the same witness was made. Blood marked the portico, people held banners on the sidewalk, children came with their own posters and banners and all the "shame" posters were planted on the lawn of the White House where, in truth, they belong.

*Epiphany Plowshares—1987*

On January 6, 1987, Fathers Dexter Lanctot and Tom McGann, Greg Boertje, and Lin Romano entered Willow Grove Naval Air Station and spilled blood and hammered on P-3 Orion aircraft, which represent an integral part of the U.S. first-strike nuclear arsenal, and on the CH 53A Sea Stallion assault helicopter, which is a tangible symbol of our intervention in wars in other lands.

*Honduran Embassy—1987*

In late February eight people including two from Jonah House flew to Tegucigalpa, Honduras. Three days later they went to the front entrance of the United States Embassy and carried out a graphic demonstration—posting an indictment on the quickly slammed-shut iron doors. They splashed the sandstone walls with bottles of blood to symbolize the blood of the people being spilled across the region; they unfurled a banner that read in Spanish and English: "STOP THE KILLING," and they blockaded the entrance. The action caught embassy personnel and the Honduran security forces by surprise ... press was everywhere and the officials' hands were tied. No legal charges were lodged—the protesters were flown home. The media coverage was extensive in Latin America but scant in the States.

*Holy Week—1987*

On Holy Thursday the group—about 120 including a group of college and university students from the Midwest—went to the Pentagon and began with a blockade and the symbol of blood at the South Entrance. Despite both actions, police made no arrests. On Good Friday the place of the witness was the White House. Two groups went through the tour proclaiming a litany and singing as they went. Greg Boertje, Brian Barrett, and Tom Joseph poured blood on the gate pillars and were arrested. Three others held banners in the restricted zone and were arrested. The main group enacted a Way of the Cross on the Lafayette Park side of Pennsylvania Ave. after the sidewalk in front of the White House was cordoned off by police.

*National Guard Actions June–July 1987*

The Maryland National Guard was sent to Honduras during the summer of 1987 but not without opposition. Two people from Jonah House joined with seven others to see the governor and halt this tyranny. They didn't see him and were arrested instead after awaiting him a full day (June 29). On July 4, as the guard was being shipped, four people from Jonah House were among fourteen arrested—ten for blocking the gates to the base, four for standing on the runway even as the planes were ready to take off.

*August 5 through 9—1987*

Between thirty and fifty people gathered to remember the anniversaries. On the 6th the groups went to the Pentagon and blockaded employees going to work through the Metro entrance. The blockade went on for an hour as Federal Protective Service police insisted on keeping access open even at the risk of bone and muscles of the blockers. Then Metro police arrested ten people and took them to Arlington County Jail. They were tried on September 17 and given suspended sentences. On the eighth the group went to the White House. While some went through the tour, others remained in front of the White House carrying signs that each, in turn, explained to passers-by. At the end of the vigil, all the signs (each with an aspect of the terror of nuclear weapons painted over a "nuclear shadow") were left on the White House lawn while two of the group poured blood and painted shadows on the sidewalk. After emptying a full can of paint, they knelt and prayed. No police appeared and no arrests were made.

*APL hosts Military Symposium—October 1987*

The Kasiakoff Center at the Applied Physics Lab is used frequently for symposia attended only by those with high-security clearances. One such symposium in October came to the attention of the nucleus of people who vigil, leaflet, and banner there regularly and act when possible. Four people blocked the entrance to the symposium and were arrested. They were given suspended fines.

*Thanksgiving—1987*

The day before Thanksgiving, the Baltimore community went to The Johns Hopkins University Administration Building. Three people entered the office of University President Muller and poured blood on his desk and on a small Thanksgiving turkey they brought with them. About twenty people bannered, leafleted and vigiled outside, handed bread to those who came and went, and recalled the meaning of Thanksgiving. No arrests were made at the time but the three were subpoenaed and tried for destruction of property and trespass. They may serve eighteen months in jail for this action.

*Feast of the Innocents—1987*

About sixty people gathered at the Pentagon to resist the on-going massacre of the innocent. On the parade ground in front of the River Entrance, the group placed grave markers for the children who are no more, and dug a grave in which a coffin was interred containing hundreds of names of innocent children. Police failed to see the six diggers and no one was arrested. Then the group blockaded the South Entrance to the building.

On the twenty-ninth the group visited the Air and Space Museum where, amid an enactment of the death of nuclear weapons, John Pendleton poured blood on the Minuteman missile on display. He was arrested but acquitted on a technicality.

On the thirtieth, we went to the White House where four people attempted to label it with blood. Some were excluded from the tour, but two women were passed over by security and labeled that Whitened Sepulchre with blood. The women were supported by a small group that was able to stay with the tour. Outside demonstrators used a megaphone to express individually to passers-by and tourists why they were there. We ended by placing our "SHAM" placards on the White House lawn. One person was arrested for littering though nine others were passed over.

*Martin Luther King Jr.'s Birthday—1988*

Five children and three adults mounted the roof of The Johns Hopkins University Applied Physics Lab and displayed a banner the children had made. Friends on the ground distributed a leaflet the children had drafted. All five children were served with tickets indicating that they would be informed of the date they must appear in juvenile court (that never happened). The adults were arrested, tried, and given suspended fines.

## No Contra Aid—February 2-4, 1988

Some members of Jonah House joined the series of actions in Washington, D.C., against further funding for the Contras. Dale Ashera-Davis, after the funding was turned down, learned of a Contra Press Conference to initiate a private fund-raising campaign, and, with several others, brought into the press room the bloody meaning of funding Contras. They were removed but not arrested.

## Valentine's Day—1988

Members of the Atlantic Life Community came to Baltimore for a weekend of reflection and action at the Applied Physics Lab. Sixteen people were arrested for blocking the entrances to the lab. Repeaters from Baltimore were given fifteen days in jail after they refused to pay a fine; people from out of town were given suspended fines.

## Holy Week—1988

Using the theme of *The Never Ending Story,* a group gathered for the Holy Week remembrance—the never ending story of greed and its fruits and the never ending story that could and should be ours. People vigiled around the clock at the Pentagon. On Holy Thursday we made of the Parade Ground a cemetery complete with "dead" and crosses; we enacted a foot-washing on the steps of the River Entrance as a reminder of the compasionate service to which we are summoned. On Good Friday, we blockaded the South Entrance for about an hour and marked it with blood before beginning to meditate together on the Sorrowful Mysteries of the Rosary, one for each side of the Pentagon as we circled it. One person was arrested for defacing the Pentagon and served thirty days in jail.

## Easter 1988—"The Nuclear Navy Plowshares."

Four people, including three from Jonah House, boarded the Battleship, the USS Iowa, on display for tourists at the Norfolk,

Virginia, Naval Base after it had been on a six-month alert in the Persian Gulf. They poured their blood on two Box Launchers—launching systems for the Tomahawk Sea Launched Cruise Missiles (SLCM) and hammered on them. And they hung two banners from the railings of the ship: "Tomahawks to Plowshares" and "Seek the Disarmed Christ." The four were charged with trespass. The state determined to squash their protest by denying them a jury trial. They were held in jail through bench trial and sentencing. Sr. Margaret McKenna served more than three months; Andrew Lawrence served four months; Phil Berrigan and Gregory Boertje each served six months.

*Catonsville—Twenty Years Later, May 17, 1988*

A vigil at the site of the "Catonsville 9" action, May 19, 1968, was held on the twentieth anniversary. More than a hundred people came to commemorate that event and to state our commitment to resist any future Vietnam wars. A party was held that night and the following day many of the participants left in caravans for the Festival of Hope and the trial of the Nuclear Navy Plowshares.

*Martin Airfield Protests—May to June 1988*

On each of the three Saturdays, May 21 through June 4, we acted, in protest and hope, at the airfield from which the Maryland National Guard departed for Central America.

*An Assault on Truth—June 1988*

Attending the civil trial that purposed to close the Lexington Prison Control Unit, John Heid was forcibly removed from the courtroom for failure to stand for the judge, dragged down a stairway, and beaten by the U.S. Marshals. B. Wardlaw intervened and was also beaten. Both were placed under arrest and charged with assault on Federal Officers. They were tried in

September; B. was acquitted and John was convicted. (As of this writing, John is awaiting sentencing.)

*August 5 through 9—1988*

Using the theme, Homes not Bombs, about thirty people gathered to make clear and public the connections between militarism and human suffering, at home and abroad. A shelter and a street theater production were brought to the Air and Space Museum, and then to the Pentagon where people reconstructed the shelter on the Parade Ground and stayed with it for more than twenty-four hours.

*APPENDIX C*
*Resources*

# PEACE AND DISARMAMENT GROUPS[1]

Groups Working on an International, National, and Regional Level for Disarmament and Social Justice

The following is a list of groups that might be helpful in assisting new and established groups in their work of peace and justice. This is not a comprehensive list; it would be extremely difficult to list all the numerous anti-nuclear groups, which vary greatly in emphasis and action. Many of the groups below have information concerning regional groups with which they are affiliated.

*Agape Communities.* A network of spiritually based communities in the Northwest, West, Southwest, and South who are involved in a nonviolent campaign to stop the transport of nuclear weapons by the "nuclear train." Contact Ground Zero Center for Nonviolent Action, 16159 Clear Creek Rd. NW, Poulsbo, WA 98370.

*American Friends Service Committee (AFSC).* An organization with regional offices around the United States involved in education and nonviolent action for nuclear disarmament and social jus-

---

[1] This list is reprinted and updated from *Swords into Plowshares: Nonviolent Direct Action for Disarmament.* Edited by Arthur J. Laffin and Anne Montgomery. Harper and Row. San Francisco. 1987.

tice. It publishes a wide variety of resources on peace and disarmament. 1501 Cherry St., Philadelphia, PA 19102.

*Association for Transarmament Studies (ATS).* A worldwide organization providing resources for the study and discussion of civilian-based defense. It sees "transarmament" as a desirable future possibility for nations if and when they are able to rely on prepared nonviolent action to deter and resist aggression. 3636 Lafayette, Omaha, NE 68131.

*Atlantic Life Community (ALC).* A network of individuals and spritually based resistance communities throughout the eastern United States involved in nonviolent direct action for disarmament at the Pentagon, the White House, and nuclear weapons facilities. Contact Jonah House, 1933 Park Ave., Baltimore, MD 21217.

*Catholic Worker.* A Catholic network of over fifty communities in the United States committed to the "works of mercy and peace" from a gospel-pacifist perspective. It publishes a monthly newspaper. For Catholic Worker houses in your area contact The Catholic Worker, 36 E. First St., New York, NY 10012.

*Center Peace* (formerly known as the National Center on Law and Pacifism). An ecumenical pacifist group focusing on theological and legal counseling for war-tax resistance and providing books and other resources on conscientious objection to war. It published *People Pay for Peace,* an excellent guide on war-tax resistance, by William Durland and it publishes a newsletter. c/o Chrysalis, 70 Adams Street, Burlington, VT 05401.

*Clergy and Laity Concerned (CALC).* An interfaith organization with local chapters throughout the United States dedicated to religious political action for peace and justice. It distributes a wide range of disarmament and justice resources. 198 Broadway, New York, NY 10038.

*Coalition for a New Foreign and Military Policy.* A coalition of social action, religious, labor, and peace groups working for a peaceful, demilitarized U.S. foreign policy. It distributes a variety of resources. 712 G St. SE, Washington, DC 20003.

*Disarmament Campaigns.* A Dutch groups that distributes information about disarmament campaigns occurring worldwide. Anna Paulownaplein 3, PB 18747, 2502 ES The Hague, Netherlands.

*Educators for Social Responsibility.* An organization with local chapters working with educators, parents, and students to introduce a war and peace curriculum into the school systems. 23 Garden St., Cambridge, MA 02138.

*Fellowship of Reconciliation (FOR).* A religious pacifist organization working for disarmament and social justice. It has numerous local and denominational fellowships, a "U.S.-U.S.S.R. Reconciliation Program," and a "Children's Conflict" program. It publishes *Fellowship,* a monthly magazine. Box 271, Nyack, NY 10960.

*Infact.* This national grassroots organization, which led the successful seven-year Nestle boycott, is now coordinating a nationwide boycott against General Electric for its role in producing nuclear weapons. 186 Lincoln Street, Room 203, Boston, MA 02111.

*International Physicians for the Prevention of Nuclear War.* An international organization of doctors from the United States, the Soviet Union, and other countries working to reverse the arms race. It provides audiovisual and other educational resources on the medical aspects of nuclear war. It won the Nobel Peace Prize in 1985. 225 Longwood Ave., Boston, MA 02115.

*International Fellowship of Reconciliation (IFOR).* A transnational religious community of different faiths committed to nonviolence as a principle of life for a world community of peace and justice. It has affiliates in over thirty countries and publishes a magazine five times a year with a strong focus on human rights and disarmament. It disseminates information about nonviolent movements worldwide. Hof Van Sonoy 15-17, 1811 LD, Alkmaar, The Netherlands.

*Jobs with Peace.* A group concerned about connecting militarism and human needs and the people suffering from this nation's eschewed priorities. 110 S. Wolfe St., Baltimore, MD 21231.

*Lawyers' Committee on Nuclear Policy.* A nonpartisan organization involved in educating the legal community and the public about the illegality of nuclear wapons under international law. It acts as legal counsel to Nuclear Free Zone campaigns and efforts to oppose naval homeporting. 225 Lafayette St., Suite 513. New York, NY 10012.

*Mobilization for Survival (MFS).* A coalition of groups emphasizing grassroots action toward reversing the arms race and meeting human needs. It provides information and resources on disarmament and groups working around the country to resist U.S. nuclear military policy. It is the contact for the National Weapons Facility Network. 853 Broadway, Room 418, New York, NY 10003.

*New Call to Peacemaking.* A coalition of the historic peace churches—Quaker, Mennonite, and Brethren—involved in work for peace and disarmament. Box 1245, Elkhart, IN 46515.

*National Inter-Religious Service Board for Conscientious Objectors (NIBSCO).* A coalition of religious groups who oppose all forms of compulsory service. It provides resources on countering military recruiting and on draft counseling, including a booklet, *Words of Conscience: Religious statement on Conscientious Objection.* 550 Washington Building. 15th and New York Ave. NW, Washington, DC 20005.

*North Atlantic Network.* A Network of peace groups in countries facing the North Atlantic, Norwegian, and Baltic Seas. It is committed to facilitating a greater understanding of the region's rapidly expanding naval arms race. It coordinates international days of action to draw attention to the dangers of war at sea.

It conducts conferences and provides educational resources. 853 Broadway, Room 418, New York, NY 10003.

*Nukewatch.* A national project coordinating nonviolent vigils and helping raise public awareness about the transportation of nuclear warheads and components by truck over U.S. roads and highways. (Eighty percent of all nuclear warheads are transported by truck.) 315 West Gorman St., Madison, WI 53703.

*Pacific Concerns Resource Center.* Network center for Nuclear Free and Independent Pacific Movement. P.O. Box 27692, Honolulu, HI 96827.

*Peacework Alternatives.* A group promoting discussion of the ethical questions of employment in weapons work and providing a network of services (i.e., counseling, workshops, finding nondefense jobs) for defense workers considering leaving their jobs for conscience reasons. 3940 Poplar Level Rd., Louisville, KY 40213.

*Physicians for Social Responsibility (PSR).* A groups of health and medical professionals who provide information about the health hazards of nuclear weaponry and nuclear power. Box 295, Cambridge, MA 02236.

*Prolifers for Survival.* A network of women and men committed to nonviolence who support alternatives to nuclear arms and abortion. P.O. Box 3316, Chapel Hill, NC 27515.

*Promoting Enduring Peace.* An educational organization that offers free reprints of articles on peace and disarmament on a quarterly basis. Box 5103, Woodmont, CT 06460.

*Religious Task Force.* An interfaith group affiliated with MFS organizing primarily in the religious community for peace and disarmament. It organized the "Children of War" tour in 1985 and distributes an array of resources to the religious community on disarmament. 85 South Oxford St., Brooklyn, NY 11217.

*Riverside Church Disarmament Program.* An organization based at Riverside Church providing speakers and resources on Christian peacemaking and disarmament. It published *Peace in Search of Makers* and publishes a newsletter. 490 Riverside Dr., New York, NY 10027.

*Sane/Freeze.* A new group resulting from the merger of SANE and The Nuclear Weapons Freeze Campaign. It is a national organization composed of local groups committed to a bilateral nuclear weapons freeze. Members do door to door canvassing and the organization provides resources on nuclear arms control. 220 I St., Suite 130. Washington, DC 20002.

*Sojourners Community.* An evangelical and ecumenical Christian community that through its Peace Ministry offers resources and help to those who are raising peace issues as central to the Church's life. It publishes a monthly magazine and distributes books, audiovisual resources, and other materials on disarmament. P.O. Box 29272, Washington, DC 20017.

*Students/Teachers Organization to Prevent Nuclear War (STOP).* A group of high-school students and teachers involved in education and action for disarmament. Activities include attending nonviolent protests, seminars, and trips to the Soviet Union. It helps organize local groups. Box 232, Northfield, MA 01360.

*Vietnam Veterans Against the War.* An organization of Vietnam veterans, formed in 1967 to help end U.S. involvement in Indochina, which actively opposed U.S. and Soviet military intervention and increased military spending. It is an advocate for veterans rights. It coordinates veteran support groups, and it publishes the newsletter, *The Veteran.* P.O. Box 25592, Chicago, IL 60625.

*War Resisters League (WRL).* A pacifist groups that opposes armaments, conscription, and war. It publishes *The Nonviolent Activist* ten times a year as well as an annual peace calendar and disseminates a variety of resources on disarmament and social justice, including an excellent guide on war-tax resistance. It has regional chapters nationwide. 339 Lafayette St., New York, NY 10012.

*Women's International League for Peace and Freedom (WILPF).* An international women's organization working for disarmament and social justice and nonviolent solutions to domestic and international problems. It publishes a magazine, *Peace and Freedom.* 1213 Race St., Philadelphia, PA. 19107.

*World Peacemakers.* A mission group of the Church of the Savior that seeks to establish local groups both in their own Churches and across denominational lines. It publishes a variety of resources on the Christian response to the arms race. 2025 Massachusetts Ave. NW, Washington, DC 20009.

NOTE: For a complete listing of 5,700 peace and justice groups and other resources see: Peace Resource Book—*A Comprehensive Guide to Issues, Groups, and Literature.*, edited by Elizabeth Bernstein et al (Cambridge, MA: Ballinger, 1986). Also see *The Peace Catalog,* edited by Duane Sweeney (Press for Peace, 5621 Seaview Ave. NW, Seattle, WA 98107; 1984.)

*Local Groups Involved in Nonviolent Resistance Actions*

The following is a partial list of groups in the United States and Canada involved in organizing a variety of nonviolent resistance actions at nuclear weapons facilities, military bases, companies involved in nuclear weapons production, federal buildings, and other sites. For further information about other nonviolent resistance groups in your area contact: ALC, MFS, FOR, WRL (see preceding list) and the "Nuclear Resister," P.O. Box 43383, Tucson, AZ 85733.

Act for Disarmament Coalition, 139 Robert St., Toronto, Ontario, M5S 2KG, Canada

Ahimsa, Box 494, Forge Hill Rd., Voluntown, CT 06384

Ailanthus Community, c/o Haley House, 23 Dartmouth St., Cambridge, MA 02116

American Peace Test, Box 26725, Las Vegas, NV 89126

Ann Arbor Peace Community, 2122 Geddes, Ann Arbor, MI 48104

Bemidji Friends for a Nonviolent World, 1517 American Ave., Bemidji, MN 56601
Brandywine Peace Community, Box 81, Swarthmore, PA 19081
Brattleboro Atlantic Life Community, 80 Birge St., Brattleboro, VT 05301
Casa Maria, 401 E. 26th St., Tucson, AZ 85713
Catholic Action—Hawaii, 1918 University Ave., Honolulu, HI 96822
Chrysalis, 70 Adams Street, Burlington, VT 05401
Citizens for Alternatives to Trident and ELF, Box 364, Webster, WI 54893
Community for Creative Nonviolence, 425 2nd St. NW, Washington DC 20001
Coalition for a Nuclear Free Harbor, 135 W. 4th St., New York, NY 10012
Coalition to Stop Trident, Box 411, New Haven, CT 06502
Chicago Life Community, 1020 S. Wabash St., Room 401, Chicago, IL 60605
Covenant for Peace, Box 1831, East Lansing, MI 48823
Cruise Missile Conversion Project, 730 Bathurst St., Toronto, Ontario M5S 2R4 Canada
Detroit Peace Community, c/o Day House, 2640 Trumbull St., Detroit, MI 48216
Disarm Now Action Group, 407 Dearborn #370, Chicago, IL 60605
Faith and Resistance Retreat, c/o Catholics for Justice, 3125 Chestnut, Kansas City, MO 64128
First Strike Prevention Project, P.O. Box 1960, San Jose, CA 95109
Florida Coalition for Peace and Justice, P.O. Box 2486, Orlando, FL 32802
Greenfields Community, 4216 Grant, Omaha, NE 68111
Ground Zero Center for Nonviolent Action, 16159 Clear Creek Rd. NW, Poulsbo, WA 98370
Groundwork for a Just World, 11224 Kercheval, Detroit, MI 48214

Honeywell Project, 1519 E. Franklin Ave., Minneapolis, MN 55404
Immanuel House, 2130 Burlington Ave. N, St. Petersburg, FL 33713
Isaiah Peace Community, 66 Edgewood Ave., New Haven, CT 06511
Jeremiah House, 2016 W. Moore St. Richmond, VA 23220
Jeremiah House, 1826 E. Lehigh St., Philadephia, PA 19125
Jonah House, 1933 Park Ave., Baltimore, MD 21217
Kairos Community, 225 Lafayette St., Suite 207, New York, NY 10012
Knolls Action Project, 221 Central Ave., Albany, NY 12206
Livermore Action Group, 3126 Shattuck Ave., Berkeley, CA 94705
Long Island Catholic Peace Fellowship, 34 Jamaica Ave., Wyandanch, NY 11798
Los Angeles Catholic Worker, 632 N. Brittania St., Los Angeles, CA 90033
Nevada Desert Experience (NDE), P.O. Box 4487, Las Vegas, NV 89127-0487
New Hampshire Seacoast Clamshell, Box 734, Concord, NH 03301
Olive Branch Catholic Worker, 1322 Kenyon St. NW, Washington DC 20010
Pax Christi Syracuse, 208 Slocum Ave., Syracuse, NY 13202
Peace House, 431 S. Weber, Colorado Springs, CO 80903
Peace Witness at GTE, c/o 136 Austin St., Worcester, MA 06109
Peacemakers of the Tri-Counties, c/o 126 N. Weadock, Saginaw, MI 48607
Resource Center for Nonviolence, P.O. Box 2524, Santa Cruz, CA 95063
Rhode Island Mobilization for Survival, Box 2534, Providence, RI 02906
River City Nonviolent Resistance Campaign, c/o Thomas Merton Center, 5125 Pennsylvania Ave., Pittsburgh, PA 15224
Rocky Mountain Peace Center, 1520 Euclid, Boulder, CO 80302

Save All Living Things, Box 810, Great Falls, MT 59403
San Jose Peace Center, 520 S. 10th St., San Jose, CA 95112
Silence One Silo, Box 9203, Missoula, MT 59807
Strategies and Action for Conversion, P.O. Box 283, Omaha, NE 68101
Witness for Peace at AVCO, Box 736, Wilmington, MA 01887
Witness for Disarmament, P.O. Box 181, New Haven, CT 06501
Women Rising in Resistance, P.O. Box 2096, Station A., Champaign, IL 61820
Women's Peace Encampment for a Future of Peace and Justice, 5440 Rt. 96, Romulus, NY 14541
Women of Faith, P.O. Box 14785, Hartford, CT 06114
Vandenburg Action Coalition, 273 Frederick St., San Francisco, CA 94117

*Denominational and Religious Peace and Justice Groups*

*Baptist*
Peace Concerns Program, American Baptist Church, P.O. Box 851, Valley Forge, PA 19482-0851
Baptist Peace Fellowship, 222 East Lake Dr., Decatur, GA 30030

*Brethren*
Brethren Peace Fellowship, Box 455, New Windsor, MD 21776

*Buddhist*
Buddhist Peace Fellowship, c/o Fellowship of Reconciliation, Box 271, Nyack, NY 10960
Monks and Nuns of Nipponzan Myohoi, New England Sangha, 100 Cave Hill Road, Leverett, MA 01504

*Catholic*
Catholic Peace Fellowship, 339 Lafayette St., New York, NY 10012
Pax Christi USA, 348 East Tenth St., Erie, PA 16503
U.S. Catholic Conference, Office of International Justice and Peace, 1312 Massachusetts Ave. NW, Washington, DC 20005

*Disciples of Christ*
Shalom Congregation Program, Christian Church (Disciples of Christ) 222 S. Downet St., Box 1986, Indianapolis, IN 46206

*Episcopal*
Episcopal Church Center, Public Issues Office, 815 Second Ave., New York, NY 10017
Episcopal Peace Fellowship, Hearst Hall, Wisconsin Ave. & Woodley Rd. NW, Washington, DC 20016
Evangelicals for Social Action, 712 G St. SE, Washington, DC 20003

*Jewish*
Jewish Peace Fellowship, Box 271, Nyack, NY 10960
New Jewish Agenda, 14a Church St., Suite 2 N, New York, NY 10007
The Shalom Center, Church Road & Greenwood Ave., Wyncote, PA 19095

*Lutheran*
American Lutheran Church, Office of Church and Society, 422 South Fifth St., Minneapolis, MN 55414
Lutheran Peace Fellowship, 2481 Como Ave. West, St. Paul MN 55108

*Methodist*
General Board of Church and Society, The United Methodist Church Department of Peace and World Order, 100 Maryland Ave. NE Washington, DC 20002-5664
United Methodist Peace Fellowship, 5123 Truman Rd., Kansas City, MO 64127

*Presbyterian*
Presbyterian Peacemaking Program, 475 Riverside Dr., Room 1101, New York, NY 10115
United Presbyterian Peace Fellowship, Box 271, Nyack, NY 10960

*Reform*
Reformed Church in America, Office of Social Witness, 475 Riverside Dr., Room 1822, New York, NY 10115
Reformed Peace Fellowship, 31 Shull Dr., Newark, DE 19177
Unitarian Universalist Peace Network, 5808 Green St., Philadelphia, PA 19144
United Church of Christ, Office for Church in Society, 110 Maryland Ave. NE, Washington, DC 20002

*Groups Involved in Nonviolent Action Against U.S. Military Policies in Central America*

*Inter-Religious Task Force on Central America.* A New York-based interfaith group involved in organizing the religious community to oppose U.S. military policy in Central America. It publishes a newsletter and distributes an array of resources on Central America. 475 Riverside Dr., Room 563, New York, NY 10115.

*Pledge of Resistance.* Begun in 1983 by a group of Christian peacemakers opposed to U.S. policy in Nicaragua, it is a network of over seventy thousand people across the United States who have pledged to engage in acts of nonviolent resistance if the United States invades, bombs, sends combat troops, or otherwise significantly escalates its intervention in Nicaragua or El Salvador. Many local groups have organized local nonviolent actions to protest U.S. military policy in Central America. Contact National Resource Center of the Pledge of Resistance, P.O. Box 53411-3411, Washington, DC 20009-3411.

*Sanctuary Movement.* Begun in 1981, it is an interfaith network of over two hundred Churches and synagogues that, in defiance of U.S. immigration laws, have publicly stated their intention to shelter and transport "illegal" Central American refugees—mostly from El Salvador and Guatemala—who have fled their countries because their lives are endangered. For information about sanctuary and the legal status of refugees and sanctuary workers who have been indicted, contact Chicago Religious

Task Force on Central America, 407 S. Dearborn St., Room 370, Chicago, IL 60605.

*Witness for Peace.* An ecumenical network of faith communities throughout the United States that, over the last six years, have organized ongoing nonviolent vigils in war zones throughout Nicaragua in prayerful solidarity with the Nicaraguan people, who are opposed to the U.S.-backed *contras'* attempt to overthrow the existing government. For further information contact Witness for Peace, Box 29241, Washington, DC 20017.

*Groups Involved in Nonviolent Action in Latin America*

*Servicio Paz y Justicia (SEPAJ)*—Service of Peace and Justice. An ecumenical organization based in Argentina working for the promotion and support of nonviolent movements for liberation in Latin America. For more information contact SERPAJ, Casa De La Paz, Mexico 479, 1097 Buenos Aires, Argentina.

*Groups Involved in Nonviolent Resistance to Apartheid*

For information concerning the nonviolent campaign in the United States to end all U.S. support for the racist South African government and abolish apartheid contact Free South Africa Movement, c/o TransAfrica, 548 8th St., SE, Washington, DC 20003

*Plowshares Disarmament Support Groups*

For more information concerning ongoing Plowshares disarmament support activities contact:
Griffiss Plowshares, 106 Maywood Dr., Syracuse, NY 13205
Isaiah Peace Ministry, 66 Edgewood Ave., New Haven, CT 06511
Jonah House, 1933 Park Ave., Baltimore, MD 21217
New York Plowshares, 225 Lafayette St., Suite 207, New York, NY 10012

Richard Miller—Pantex Disarmament Action, c/o Kindred Community, 1337 6th Ave., Des Moines, IA 50314
Pershing Plowshares Support Committee, P.O. Box 585, Orlando, FL 32802
Silo Plowshares Support Group, 5219 Lydia, Kansas City, MO 64110
Silo Pruning Hooks/Woodson Family Support Group, Gaudete Peace and Justice Center, 634 Spruce St., Madison, WI 53715
Trident II Plowshares/Pruning Hooks Support Groups, Box 3291, Wayland Square, Providence, RI 10906
Witness for Peace at AVCO, Box 736, Wilmington, MA 01887

## PERIODICALS

Articles on the arms race, nuclear disarmament, United States intervention policy, and nonviolent resistance can be found in the following publications.

*Catholic Agitator,* 632 N. Brittania St., Los Angeles, CA 90033.
*Christianity and Crisis,* Bob Hoyt, 537 W. 121 St., New York, NY 10027.
*Fellowship.* Box 271, Nyack, NY 10960.
*Greenpeace,* Andre Carothers, 1611 Connecticut Ave., NW, Washington DC 20009.
*In These Times,* Institute for Public Affairs, 1300 W. Belmont, Chicago, IL 60657.
*Mobilizer,* 853 Broadway, Suite 418, New York, NY 10003
*Mother Jones,* 1663 Mission St., 2nd Floor, San Francisco, CA 94107
*National Catholic Reporter,* 115 E. Armour, Box 419281, Kansas City, MO 64141
*Nuclear Times,* 1601 Connecticut Ave., Washington, DC 20009
*Peace Magazine,* 736 Bathurst St., Toronto, M5S 2R4, Canada
*Sojourners,* Box 29272, Washington, DC 20017
*The Bulletin of Atomic Scientists,* 1020-24 E. 58th St., Chicago, IL 60637
*The Nation,* 72 5th Ave., New York, NY 10011

*The Other Side,* 300 W. Apsley St., Box 12236, Philadelphia, PA 19144

*The Progressive,* Erwin Knoll, 409 E. Main St., Madison, WI 53703

*Zeta Magazine,* 116 Botolph St., Boston, MA 02115

*APPENDIX D*
*Suggested Readings*

## SUGGESTED READINGS

Aldridge, Robert and Janet. *Children and Nonviolence.* Hope Publishing House. Pasadena, California. 1987.

Aldridge, Robert. *First Strike: The Pentagon's Strategy for Nuclear War.* South End Press. Boston, Massachusetts. 1983.

Aldridge, Robert. *The Counterforce Syndrome: A Guide to U.S. Nuclear Weapons and Strategic Doctrine.* Transnational Institute. Washington, D.C.. 1978.

Berrigan, Daniel. *The Book of Uncommon Prayer.* Seabury. New York. 1978.

Berrigan, Daniel. *The Nightmare of God.* Sunburst. Portland, Oregon. 1983.

Berrigan, Daniel. *To Dwell in Peace.* Harper and Row. New York. 1987.

Berrigan, Philip. *Of Beast and Beastly Images.* Sunburst. Portland, Oregon. 1978.

Berry, Wendell. *Standing by Words.* North Point Press. San Francisco. 1983.

Berry, Wendell. *A Part.* North Point Press, San Francisco. 1980.

Brueggemann, Walter. *Prophetic Imagination.* Fortress Press. Philadelphia, Pennsylvania. 1978.

Day, Dorothy. *The Long Loneliness.* Harper and Row. San Francisco, California. 1952.

Douglass, James. *Resistance and Contemplation: The Way of Liberation.* Dell. New York. 1972.

Ellis, Marc. *Peter Maurin; Prophet in the 20th Century.* Paulist Press. 1981.

Ellul, Jacques. *Apocalypse, The Book of Revelation.* Seabury Press. New York. 1977.

Ellul, Jacques. *Hope in a Time of Abandonment.* Seabury Press. New York. 1973.

Erikson, Erik. *Gandhi's Truth.* W.W. Norton. 1969.

Falk, Richard and Lifton, Robert. *Indispensable Weapons: The Political and Psychological Case Against Nuclearism.* Basic Books. New York. 1982.
Fischer, Louis. *The Life of Mahatma Gandhi.* Collier Books Edition. 1962.
Fromm, Eric. *Let Man Prevail: A Socialist Manifesto and Program.* A Doubleday Anchor Book. New York. 1961.
Gutierrez, Gustavo. *The Theology of Liberation.* Orbis Press. Maryknoll, New York. 1973.
Herman, Edward S. *"Atrocities" in Vietnam: Myths and Realities.* Pilgrim Press. Boston. 1970.
Johnson, Paul. *Modern Times: The World from the Twenties to the Eighties.* Harper and Row, Publishers. New York. 1983.
Kim Chi Ha. *The Gold Crowned Jesus and other Writings.* Orbis Press. Maryknoll, New York. 1978.
Laffin, Arthur J. and Montgomery, Anne. *Swords into Plowshares: Nonviolent Direct Action for Disarmament.* Harper & Row, Publishers, San Francisco. 1987.
Lens, Sidney. *The Day Before Doomsday.* Doubleday and Company. New York. 1977.
Mayer, Milton. *They Thought They Were Free: The Germans 1933-45.* University of Chicago Press. 1955.
Merton, Thomas. *Faith and Violence.* University of Notre Dame Press. 1968.
Merton, Thomas. *The Seven Storey Mountain.* Harcourt, Brace and Company, New York. 1948.
Miller, William D. *Dorothy Day, A Biography.* Harper and Row. New York. 1982.
Miranda, Jose. *Being and the Messiah.* Orbis Books. Maryknoll. New York. 1977.
Miranda, Jose. *Marx and the Bible.* Orbis Books. Maryknoll. New York. 1974.
Peguy, Charles. *Basic Verities.* (French-English Edition by Ann and Julian Green.) Pantheon Books. New York. 1943.
Priestley, Denise. *Bringing Forth in Hope: Being Creative in a Nuclear Age.* Paulist Press. New York. 1983.
Sampson, R.V.. *The Discovery of Peace.* Pantheon Books. 1973.

Sheer, Robert. *With Enough Shovels.* Vintage Books. 1983.
Sider, Ronald and Taylor, Richard. *Nuclear Holocaust and Christian Hope.* Inter Varsity Press. 1982.
Sollee, Dorothy. *Choosing Life.* Fortress Press. Philadelphia, Pennsylvania. 1981.
Stringfellow, William. *An Ethic for Christians and Other Aliens in a Strange Land.* Word Books. Waco, Texas. 1976.
Zinn, Howard. *A People's History of the United States.* Harper Colophon. New York. 1980.
Zinn, Howard. *The Twientieth Century.* Harper Colophon. New York. 1980.

www.ingramcontent.com/pod-product-compliance
Lightning Source LLC
Chambersburg PA
CBHW071231230426
**43668CB00011B/1393**